Also available at all good book stores

9781785315466

9781785313929

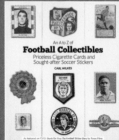

9781785315602

9781785315671

9781785311581

9781908051349

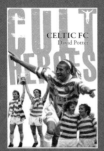

9781848181090

9781848182035

9781785313318

THE
SCOTTISH
CUP

DAVID POTTER

THE
SCOTTISH
CUP

CELTIC'S FAVOURITE TROPHY

First published by Pitch Publishing, 2020

Pitch Publishing
A2 Yeoman Gate
Yeoman Way
Worthing
Sussex
BN13 3QZ
www.pitchpublishing.co.uk
info@pitchpublishing.co.uk

A CIP catalogue record is available for this book
from the British Library.

ISBN 978 1 78531 689 0

Typesetting and origination by Pitch Publishing
Printed and bound in India by Replika Press Pvt. Ltd.

Contents

INTRODUCTION

THERE IS a special relationship between Celtic and the Scottish Cup. Celtic have won the Scottish Cup 39 times, six more than Rangers who have had several periods of missing out on the trophy, not least the years between 1903 and 1928 when a whole quarter of a century elapsed without Rangers winning the Scottish Cup. They were able to win the Scottish League but not the Scottish Cup. Third, incidentally, comes Queen's Park who, of course, ruled the roost in the 19th century but could not cope with professionalism. Then a fairly long way behind come clubs like Aberdeen, Hearts and Hibs – all of whom really should have done an awful lot better.

But the sight of the Scottish Cup draped in green and white ribbons remains for Celtic fans one of the greatest sights of them all; 'When the Celts go up, to get the Scottish Cup, we'll be there' is sung with gusto on appropriate occasions, and on at least three occasions in history – 1951, 1965 and 1995 – a trophy famine was symbolically ended by Celtic lifting the Scottish Cup!

The Scottish Cup is the second-oldest football competition in the world, second only to the English (or

FA) Cup, but then again there have been three different English Cup trophies. The original Scottish one is now without doubt the oldest trophy still played for in the football world. It is too frail to be carried about, so it stays at Hampden, is duly presented to the winning captain (almost exclusively Scott Brown in recent years!) on cup final day, then exchanged for a replica while the original is put back into its case.

Since 1873 it has engendered an incredible amount of annual interest, excitement, enthusiasm, ecstasy and heartbreak with huge crowds. It has also created an awful lot of money. In 1955, 1957 and from 1977 onwards, the Scottish Cup Final has been televised live and to many countries. It is virtually impossible to quantify how many people actually watch the Scottish Cup Final – but it is a lot – and it is not uncommon to hear claims from some US, Australian and Canadian television companies that the Scottish Cup Final, especially when Celtic are involved, attracts more television spectators than the English Cup Final.

Another team that attracts a lot of attention in the new world are not Rangers, funnily enough (although they too have a sizeable following), but Aberdeen. Like Celtic, the ancestors of Aberdeen supporters had a fairly large diaspora in the 19th and early 20th centuries. Therefore, a Celtic v Aberdeen pairing on Scottish Cup Final day creates a tremendous amount of interest in the lands beyond the wave.

The Scottish Cup, being some 17 years older than the Scottish League, was, until the arrival of the European Cup in the mid-1950s, considered to be the more important of the two trophies. (The Scottish League Cup, which really only started after the Second World War, is a lot younger and still to this day suffers a little sneering, especially from the supporters of teams who have suffered early exits!) The Scottish Cup was called the 'Blue Riband' (a Victorian term for the best honour of them all) and the final at Hampden, usually on a sunny day in April until the 1960s, then May from the mid-1970s onwards, was (and rightly) looked upon as one of the highlights of the season. In the 1950s, when people were less partisan in their allegiances, fans would make a point of going to the Scottish Cup Final, no matter who was playing, and Hampden was, of course, always big enough to accommodate everyone.

And there is so much more to it than simply the final. The early rounds are before the new year, the first round containing the top league teams is usually in January and then each subsequent month has a round. There are, of course, no second chances in the Scottish Cup as there are in the Scottish League, and therein lies the attraction. It is always possible for big teams to go out on the day to smaller teams. Celtic have suffered at the hands of Inverness, Clyde, Arthurlie and a few others. Thankfully, the Scottish Cup has not been devalued as the English Cup has been in recent years.

It has been argued that it was the winning of the Scottish Cup by Hibernian in 1887 which played a large part in the history of Celtic. Hibs, the self-proclaimed Irish team of Edinburgh, beat Dumbarton in February 1887 to become the first eastern team to lift the trophy. 'Eastern' was a big enough shock, but 'Irish' had the

9

longer-lasting indirect effect. It was possibly a blow and a wake-up call to Queen's Park and the middle-class establishment, but the fact that the Edinburgh Irishmen could win the Scottish Cup may well have – in fact almost certainly – planted a few seeds in the minds of some Glasgow Irishmen that they could found a team which could do the same thing. By the end of 1887, a decision had been taken that a football team would be established to provide food for poor children.

Two years later in 1889, the Glasgow Irishmen's team had reached the final and in 1892, they won the trophy. If we can imagine (or in some cases, if we are old enough, recollect) 26 and 27 May 1967 when Celtic came back with the big, beautifully ugly, European Cup from Lisbon and the prolonged celebrations in Celtic enclaves all over Scotland, then we can get some idea of what 1892 did to the East End when Celtic won the Scottish Cup. The Irish, despised, ridiculed and blatantly discriminated against by some, could now do something. They could play football! There was now no need for violence to make any political point. They had done it on the football field, and the Scottish Cup was there to prove it!

Celtic won the trophy again in seven years' time, and from that day to this (if we ignore war years and the acknowledged lean years between 1954 and 1965) seven years have not passed without Celtic winning the Scottish Cup. Even in the awful years between 1954 and 1965, Celtic reached four Scottish Cup Finals and the lamentations of the Celtic support plummeted to biblical depths – but it still did a lot to illustrate the affinity that Celtic supporters had with the Scottish Cup.

So many Celtic players have been defined by the Scottish Cup. One thinks of Sandy McMahon with a glorious header in 1892, Jimmy Quinn's hat-trick in 1904, Patsy Gallacher in 1925, Billy McNeill in 1965, Dixie Deans (also with a hat-trick in 1972), Frank McAvennie in 1988, Henrik Larsson in 2001 and 2004 and Odsonne Edouard in 2019.

It is also true that Celtic can be defined in a negative sense as well by the Scottish Cup. The 'lean years' between 1954 and 1965, as we have said, saw four dreadful Scottish Cup Finals. Three went to replays, and in every single one of them, dreadful team selection played a part, the one in 1956 in particular defying belief.

Spite against one particular player and a misguided attempt to be seen to gain the moral high ground played a part in 1955, 1961 was just plain silly and the 1963 replay must be one of the earliest surrenders on record. In each of the four cases, the benefitting club simply could not believe their luck, and the defeat and the manner of the defeat left a virtually indelible pain in the hearts of the Celtic supporters.

It was once said by Billy McNeill that if Celtic and Rangers had been in the English Civil War, Celtic would have been the Cavaliers. Rangers would have perhaps been the more technically correct, orthodox, solid Roundheads but Celtic would have been the romantic, quixotic, spectacular Cavaliers. It is a reasonable analogy and possibly explains why Rangers have won the league more often, whereas Celtic have had more panache and flamboyance to win the Scottish Cup.

The Scottish Cup is – and should be – Celtic's favourite trophy. Celtic have competed in it 119 times and won it 39 times, and that is a success rate of something like once every three years. That is not bad.

CHAPTER ONE

THE 19TH CENTURY
1888/89–1898/99

THE SCOTTISH Cup had been in existence since the 1873/74 season. In the early years it had been more or less the exclusive property of Queen's Park, but Vale of Leven, Renton and Dumbarton had had their moments of glory as well, and, of course, when Hibs won the Scottish Cup in 1887, it galvanised the Glasgow Irishmen into starting a football club on the grounds that whatever the Edinburgh Irishmen could do, the Glasgow Irishmen could also do.

Celtic's first Scottish Cup tie was played at Old Celtic Park against near neighbours Shettleston on 1 September 1888. It was only natural that the first Scottish Cup tie of this new, and already well-supported, team should attract a great deal of attention, and the fact that it was a local derby added to the occasion. The rain had stopped by the time the game began, but there had been an awful lot of it, and the pitch is described as 'greasy' in *The Scotsman*.

The Courier in Dundee, a newspaper which would in later years become very well disposed to the new Celtic team, is rather offhand when it bemoans the fact that some players can join other teams almost at will and laments the fact that the great Renton side which won the Scottish Cup in 1888 have lost two men, Neil McCallum and James Kelly, to Celtic, 'a club composed of players of the Catholic persuasion'. This rather unflattering introduction (indeed, it is a rather offensive racial or sectarian slur which is not necessarily true in any case) of Celtic to the Dundee readers may well have had the effect of rallying the large and burgeoning Dundee Irish population to the cause of the Celtic, but in any case the new club already had a large support. Today they won 5-1 to progress to the next round.

All goals were scored, apparently, by an otherwise obscure character called John O'Connor, but one must be very careful about this. Newspaper reporting in 1888 was far from an exact science. There were no such things as press boxes or football correspondents, and often a report was composed by asking a spectator 'Who scored that one?' or even by making it up! Possibly, he was not even at the game and found out the goalscorers and other details of the game 'by word of mouth'. But the Celtic team for the first of their many cup ties was Dunning, McKeown and James Coleman; Gallagher, Kelly and McLaren; McCallum, John Coleman, Groves, Dunbar and O'Connor.

So it was onwards and upwards for Celtic as they moved into the next round. This game took place three weeks later, again at Old Celtic Park. Once more it was against near neighbours, this time Cowlairs, and the score was a spectacular 8-0 – a surprise, because Cowlairs had defeated Celtic in the Glasgow Exhibition Cup Final two weeks earlier. This result energised the 7,000 supporters (a huge crowd for 1888 and a potent indication of just how many followers this new club could command) and gave the new club a huge boost. This time the goals seem to have been scored (although accounts disagree) by Mick Dunbar who had a hat-trick, two from Neil McCallum and one each from Tom Maley, James Kelly and Willie Groves, who had joined Celtic from Hibernian and rejoiced in the nickname 'darlin' Willie'.

For the third time in a row, Celtic had a home tie, this time against a team called Albion Rovers from Coatbridge described as a 'crack Lanarkshire club'. Like Celtic, their supporters tended to be of Irish origin, but today in front of a poor crowd of 600 (even though it was a nice sunny day) Celtic beat them 4-1 – Mick Dunbar, Tom Maley, Willie Groves and Paddy Gallagher (no relation to the famous Patsy Gallacher of the future) scoring the goals for the team variously described as 'the Irishmen', 'the Celts', 'the Glasgow Irishmen' or 'the green shirts'.

At long last an away tie followed, and this time it was a trip to Edinburgh to play St Bernard's at Powderhall. 'Great satisfaction was evinced' in Edinburgh when the draw was made. By this time, reports of the Celtic had spread. In spite of some terrible weather, some 6,000 (a huge crowd for Edinburgh with many having travelled through on the train along with the team from Glasgow) came to see this team who 'passed brilliantly' to each other. Willie Groves and James Kelly were outstanding for the 'famous green jerseys' (interesting that the jerseys are 'famous' less than six months after they were first worn!) and this time 'darlin' Willie' scored two and Tom Maley and Mick Dunbar one each. St Bernard's were much commended for scoring once against this mighty side and for restricting them to 4-1.

It is not exactly clear what type of 'green jersey' it was. It may have been green and white vertical, or it may have been pure green, or it may have been white with green trimmings and a green badge, but there seems to have been little doubt that it was famous at the time.

But then on 24 November at Celtic Park in another east of Glasgow derby before 9,000, Celtic lost – or at least they appeared to. Clyde won 1-0, but the game had to be shortened and even so, it finished in darkness for the bizarre reason that Clyde were wearing illegal footwear and were dilatory in changing their boots!

Not unnaturally Celtic protested. Rather destroying the beliefs of the nascent 'everyone hates Celtic' paranoia, the SFA upheld the protest and ordered the game to be played again on 8 December, once more at Celtic Park. Clyde played the game under protest although the edge was taken off their outrage when they saw the huge 9,000 crowd and they contemplated their share of the large gate. This time Celtic simply took control, played sparkling football and won 9-2 – with hat-tricks from Tom Maley and darlin' Willie, two from Neil McCallum and one from James McLaren, commonly known as the 'auld giniral'.

And before the year of 1888 was out, the infant club had made further progress in the Scottish Cup, this time on 15 December at Merchiston near Falkirk, the home of East Stirlingshire. This time it would have to be said that Celtic were rather fortunate and for a long time it looked as if they were going out of the Scottish Cup thanks to a goal scored late in the first half by the 'Shire. But within the last five minutes Neil McCallum equalised, and Celtic then scored the winner to a great feeling of relief from the surprisingly large number of those who had once again followed the team on the train from Glasgow. Some had already departed for an early train, convinced that the team were out of the cup, but those who stayed got their reward.

And this ended 1888. The new team had made astonishing strides to reach the semi-final of the Scottish Cup after little more than six months' existence, but, of course, most of the players had been around for some time – McCallum and Kelly were already cup winners with Renton, for example, and McLaren and Groves with Hibs. But there was also an enthusiasm about the green jersey and it was clear that the word 'Celtic' already meant an awful lot to an awful lot of people. For the Irish in the East End of Glasgow, there was now a rallying point.

They were also all about professionalism. Professionalism had been legal in England from 1886 but Scotland still lagged behind with Queen's Park, the leading club in Scotland and indeed founders of the game, absolutely obdurate on this issue. It did not take a huge amount of thinking, however, to work out that players from Renton and Hibs would not go to this new Glasgow club for reasons of nationality and religion. There was a certain amount of money changing hands as well, it was felt, and this new ambitious club had the wherewithal to pay their players, albeit illegally.

The rest of Scotland sat up and took notice as well. It is often said that every action has a reaction. There was a definite reaction to this new team and their success. Other clubs tended to welcome the success of the Celts and their large support (after all, it meant that there was more money about for everyone), but some of the supporters of other clubs were less keen, tapping into the latent xenophobic and sectarian bile that the Orange Lodges, sometimes with subtlety but sometimes not, peddled. Funnily enough, this intolerance did not as yet reach Rangers to any large extent, but it was more obvious at out-of-Glasgow grounds like Airdrie and St Mirren.

At a different level, the lofty, patrician Queen's Park also trembled. There was now a club with the resources to challenge them – and within Glasgow itself! In recent years, there had been a challenge from Edinburgh from Hearts and Hibs in addition to the more established challenges of the Dunbartonshire villages of Renton and Alexandria. But now a new club had arrived, tapping into the support of a huge and already well-established ethnic minority.

The semi-final of the Scottish Cup took place on 12 January at Boghead, Dumbarton before 6,000 spectators, believed to be the biggest crowd up till this time at Boghead with Celtic once again giving a huge boost to the finances of the railway companies. Several trains brought supporters from Glasgow. Those who were there saw just why the new team had taken the country by storm, for they won 4-1 with two goals from

Groves and two from Dunbar. *The Scotsman* says that the 'beautiful passing of the Celts was a matter for general admiration' and that their 'swiftness and general ability' were superior. Dumbarton, who had won the Scottish Cup in 1883, were simply swept aside, and as the Third Lanark Rifle Volunteers had beaten Renton in the other semi-final, it was to be an all-Glasgow Scottish Cup Final, scheduled for Hampden Park, the home of Queen's Park, on 2 February. (This ground was not, of course, the Hampden as we know it today. It was the ground that became known in later years as Cathkin.)

Great was the enthusiasm throughout Glasgow and indeed all of Scotland about this game. Third Lanark had twice before reached the Scottish Cup Final, losing to Queen's Park and Vale of Leven in the 1870s, but they had never won it and their supporters (generally ex-soldiers and those who lived in the south of Glasgow but considered themselves not rich enough to support Queen's Park!) were there in strength. But so too were those of Celtic and the crowd was given as 18,000, by some distance the biggest crowd ever at a Scottish football game, beating even Scotland v England games. But the weather took over.

Snow had fallen intermittently in the morning, but by kick-off time, it intensified and it soon became obvious that play was more or less impossible. Neither team wanted to play, but the referee Charles Campbell of Queen's Park insisted, but then relented a little to say that the game should be played as a friendly and that the fate of the Scottish Cup was not at stake. The crowd, who had paid a massive £920, were not informed, although they might have guessed, and in impossible conditions with visibility a major problem Third Lanark won a farcical game 3-0 with many in the crowd losing interest in the game and making snowmen around the ground instead. Snowballs were thrown at opposition players, the referee and the umpires (one from each side who acted as a linesman).

Half-time was a particularly entertaining occasion for the spectators. 'Those in whom the creative urge was uppermost' built a snowman or two, some of them with unnaturally huge appendages; others entertained each other by singing good-naturedly a repertoire of songs from the Victorian music hall like 'My Darling Clementine' and 'Two Lovely Black Eyes' – a salutary reminder of what can happen to a young man if he gets too friendly with another man's wife – or 'A Floppy Scottish Sausage', a reference to the relationship between the late John Brown and Queen Victoria, when the Queen was a little disappointed with John.

But in footballing terms, it didn't matter. Next week did, however. The conditions were 100 per cent better, although it was still cold and the ground was hard, and a crowd of similar size turned up. This time, although Neil McCallum scored for Celtic in the second half, Third Lanark had already scored one in the first half and late in the game Oswald scored the winner. The consensus of opinion in the press was that Thirds were the better team.

The defeat was obviously very disappointing, but it was nevertheless a great achievement for the infant Celtic club to reach the final of the Scottish Cup in their first year of existence. The team on that bittersweet day of 9

February 1889 was John Kelly, Gallagher and McKeown; W. Maley, James Kelly and McLaren; McCallum, Dunbar, Coleman, Groves and T. Maley. There were enough players in that team wise enough to learn a lesson or two. More importantly, they had tasted the 'big time'. They wanted some more.

The new team, 'the Celts', 'the Irishmen', 'the Green and Whites', were less successful in the Scottish Cup of 1889/90. Indeed, they did not survive September. Their home tie against Queen's Park on 7 September highlighted the inadequacy of Old Celtic Park when about 25,000 turned up clamouring for admission at the ten entrances. Not all the crowd were allowed in; some had to be turned away, others climbed the walls to get in, but at least they never turned nasty. However, frequent encroachments on to the field by the panicking crowd who feared being crushed to death meant that the play was seriously disrupted, and at one point in the second half, referee Mr Sneddon called the captains together and said he wanted to abandon the game. Nevertheless, it was decided to play the game out, and it finished a 0-0 friendly.

The SFA (who generally showed a remarkable tendency to decide in favour of Queen's Park in any given dispute) then decided that the game should be played next week at the much larger Hampden Park, and that the admission charges should be doubled from last week's already high one shilling. One did not need to be a genius to work out that all this turned out very much in favour of Queen's Park, whose wealthy supporters were more able to afford the staggering two-shilling entrance fee. Ten thousand, still a huge crowd, saw a very even game with Groves equalising for Celtic after Hamilton had put the home side ahead, but then with only minutes left, Berry scored the winner and Celtic were out. Queen's Park went on to win the Scottish Cup (their ninth) in 1890.

Celtic lasted in the Scottish Cup a little longer in 1890/91, but even so exited the tournament some ten days before the new year. It would have to be described nevertheless as one of the more interesting, although not necessarily one of the more pleasant, of campaigns with loads of bad weather, crowd problems and not a little disorder. This was also the first season of the Scottish League – a new concept where every team played each other home and away and were awarded points – but the Scottish Cup was still the number one tournament and would remain so for many decades.

Ironically to a football historian, but coming as no surprise to contemporaries, the best and most peaceful game was the first one, namely Celtic v Rangers at Old Celtic Park where 16,000 (all paying sixpence) were crammed in, and the gates were closed well before the 4pm start time, to see a good, well-fought but thoroughly sporting encounter. These two teams famously got on well together, and there was absolutely no trouble whatsoever as Celtic won 1-0, the only goal of the game coming when once again Celtic's great goalscoring hero 'darlin' Willie' finished off a good move with 'a grand shot', although some sources describe it as a 'miskick'!

Carfin Shamrock were next at Celtic Park. The 2-2 scoreline raised a few eyebrows, and not for the last time, hints appeared in several newspapers to the effect that the replay on the holiday Monday, 6 October, at Byreknowes Park, Carfin would in no way be financially disadvantageous to both sets of Irishmen! An enormous crowd gathered round the ropes and saw a good 3-1 victory for the Glasgow men with goals coming from Barney Crossan, Peter Dowds and 'darlin' Willie'.

There followed a trip to Wishaw Thistle in mid-October, but on a fine autumnal day the Lanarkshire men had no answer to the 'all-firing Celts' and lost 2-6. Celtic had to travel further afield and in far worse weather conditions to West Craigie Park, Dundee to take on Dundee Our Boys. The game on 8 November was played in torrential rain throughout but nevertheless attracted 4,000 spectators to a ground that was almost entirely exposed to the elements. Celtic scored three goals round about the half-hour mark, after the local side had had the temerity to score first. The second half was a low-key affair with Celtic clearly on top but having no desire to humiliate the Dundonians who were clearly in awe of the Celtic side that had revolutionised Scottish football in two and a half years. Dundee Our Boys, however, intended to protest about the state of the pitch (their own!) and bizarrely the studs on the boots of the Celts, but forgot to send the letter in time! Such incompetence may well explain why that club disappeared soon after!

And then things began to get murky in every sense of the word, for the next round of the draw took Celtic to Raploch Park, Larkhall to play Larkhall Royal Albert. The events that took place over the three weeks at the end of November and beginning of December may well have been an early example of sectarian hatred at football matches (1890 was certainly a year when Home Rule for Ireland was in the news, with even a little sexual spice for the prurient added with the divorce case of Charles Stewart Parnell!) but this may be looking at matters through more modern eyes. Yet certainly, Celtic were undeniably Irish, and Larkhall Royal Albert's very name gives an indication of where their sympathies and loyalties lay. This all may well have played a part in what happened.

29 November saw a severe frost. An agreement was reached that the cup tie should be postponed and a friendly played in its place. A civilised 2-2 draw was played out, although it was not impossible that a few things might have happened, possibly things said, which would be carried on next week. The events of the following Saturday, 6 December, were, frankly, a disgrace and although the evidence is scant, it is difficult to avoid the conclusion that one prominent Celt was very lucky not to be on the wrong end of serious trouble.

The game was one-sided, and Celtic, 4-0 up with goals from Jimmy McLaren, Johnny Madden and two from the rising star left-winger Johnny Campbell, were coasting. They should have been allowed to coast, but when a Larkhall player called Frame fouled Johnny Madden, Celtic's linesman/umpire Tom Maley not only awarded the foul but entered the field of play, remonstrated with Frame and ended up hitting him with his flag, or punching him depending on what account one reads. This incited the crowd, who invaded the park, were persuaded to go back, but then returned a few minutes later when Jerry Reynolds showed his pugilistic skills by punching someone. *The Scotsman*, in a breathtaking euphemism, describes this as a 'slight accident'! The referee was compelled to cut the game short some 12 minutes early.

Larkhall then argued for a replay. It was unlikely (even impossible) that they could have scored four goals in 12 minutes and in any case they should have exercised more control over their own supporters. (The two policemen on duty did a marvellous and courageous job and were much praised for their bravery and devotion to duty, but two against 4,000 is impossible odds.) On the other hand, the conduct of Tom Maley could not be excused, and it was he, and only he, who was responsible for the riot. Celtic opposed a replay, suggesting that Larkhall were now sniffing extra money (a reasonable assumption, one feels) but the SFA then came to the incongruous decision that no action should be taken against Tom Maley, but that the game should be replayed next Saturday at, of all places, Ibrox. Those who suspect that the SFA have an innate bias against Celtic might find it difficult to explain away the exoneration of Maley, but those who suspect that the SFA suffer from endogenous insanity possibly have more ammunition in this case!

Be that as it may, the replay at Ibrox on 13 December passed rather uneventfully with a routine and predictable 2-0 win for Celtic with second-half goals from Crossan and Campbell. Everyone seems to have behaved on the field, and 5,000 spectators turned up and left similarly becalmed after last week's events described in some newspapers as 'thrilling'! This one was more routine.

And so to 'fatal' Boghead, Dumbarton for the next round on 20 December. Referee Mr Dunn of Cambuslang was of the opinion that the ground was suitable for play, but he was the only one of that persuasion. Nevertheless, the snow had been cleared and to the delight of the huge 14,000 crowd disgorging from the Glasgow trains, the game went ahead. The conditions were certainly less than ideal (both teams emphatically said so) but Dumbarton played better than Celtic did and duly won 3-0. A few crowd disturbances were in evidence and some Celtic fans tried to get the game abandoned by invading the field (after all, Larkhall fans had succeeded in that a few weeks back!), but the ground was cleared and the game finished.

Early in the new year of 1891, Celtic made their protest about the conditions (Dumbarton intended to join them, but withdrew their protest after they had won the game!) but the decision on the casting vote of the chairman of the SFA committee was that the referee's decision should be upheld. There would thus be no Scottish Cup for Celtic in 1891, the trophy this year going eastwards to Heart of Midlothian.

But 1892 changed all that, and was the first great year in the history of our club. The Scottish Cup had been streamlined – a necessity because the Scottish League was now taking up more fixture dates – and Celtic's first game was against St Mirren at Westmarch in Paisley on 28 November 1891, and they won comfortably 4-2, but the scorers of the goals are uncertain. What was certain, however, was that Celtic now had a great forward line with the left-wing pair of Sandy McMahon and Johnny Campbell outstanding.

In the next round Kilmarnock Athletic (not the Kilmarnock team that we now know to play at Rugby

Park) presented few problems on 19 December when Celtic won 3-0. Cowlairs were then similarly dispatched 4-1 on 23 January to put Celtic into the semi-final, where they found themselves up against Rangers again at Old Celtic Park. New Celtic Park was now being built – indeed, it was well advanced – and this would be the last big game at the original ground (if we exclude the Scotland v Ireland international on 28 March). The semi-final was not as big a game attendance-wise as might have been expected, for heavy rain on 6 February 1892 cut the crowd to a slightly disappointing but still respectable 11,000. To put things into the perspective of 1892, however, Hearts were playing Renton at Hampden and attracted a larger crowd! Clearly in 1892, a Celtic v Rangers game did not necessarily make the whole world stop and wait for it.

The crowd at Old Celtic Park saw a great Celtic performance and a 5-3 win over Rangers. Indeed, Celtic were 5-0 up early in the second half with McMahon and Campbell absolutely rampant. They then must have tired a little, for Rangers pulled three back but Celtic were never seriously threatened, and in four years, they had now reached two Scottish Cup Finals – and this time they were to face the team with the best Scottish Cup record of them all – Queen's Park.

In 1892 Queen's Park were the real rivals. The Scottish Cup Final of that year was therefore relished and looked forward to. It was the old v the new, the Scottish establishment v the Irish immigrants, the rich v the poor – it was all these things, and Queen's Park, the founders of the game in Scotland, were now being challenged within Glasgow itself by a group of determined 'ethnic' people who were in the throes of building a new stadium big enough to house the Scotland v England international games, and who were supporters of the subversive (as Queen's Park saw it) idea of professionalism – which was still illegal but nevertheless widely practised. This new club also had supporters who made no bones about their political support for Home Rule for Ireland! Yes, there was a lot at stake on 12 March 1892 at Ibrox in the Scottish Cup Final.

But it didn't really happen. It might have been better if the frost and snow had stayed a little longer and prevented the game from taking place at all, but it had begun to thaw, the snow was melting and the pitch was playable in the opinion of the referee Mr Sneddon of Edinburgh University. Seaweed and sand were used to give players a foothold, but even so, not all newspapers or players agreed with Mr Sneddon's decision.

But that was the lesser of the problems. The major problem was the sheer size of the crowd. The game started at 4pm. The gates were opened at 12 and for the next few hours the crowds poured in with the Celtic crowd and their green favours predominant. Rangers had erected a couple of extra temporary stands, but they were quickly filled, and even though the gates were belatedly closed, something like 40,000 were in the ground which was really only built for less than half of that number. Even before the start, the crowd were encroaching on the pitch to avoid being crushed to death – they were pushed back but came on time and time again, so that, early in the first half, it was agreed that, given the size of the crowd and the state of the pitch, now rapidly deteriorating because of the number of spectator encroachments, the game would be played as a friendly. Celtic actually won 1-0 through a Johnny Campbell goal, but it did not matter.

It did not escape the notice of anyone that all this meant another big gate and more money. To their credit both Celtic and Queen's Park made charitable donations (in Celtic's case, on the suggestion of Michael Davitt, the Irish patriot, to evicted Irish tenants) but what really riled the Celtic support was the doubling of admission prices for the replayed cup final on 9 April. This was 'to deter so many people from attending', but that specious nonsense fooled no one. It was all for money, and there was again the not particularly subtle issue here that Queen's Park supporters, middle class, well-heeled and affluent, would find it easier to find two shillings to get in than would the under-privileged supporters from the East End.

Be that as it may, 23,000 turned up at Ibrox, and Celtic were by no means unrepresented. Not only was that the case, but the streets outside were thronged with Celtic fans who turned up to follow the game by the noise of the crowd. They had little to shout about at half-time when they were 1-0 down, but at the turnaround, this fine Celtic team, with the wind now in their favour, simply took charge and won 5-1. The scorers are given differently in different sources.

It may be that Sandy McMahon scored a hat-trick, Johnny Campbell scored another and there was an own goal. Other sources agree that there was an own goal, but say that McMahon and Campbell scored two each. Certainly one of McMahon's goals was a glorious header, and another was an overhead shot. The balance of evidence is in favour of 'two each' and one is inclined to back that view on the grounds that more would have been made of a McMahon hat-trick, if he had scored one. There was certainly no mention of any 'McMahon hat-trick' in the context of Jimmy Quinn's spectacular feat of that nature 12 years later. One curses TV and video for being so late in arriving on the scene! This argument could so easily have been settled!

What is not in the slightest doubt, however, is that this was a great day for the club and for Cullen, Reynolds and Doyle; Maley, Kelly and Gallagher; McCallum, Brady, Dowds, McMahon and Campbell. The Scottish Cup was presented at the banquet in the Alexandra Hotel, Bath Street and in the East End, singing and dancing were the order of the day and night. 'Our Bhoys Have Won the Cup' was the cry, and Scotland would never be the same again. The result was hailed in Irish communities in Edinburgh and Dundee and even in England and throughout the world, except perhaps, funnily enough, Ireland itself which was not yet a great football-playing country. Celtic had taken off, and the impoverished urchins and their emaciated mothers and fathers had something to cheer about. Bands paraded the streets of the East End that night with drums, bugles and flutes (!) very much in evidence.

Celtic had certainly given Scotland something to think about. Much of the reaction was disparaging and it is hard not to feel that there was a certain amount of 'feeling threatened' in some newspaper offices. The usually respected *Scottish Referee*, for example, talks about a 'Pyrrhic victory' for the benefit of those of its readers who had a classical education, for they say 'Queen's had a skeleton team'. Both of these statements are utter rubbish, for there was no great injury crisis at Queen's Park, and in any case, a 'Pyrrhic victory' (named after Rome's enemy King Pyrrhus of Epirus in the third century BC) is one in which many casualties are sustained by the winning side. This was emphatically not the case. It was a great Celtic victory commemorated up to this day.

Clearly the new Celtic club had started something. Little else went right for their supporters in their lives, but now they had something to cheer about. Home Rule for Ireland was now confidently predicted by the illogical, and now there was at least some payback for the landlords, the gombeen men, the British Army, the coffin ships and the potato famine. There was at least one part of the world in the evergrowing Irish diaspora where the wearing of the green would be something associated with pride and achievement.

Willie Maley himself played in the game and would often say that the scenes that he saw that day as the Scottish Cup was brought back in the horse-drawn charabanc from the Alexandra Hotel in Bath Street to the Calton in the East End changed his life and made him decide that from now on he would dedicate himself to the cause of this great club. He saw the destitute, the paupers, the children with no shoes, the beggars – he had seen all this before – but this time they had smiles on their faces, and he had helped to put the smiles there. 'Our Bhoys Have Won the Cup' was the cry. They were 'the risen people'.

As for the effect that this victory had on Celtic's supporters, we, of course, also have this brilliantly graphic description from the *Scottish Referee* of the celebrations in the streets of the Celtic heartland that night. 'Even the women lent a hand, and helped in no small measure to make the rejoicings hearty. But it was when the boys came marching home from the aristocratic Ibrox that the fun began in earnest ... Bands? You ought to have seen them. They perambulated the whole district until well on in the evening ... Truly the East End was a perfect turmoil until the very early hours of the Sunday, and many of the crowd won't be able to get over the rejoicing racket for days to come.'

Perhaps the only modern parallel to this would be 1967. Those of us who recall the homecoming on Friday, 26 May 1967 when the bus came along London Road, big Jock famously emerged with the big cup, then a lorry (!) took the players round the ground to show off the beautifully ugly trophy to the huge appreciative crowd. This was, once again, 'the risen people', and the euphoric glow lasted for months. Tellingly, so many people now began to say, 'Of course, I have always been a Celtic supporter ...' when the facts of their past life did not really support such a contention. And there was now a slow but significant trickle to the banners of the club of those who were neither Irish nor Catholic but who simply enjoyed good football.

The following year's campaign, with the new Celtic Park now up and running, began in late November with a routine 3-1 win over Linthouse. The week before Christmas saw a 7-0 defeat of inferior opposition in the Fifth King's Royals. Following the turn of the year, more difficult opposition in Third Lanark came to Celtic Park but Celtic disposed of them 5-1, and even the semi-final in early February brought few problems as Celtic beat St Bernard's 5-0, the overawed Edinburgh side playing their first-ever game at this advanced stage of the competition.

So far, no problem (and cup success was achieved parallel to victories in the Scottish League as well), but it was Queen's Park again in the final at Ibrox. This was one of the first Scottish Cup Finals in which Celtic left the competition with a nasty taste in their mouth – twice! The final was scheduled for Ibrox on 25 February. The weather was fine and dry, but the Ibrox pitch was hard and the decision was taken to play the game but only as a friendly and NOT to tell the large crowd (30,000 according to one report) until after the game! It was a familiar leitmotif. This sort of thing had happened before and really lacked logic, for if the conditions were not suitable for a Scottish Cup Final, it was difficult to understand why they were suitable for a friendly. It was seen, once again, as a way of making extra money.

The game began with only a select few knowing that it was a friendly, but tongues always wag in Glasgow, a place where it is difficult to keep a secret. Rumours spread rapidly round the puzzled crowd that it was only a friendly, a supposition strengthened by the demeanour of the players who did not seem to be exerting themselves too much. Tom Towie scored the only goal of the game for Celtic, but this excellent player's moment of glory was in vain – even though many of the crowd had gone home convinced that Celtic had won the Scottish Cup!

The Scotsman newspaper pulled no punches, saying that this was 'discreditable to the officials of the Association, inconsiderate to the members of the public and detrimental to the best interests of the game'. It most certainly was, and the wonder was that there was not more protest or even disorder about this, and that 13,329 were persuaded to turn up to the replay on 11 March. Possibly there was some kind of unofficial boycott, for the attendance was disappointing. It would surely have made more sense and been more considerate to the eager public simply to say that the game was off at an earlier stage and not to have taken money from people under false pretences.

Celtic supporters were entitled to feel sore about 25 February, and they were a great deal sorer after the somewhat ludicrous events of 11 March, Queen's Park's tenth Scottish Cup victory and their last. This time the weather was acceptable and the pitch was fine. Before the game, there had been a difference of opinion about goal nets. They had been in use for some time now, but when Celtic suggested that they might be deployed here, Queen's Park vetoed the idea and Celtic, to their cost as it turned out, did not pursue the matter. Maybe goal nets too 'smacked of professionalism'!

The game was a tough one. Willie Maley sustained a bad facial injury and had to retire and one or two other Celtic players were on the wrong end of coarse challenges. Queen's Park, with the wind behind them, scored first through Sellar, but then came the moment that defined this final. Ten-man Celtic were under pressure and Dan Doyle was compelled to concede a corner kick, as he thought. But the referee thought that the ball might have gone between the posts – and, of course, there were no goal nets! Mr Harrison of Kilmarnock was influenced by Queen's Park (all honourable middle-class amateurs, of course, as distinct from vulgar Irishmen!) who said 'It's a goal, Mr Harrison! It's a goal!' The goal was awarded. Doyle and Kelly protested, but a goal it was and Celtic were 0-2 down and it was not yet half-time.

Things improved in the second half. The wind was now behind Celtic, Maley returned and then Jimmy Blessington scored with a header from a corner kick, and for a long time, it looked as if a fightback was going to happen. But the Queen's Park tackling was robust, and the defence was tight. As a desperate measure Dan Doyle went into the forward line, but the final whistle came with the score still at 2-1. This signalled disappointment for Cullen, Reynolds and Doyle; Maley, Kelly and Dunbar; Towie, Blessington, Madden, McMahon and Campbell, who had probably done well enough to deserve to win. For the supporters, there was the feeling of being cheated. Those of us who recall the Scottish Cup Finals of 1970 and 1984 will have an idea of how our forefathers felt in 1893. Things were hardly helped by the press singing the praises of Queen's Park, including a statement that they won because 'of the excellence of their charging'!

There was consolation when Celtic won the league in 1893, a feat repeated in 1894. 1894 also saw another appearance in the Scottish Cup Final. Hurlford and Albion Rovers were more than competently disposed of before the new year, then St Bernard's came to Celtic Park, were comprehensively hammered 8-1 and blamed it all on Celtic's admittedly primitive floodlighting system, with lights strung up all over the park, but only 15 feet in the air. The game itself was played in daylight, of course, but the lights and the wires still got in the way, according to the Edinburgh men. Their appeal was dismissed, on the grounds, presumably, that electric wires and lights, however deplorable, could hardly explain giving away eight goals!

This brought Celtic to the semi-final against Third Lanark at Old Cathkin Park, and the 12,000 crowd on a fine day in early February saw a really good game with loads of goals and Celtic winning 5-3. Sandy McMahon scored a hat-trick and the other two goals were scored by Jimmy Blessington and Joe Cassidy.

Celtic were thus favourites for the Scottish Cup Final on 17 February 1894 against Rangers. Rangers, founded in 1873, had yet to win the Scottish Cup, something that was already becoming a music hall joke in Glasgow, for their history included a refusal in 1879 to turn up for the replay of the final after they had not got their own way in the first game! This is hard to imagine today and it was hard to imagine in 1894 as well, for this was a new, determined Rangers team.

The weather was wet, the pitch was heavy and Willie Maley, pig-headedly, insisted on playing against doctor's advice. The heavy pitch seemed to militate against Celtic's two tall star forwards, McMahon and Campbell, and although the game was goalless at half-time, Rangers came out in the second half and took command, scoring three goals, while Celtic's solitary counter came from the ailing Maley after the game was more or less over. It was simply one of these occasions where the Celtic historian, however painful an experience it is, must simply hold up his hands and say 'Rangers were the better team'.

There were consolations though. The cosy relationship between the two clubs meant that there was little bitterness (again, hard to imagine today!) and there was not the feeling of having been cheated as there had been the previous year against Queen's Park. In any case, Celtic got their revenge the following week by beating Rangers 3-2 and in so doing, winning the Scottish League. Both clubs congratulated each other on their successes, and as far as we can imagine, the poisonous, toxic element of sectarianism had not yet arrived at Ibrox. It had at a few provincial clubs like St Mirren and Airdrie, but not yet at Rangers.

The next four years of Celtic's Scottish Cup history contained three disappointments and one disaster as the club struggled to find its identity, after its heady early success. The 1897 disaster possibly had to happen in order to bring about changes in the same way as the 2000 disaster with Inverness Caledonian Thistle did in fact bring some good in the long term. But the 1890s were characterised by internal squabbles and did little to dispel the commonly held perception that the problem with the Irish was that they were natural fighters and didn't like each other, let alone the Scots. The 1890s, however, were a learning process, and intelligent men like John Glass, John H. McLaughlin, James Kelly and Willie Maley did the learning. It was also the era of the great Sandy McMahon, Celtic's first real goalscoring hero.

1894/95 saw a strange campaign. It began with an excellent 4-1 defeat of Queen's Park in late November and this was the week after Celtic had won the Glasgow Cup by beating Rangers. Things looked good in spite of a bad injury to Sandy McMahon. They then travelled to Easter Road on 15 December to play Hibs, a club nursing a massive inferiority complex about Celtic in those days. It all centred on the way that Celtic had 'stolen' (if you lived in Edinburgh) players from Hibs when they were in a bad way in 1890 and 1891. Jealousy of Celtic remains, one feels, a large part of the DNA of Hibernian – once again it is Irish v Irish – but it is a complex relationship.

Celtic played badly this day of 15 December 1894 and Hibs won 2-0, but Celtic protested about the eligibility of two Hibs players, Bobby Neil and Michael Murray. The SFA upheld the protest, a replay was ordered two weeks later on a snowy day and John Divers and Dan Doyle scored the goals as Celtic won 2-0. Hibs protested about the second goal which came from a free kick – and in 1895 all free kicks were indirect and a goal could not be scored from them. They threatened a walk-off, and later protested about the eligibility of Charlie McEleny and added a bizarre rider that Celtic's umpire, Paddy Gallagher, had been coaching the side throughout the game. This time the SFA decided that they had had enough protests and declared in favour of Celtic. The bitterness of Hibs towards Celtic intensified.

This result took Celtic to Carolina Port, Dundee to meet Dundee FC, a new club with fairly spectacular financial problems. The first game was frosted off, but the second on 19 January 1895 was possibly the game that resurrected football in Dundee. In front of a massive crowd of 12,000 and many more watching from the hill overlooking the park which gave a virtually uninterrupted view of proceedings, Sawers scored early for the home side and Celtic, without the injured Sandy McMahon, were unable to get an equaliser, although there were several close things. The disappointment of the large local Celtic support and those who had travelled through from Glasgow was keen, but Dundee talked about it for years. Not that it did them a great deal of good, for it was St Bernard's of Edinburgh who won the cup that year.

1896 saw Celtic play only one Scottish Cup tie, and it was a sore one – a 4-2 defeat to Queen's Park before 28,000 at Celtic Park. Celtic were already the winners of the Glasgow Cup and the Scottish League (which was finished before the new year) and were expected to beat Queen's Park. But they were without Barney Battles. Barney had been an excellent defender this year, but had got himself ordered off in a friendly (!) match v Rangers on New Year's Day. His hearing was scheduled for 14 January, three days after the Scottish Cup game with Queen's Park.

But fate took a hand. Hard frost postponed the game on 11 January – a decision much criticised as being 'premature', for a thaw had set in and other games were played that day – and the game was rearranged for 18 January. Barney was suspended for a month (a somewhat draconian decision, for the game in which he was sent off was only a friendly, but then again Barney was not without a little 'previous') and this meant he could not now play against Queen's Park. Celtic supporters, as is their wont on occasion, detected conspiracies here, but in fact, Queen's Park simply played better than Celtic did and Celtic, without the influential Battles, lost 2-4, in spite of having been 2-1 up at half-time.

And now we come to the game that sent shudders up and down Celtic spines for the next 60 or 70 years. Arthurlie on 9 January 1897! Celtic, frankly, were on the point of collapse. Three players, Battles, Meehan and Divers, were suspended for their part in the strike of November 1896, Maley had retired, McMahon, Madden, Dunbar and McEleny were injured, Doyle and Gilhooly did not turn up for reasons still unexplained and Celtic started the game with only seven men as a result of the malfunctioning of trains and the general incompetence of the committee. Eventually another four were able to take the field, but the damage was already being done.

The pitch at Dunterlie Park, Barrhead had a distinct slope (although it is difficult to go along with *The Celtic Story*'s hyperbole that 'a player taking a corner kick had much the same view of the goalmouth as a person leaning from a second storey window would have of the scene below') and Arthurlie won 4-2. This result imperilled the very existence of Celtic, and the only good thing that could be said about this game was that it led to the necessary changes at Celtic Park, which, of course, included, on the playing side, the appointment of Willie Maley as 'secretary' in the first instance but de facto manager, and indeed, according to his enemies, 'dictator'!

In one of these coincidences that no one could quite believe, Celtic were drawn once again at Arthurlie the following year, 1898. In spite of much talk about conspiracies, lightning striking twice and there being a hex on Celtic in the Scottish Cup, everyone turned up this year and did their job and Celtic won 7-0 to the intense disappointment of all the pressmen who had turned up for another big scoop. But the success was short-lived, for the team went down in the next round to Third Lanark at Cathkin, an honourable defeat but a defeat nevertheless, and Celtic had now gone six years without winning the Scottish Cup. They were doing well enough in the Scottish League and the two Glasgow competitions, but the Scottish Cup was becoming elusive – and it was the most important competition of the lot.

1899, however, saw Celtic achieve their second Scottish Cup success. Celtic, en route to the final, beat Galloway Royal Volunteers at Dalbeattie, and St Bernard's, Queen's Park and Port Glasgow Athletic at Celtic Park. The Queen's Park game was started at Hampden on 18 February but was stopped because of fog and bad light after 67 minutes with Celtic 4-2 up. This did not go down well at all with the Celtic fans who had paid one shilling (double the normal charge) to get in and demanded either the continuation of the game or their money back. In the event, they got neither and had to be dispersed by the constabulary.

Celtic now suggested that only the remaining 23 minutes should be played the next Saturday. The SFA, however, ordered a full replay, but perhaps worried about crowd disorder, decreed illogically that the game should be played at Celtic Park where the admission charge would be the normal 'sicky' (sixpence, half a shilling). There might still have been trouble if the result had gone the other way, but before a huge crowd of 35,000, Celtic won 2-1, both goals coming from Sandy McMahon, now called 'the Duke', either because of a French politician called McMahon, or, more likely, because of his slight resemblance to the Duke of Wellington, the hero of Waterloo. Sometimes, he was even called Alexander the Great.

Having defeated Port Glasgow in the semi-final, Celtic now discovered that Rangers were the opponents in the 1899 final. Frankly, they were a better team than Celtic whom they had beaten twice in the Scottish League on their way to winning it with a 100 per cent record. Well organised by William Wilton (a close friend of Willie Maley), Rangers were also the cup winners for the past two years and thus had the opportunity of winning the trophy three years in a row to emulate the achievement of Queen's Park and Vale of Leven. Not only that, but no club had as yet won the Scottish League and the Scottish Cup in the same season. The 'double' had now been done twice in England by Preston North End and Aston Villa, but not yet in Scotland.

The game was played at Hampden on the pleasant, sunny, spring day of 22 April. The gates were closed at 3.30pm, half an hour before kick-off, with 25,000 inside. More might have been crammed in, but the authorities were unwilling to take any sort of risk, for the streets outside were jam-packed with spectators who had all arrived by various kinds of transport including the new craze of a 'horseless carriage'. Horses were still very much in vogue though, and we were now beginning to see the development of a 'supporters' bus' whereby individuals from any given area would join together to hire a horse-drawn charabanc to take them to and from the game. Dog carts were still used as well, but quite a lot of supporters simply walked on such a lovely day. Paddy Gallagher, one of the heroes of 1892, now suffering from tuberculosis, appeared from the Bridge of Allan Sanatorium to cheer on his old mates, even though he was now looking 'a shadow of his old self'.

Celtic had been to Loch Katrine for a few days before the game. This was very much one of Maley's ideas, and in this respect he was ahead of his time. But he believed that players would benefit from intensive training, good hotel food and fresh air, not to mention each other's company for a few days. He could also keep an eye on any alcoholic overindulgence. The son of a soldier was always likely to approve of such arrangements, and it was also good for these young men to get away from the dirt and filth of Glasgow for a day or two. He also looked upon it as a social occasion, and when staying at a hotel, his players would always be encouraged to join in the dancing and the singing soirees that were held at night, while he himself talked charmingly to rich widows. It was important to Maley that the name 'Celtic' would have good connotations.

The Scottish Cup Final turned out to be one of Celtic's best performances of their early years as they beat Rangers 2-0 with a glorious header from 'the Duke' and then a late goal from John Hodge, after the Celtic half-back line of Battles, Marshall and King had taken a grip of the game. Jack Bell had been badly injured and really should have gone off, but stayed on as nuisance value, and thus McArthur, Welford and Storrier; Battles, Marshall and King; Hodge, Campbell, Divers, McMahon and Bell carried off Celtic's second Scottish Cup. It was a sporting game according to contemporary reports with the relationship between Celtic and Rangers still an excellent one.

Both teams started brightly and both goalkeepers were soon in action with Celtic possibly having the edge on pressure. McMahon headed narrowly past, and similarly a shot from the same man was lacking only slightly in accuracy, but then a moment later McMahon was required at the other end to head off his own line when McArthur was beaten.

The game had been very even in the first half as both sides took time to settle. Things took a nasty turn, however, when Celtic's left-winger Jack Bell was badly fouled by Rangers' notorious Nick Smith. Bell wanted to come off, and in truth was of little use to his team-mates, but Maley insisted that he stayed on the field to hobble about for nuisance value, if nothing else. But Celtic were now gradually taking the ascendancy and in the 67th minute, halfway through the second half, won a corner on the right. Johnny Hodge took it, swung over a high hanging ball and up rose the Duke to head home a glorious header. It was in the tradition of the goal he had headed home in 1892 and it would become the prototype and template for future Scottish Cup Final headed goals – McGrory in 1925, McNeill in 1965 and 1969, McGarvey in 1985, McAvennie in 1988, van Hooijdonk in 1995.

This event 'created bedlam among the Celtic supporters' as they 'patted each other on the back and hurled their green favours in the air'. There was, however, more than a little tension and worry in the air over the next 20 minutes. Two things worried the support – one was whether the players would give in to commercial pressures from their directors and concede a goal to allow a replay and another big gate. The other was whether Celtic might simply not believe that they could beat Rangers and would cave in, particularly as with the injury to Jack Bell, they were virtually a man short. Their fears on both accounts were groundless.

Now Celtic took a firm grip of the game with Battles in particular winning every ball that came his way and feeding the forwards with some superb passes. Jack Bell, although badly crippled, still played a vital part in the second goal when a ball spun off a Rangers defender and came to Bell, who immediately kicked it across the field with his one serviceable foot towards Johnny Hodge. Hodge collected the ball and ran through a static Rangers defence, who appealed half-heartedly for some infringement, to score Celtic's second and decisive goal. The game finished amidst intense cheering and singing with the words of 'A Nation Once Again' being converted into 'The Scottish Cup Once Again' even though the words did not quite fit! It was a great Celtic occasion, and McMahon was the hero of the hour.

The Glasgow Herald said 'the better team won definitely', and Celtic returned to their heartlands later that night with the Scottish Cup. The celebrations recalled those of seven years earlier when the cup was last won, but there was an element of relief in the celebrations too. The so-called invincible Rangers had been beaten.

The cup had been presented once again in the Bath Street Hotel, and Celtic's director John H. McLaughlin spoke magnanimously about Rangers and claimed (somewhat prematurely, one feels!) that 'sectarianism was a dead letter' in Scottish football, and that Celtic would take anyone 'from all quarters, regardless of sect'.

Rangers, although disappointed at not having emulated the feat of Queen's Park and Vale of Leven in winning the Scottish Cup three years in a row, were in attendance and were 'perfect sportsmen'. It was a fine night for Celtic, however, and for Sandy McMahon. He now had two Scottish Cup medals, and he had scored in both, his headed goal in both cases being the talk of the fast-growing Celtic support who raised their hero worship of the Duke to ever higher and higher levels.

The Glasgow Observer the following week goes into overdrive, with 'Man In the Know' stating that it was Celtic's fitness which won the cup. Several players are singled out. James Welford, who now had the distinction of having won a Scottish Cup medal and an English one – the only Englishman to do so – was 'superb' at right-back, and of the forwards, John Divers is quixotically described thus: 'his arms move in windmill fashion and his elbows are always meeting with an opponent's ribs, accidentally of course', whereas McMahon and Campbell were 'quieter but no less effective'.

The seven years without the Scottish Cup would not recur for a long time. McMahon and Campbell had now won two Scottish Cup medals, and Campbell and Welford now each had a Scottish Cup medal to go with the English Cup medals that they had won with Aston

Villa, Campbell in 1897 and Welford in 1895. What would the new century bring?

Season 1888/89: Finalists

01/09/1888	Shettleston	home	5-1	Goalscorers untraced
22/09/1888	Cowlairs	home	8-0	Dunbar 3, McCallum 2, Kelly, T. Maley, Groves
13/10/1888	Albion Rovers	home	4-1	Groves, 3 untraced
03/11/1888	St Bernard's	away	4-1	Groves 2, McCallum, T. Maley
24/11/1888	Clyde	home	0-1	

Celtic protested

08/12/1888	Clyde	home	9-2	T. Maley 3, Groves 2, McCallum 2, McLaren, Coleman
15/12/1888	East Stirlingshire	away	2-1	McCallum 2
12/01/1889	Dumbarton	away	4-1	Groves 3, McCallum
02/02/1889	Third Lanark	Hampden	0-3	

Declared unofficial because of snow

09/02/1889	Third Lanark	Hampden	1-2	McCallum

Season 1889/90: First Round

07/09/1889	Queen's Park	home	0-0	

Abandoned because of encroachment

14/09/1889	Queen's Park	away	1-2	Dowds

Season 1890/91: Quarter-Finals

06/09/1890	Rangers	home	1-0	Groves
27/09/1890	Carfin Shamrock	home	2-2	Madden 2
04/10/1890	Carfin Shamrock	away	3-1	Groves, Dowds, og
18/10/1890	Wishaw Thistle	away	6-2	Madden 2, Dowds, Campbell, 2 untraced
08/11/1890	Dundee OB	away	3-1	Crossan 2, Coleman
29/11/1890	Larkhall Royal Albert	away	2-2	2 untraced

Game played as friendly because of weather

06/12/1890	Larkhall Royal Albert	away	4-0	McLaren, Madden, Campbell 2

Game abandoned after pitch invasion

13/12/1890	Larkhall Royal Albert	Ibrox	2-0	Crossan, Campbell
20/12/1890	Dumbarton	away	0-3	

Season 1891/92: Winners

28/11/1891	St Mirren	away	4-2	Madden, McMahon, W. Maley, og
19/12/1891	Kilmarnock Athletic	home	3-0	Brady 2, Dowds
23/01/1892	Cowlairs	home	4-1	Brady 2, Madden, McMahon
06/02/1892	Rangers	home	5-3	Brady 2, Cunningham, McMahon, Campbell
12/03/1892	Queen's Park	Ibrox	1-0	Campbell
09/04/1892	Queen's Park	Ibrox	5-1	Campbell 2, McMahon 2, og

Season 1892/93: Finalists

26/11/1892	Linthouse	home	3-1	McMahon 2, Madden
17/12/1892	Fifth King's Royal Volunteers	home	7-0	Madden 5, Blessington, Campbell
02/01/1893	Third Lanark	home	5-1	McMahon 3, Towie 2
04/02/1893	St Bernard's	home	5-0	Madden 3, Blessington 2
25/02/1893	Queen's Park	Ibrox	1-0	Towie

Game played as friendly because of hard pitch

11/03/1893	Queen's Park	Ibrox	1-2	Blessington

Season 1893/94: Finalists

25/11/1893	Hurlford	home	6-0	Blessington 2, Campbell 2, McMahon, Cassidy
16/12/1893	Albion Rovers	home	7-0	Cassidy 4, Madden 2, Blessington
13/01/1894	St Bernard's	home	8-1	McMahon 4, Madden 2, Cassidy, W. Maley
03/02/1894	Third Lanark	away	5-3	McMahon 3, Blessington, Cassidy
17/02/1894	Rangers	Hampden	1-3	W. Maley

Season 1894/95: Quarter-Finals

24/11/1894	Queen's Park	home	4-1	Campbell 3, Divers
15/12/1894	Hibs	away	0-2	

Celtic protested about ineligibility of two Hibs players

29/12/1894	Hibs	away	2-0	Campbell, Divers
19/01/1895	Dundee	away	0-1	

Season 1895/96: First Round

18/01/1896	Queen's Park	home	2-4	Blessington, Doyle

Season 1896/97: First Round
09/01/1897 Arthurlie   away   2-4   Ferguson, McIlvenny

Season 1897/98: Second Round
08/01/1898 Arthurlie   away   7-0   McMahon2, Henderson2, Allan, Goldie, Campbell

22/01/1898 Third Lanark   away   2-3   Campbell, King

Season 1898/99: Winners
14/01/1899 Sixth Galloway Royal away   8-1   McMahon 3, Hodge 2, Volunteers   King, Divers, Campbell

04/02/1899 St Bernard's   home   3-0   McMahon, Hodge, Campbell

18/02/1899 Queen's Park   away   4-2   McMahon 2, Campbell, Divers

Game abandoned because of bad light
25/02/1899 Queen's Park   home   2-1   McMahon 2

11/03/1899 Port Glasgow   home   4-1   Bell 2, McMahon, Divers

22/04/1899 Rangers   Hampden   2-0   McMahon, Hodge

CHAPTER TWO

'THE CELTS OF OLD'

1900–1914

A GLORIOUS period in Celtic's history, particularly their Scottish Cup history, now begins. In the 15 inclusive years between 1900 and 1914, Celtic won the Scottish Cup seven times, reached another three finals and reached the semi-finals another twice in addition. Their league form was equally impressive, and not without cause did Willie Maley in his old age in the 1950s keep talking and writing, particularly in the *Evening Times*, about his great team whom he always called 'the Celts of old'. The implied comparison with those of the current generation was not always appreciated.

It was also the age in which Celtic established themselves not only as Scotland's number one team, but also a great British and indeed European superpower in the game of football. Horizons were extended, and instead of wallowing in being a self-pitying, victimised, ethnic minority (although that motif was by no means entirely absent from the Celtic psyche – and arguably still exists), Celtic now showed the world how football should be played and showed in so doing that there were some things that the Scottish/Irish could do well. 'He taught them how to play football, He made them the greatest of them all' are a lot more than merely lyrics to a song. They are almost an expression of identity.

And it was now a lot more than just the Irish immigrants. To a far greater extent than in the 1890s, players from other backgrounds were employed and advanced. The best example of this is, of course, James Young, commonly known as 'Sunny Jim', a man from an undeniably Scottish Ayrshire background and with an English wife. He became as much of a hero to the Celtic fans as Scott Brown is today – and that is saying something! There were also Eck McNair, Alec Bennett, Jimmy Hay, Jamie Weir, Davie McLean, Davie Adams and many, many more men of different ethnicity but still good enough to be called a Celt.

And there was more than just the playing of football games. When his team was on tour or at some hydropathic hotel, Maley continued the tradition of insisting that his players 'did their bit' at entertaining other guests with song and recitations after the evening meal. Maley himself, sociable, genial and charming, led the way. After the break-up of his own marriage, he was by no means averse to impressing the ladies, but he also made sure that there were no scandals.

1900 saw the news dominated by the war in South Africa, but it also saw Celtic's third Scottish Cup triumph. Rangers had won the league for the second year in a row by some distance, but Celtic were determined that they would not give up the Scottish Cup without a fight. Bo'ness, Port Glasgow and Kilmarnock caused few problems for Celtic, although the Port Glasgow game at Clune Park was marked by some racial abuse about the Irish. It also saw a crater appear on the pitch in the course of the game (incredibly) on a spot where an old drain had existed! It was a good game to get out of the way as Johnny Campbell scored twice, Pat Gilhooly scored twice and almost inevitably, Sandy McMahon scored as well.

It was Rangers at Ibrox for the semi-final. Rangers, league champions in 1899 and 1900, were the favourites, but after Rangers took the lead, Celtic equalised through a penalty from Johnny Campbell, then a good strike from Jack Bell. Indeed, it was with almost the last kick of the game that Rangers equalised through McPherson. But if Rangers were surprised by Celtic at Ibrox, they must have been thunderstruck two weeks later on 10 March in the replay at Celtic Park when Celtic simply took them apart, the forward line of Hodge, Campbell, Divers, McMahon and Bell running amok and 'staggering humanity' as Sandy McMahon put it in a conscious echo of Paul Kruger, the leader of the Boers. McMahon himself scored twice, and Johnny Hodge and Jack Bell once each as Rangers were put to the sword to the delight of the 32,000 crowd.

And so it was a repeat of the 1892 and 1893 cup finals at Ibrox on 14 April 1900. Things were changing, however, now that we were into the 20th century. Professionalism now having been legalised for a few years, Queen's Park's paternalistic and not always benevolent control over Scottish football had been slackening for some time and now had been almost broken with the rise of Rangers and Celtic. This game, a 4-3 victory for Celtic, symbolised the new trend and the new century. The game was played at the recently redeveloped Ibrox on a very blustery, windy day – it became known as the hurricane final – and it was as if the age of the genteel amateur was being blown away and replaced by the world of the tough and committed professional. Queen's Park never again appeared in a Scottish Cup Final, but bizarrely still, 120 years later, remain, with ten triumphs, third in the list of Scottish Cup winners – a fact that does not say very much for teams like Hearts, Hibs and Aberdeen.

Ibrox, until they built the high terracing at the Broomloan Road end, was a rather exposed ground when the wind came from the west as it tends to do in Scotland, and today it was more than just a stiff breeze. In modern times, it would have been given a name – in 1900 Storm Sandy might have been appropriate nomenclature in honour of Sandy McMahon – but even without a name, in the circumstances, no one could really expect a great, classic game of football. Before a crowd of only 15,000 – it was a holiday weekend, a false rumour spread to the effect that the game was off due to storm damage to the ground and the admission price was, once again, a shilling, double the normal – Celtic won the toss, but initially failed to capitalise and Queen's Park scored against the wind. However, Celtic then settled and by half-time were 3-1 up with goals from Sandy McMahon, John Divers and Jack Bell.

Half-time, however, brought the realisation that Celtic now had to face the wind, but after ten minutes of hard work, Divers broke away to score and put Celtic 4-1 up. Things now looked good, but Queen's Park were not yet out of it, and they managed to score twice before the 80th minute, making the last ten minutes a desperate affair. In such circumstances, experienced men like McMahon and Battles are worth their weight in gold. Sometimes they unashamedly wasted time, but they never made the mistake of the big boot up the park (it would have come straight back again!) and they kept the ball on the ground, playing a short passing game. And they had the players who were able to do it.

Dan McArthur in the goal had a great game as well, twice at the very death bringing off saves that, had he not, might have changed the destination of the Scottish Cup and indeed the entire future of both Queen's Park and Celtic, but full time came and Celtic's team of McArthur, Storrier and Battles; Russell, Marshall and Orr; Hodge, Campbell, Divers, McMahon and Bell had won Celtic's third Scottish Cup. Rangers may have won the Scottish League for two years in a row – indeed, there were times when they looked virtually unbeatable – but Celtic had for the past two years won the trophy that really mattered, the Scottish Cup. Celtic, very definitely, had the last laugh.

Celtic opened their 1901 Scottish Cup campaign with the visit of Rangers to Celtic Park. Having lost their New Year's Day league game at Ibrox, Celtic then took their players 'doon the watter' to Rothesay for special training. It clearly worked, for having arrived back on the morning of the game, 12 January, they proceeded to beat Rangers 1-0, the only goal of the game coming from

Willie McOustra, one of the few moments of glory in this man's career. Celtic's man of the match was goalkeeper Dan McArthur, but he was carried off with a bad injury 15 minutes from time and his place was taken by John Divers, who showed equal courage in the last few minutes.

In the next round, Celtic's game against Kilmarnock was played as a friendly because the referee, having misread a telegram, thought that the game was off! To their credit, Celtic did 'the handsome thing' by giving all the crowd a ticket for the proper game which had to be delayed for two weeks because on the intervening week was the funeral of Queen Victoria. Celtic duly beat Kilmarnock 6-0, and this brought them to Dens Park, Dundee to play the Dundee side who had eliminated them from the Scottish Cup in 1895.

Dundee had moved from Carolina Port. Dens Park was still a new ground in 1901, and some 'staging' was used to give spectators a better view at the west end of the ground. It collapsed causing a few injures but only minor ones. Celtic scored early on through Rab Findlay, and then held out against furious Dundee pressure with reserve goalkeeper Willie Donnelly distinguishing himself. 'Ilka doggie has his day', and this was the 'day' of Willie Donnelly, who also had the problem of the occasional encroaching spectator to deal with!

Celtic were thus in the semi-final where they beat St Mirren at Celtic Park 1-0 in an undistinguished sort of a match to reach their seventh Scottish Cup Final in their 13 years of existence. This time their opponents were to be Hearts, who had won the cup in 1891 and 1896 and those who believed in that sort of thing were confident that they would win it again this year in 1901, some five years after the last one. They did indeed win it, but for Celtic it was heartbreak and for one great player in particular, a disaster.

The game was played at Ibrox on 6 April 1901. The weather was wet, and the SFA did themselves no favours, yet again, by charging one shilling to get in. Celtic's illustrious administrator John H. McLaughlin sagely pointed out that halving the price would have doubled the crowd, and the high charge probably favoured the better-heeled, genteel folk from Edinburgh who travelled through on the trains in great numbers.

The game was even, but Celtic's goalkeeper Dan McArthur (possibly suffering from the long-term effect of concussion, so many times brought about by his constant bravery in diving at the feet of opponents) was having a nightmare with the wet, greasy ball. He was slow to the first goal, failed to shout to defender Bob Davidson for the second and thus the ball bounced off Davidson to a Hearts attacker and then McArthur could only parry a shot which led to the third. Thus Celtic were 3-1 down with half an hour to go.

But the long tradition of fighting back in cup finals, already noticed in 1892, continued here. First of all Jimmy Quinn charged down the left wing, beat six (according to reliable newspaper reports) Hearts men and scored a goal which we can now only imagine. (Those of us alive in the 1960s saw the occasional John Hughes goal like this!) Then Sandy McMahon scored one of his trademark goals with a header from a corner kick. 3-3! Ten minutes remained and now the exit gates were opened to let the crowd out, but in so doing allowed thousands of impoverished Celtic supporters to rush in and lend their support to their favourites. Sadly all that they saw was bad. In the very last minute, after some great Celtic pressure, Hearts ran up the field, Bobby Walker shot, then yet another fumble from the luckless Dan McArthur, and a goal was scored from the rebound. In all our long history there was never a greater disappointment than this, nor any more disconsolate figure than Dan McArthur. He had been a great servant of the club, but this was his nightmare. It would stay with him until his death in 1943.

The truth of the matter, however, was that 1901 and 1902 were not vintage Celtic years, and that in 1901, even allowing for Celtic's heartbreak at the end, Hearts were probably well worth their win. Celtic were in transition as their young manager Willie Maley kept looking for emerging young talent from various parts of Scotland. He would eventually be phenomenally successful, but such operations usually take a great deal of time.

1902 brought the end of the Boer War (a despicable piece of imperialist bullying which, under the guise of 'patriotism', 'honour' and 'service' cost many British lives to steal South Africa's diamonds) and it also saw the first Ibrox disaster when 26 people were killed at the Scotland v England international match on 5 April. The Scottish Cup Final between Celtic and Hibs was due to be played there the following week, but had to be postponed and Ibrox was out of commission. The final was eventually played three weeks later as a very low-key affair at Celtic Park (now the only available venue as the new Hampden was not yet built and the old Hampden was now considered to be too risky in the circumstances).

Nevertheless, even allowing for 'the nation being in shock' (as the papers kept saying) there was little doubt that Celtic played very badly in the final and Andy McGeachan's back-heeler was the only goal of the game for Hibs who thus won the Scottish Cup for the second time. One hopes that the Hibs supporters enjoyed their triumph, for none of them would be around 114 years later when they next won the trophy! It was often said that as the gloating Hibernian players climbed on their charabanc sneering at the Celtic players and supporters, an old gypsy woman put a curse on them. If this were the case, it was a very successful hex indeed! They had adapted a Boer War musical song for the purpose:

'Goodbye Celtic, we must leave you!
Though it breaks our hearts to go!
We are off to Edinburgh,
The Scottish Cup to show!'

Celtic's route to this final had not been without its interest. First Thornliebank conceded their ground rights in favour of a substantial fee and duly lost 3-0, then Celtic made their first-ever competitive trip to Arbroath on Burns Day, 25 January. They discovered then what a bitter wind there is at the Gayfield ground where the North Sea is only a matter of feet away, and 'the snow fell in pancakes' in the slightly hyperbolic words of the local press. Arbroath had, like Thornliebank, been offered a bribe to swop grounds, but laudably refused and were rewarded with a good crowd and a great game of football. It was 2-2 at half-time, but the full-time training of Celtic told in the end with the old stagers McMahon and Campbell getting the better of the Arbroath defence, as Celtic squeezed through 3-2.

The month of February was all about Celtic v Hearts. First they played at Parkhead in the despised Inter City League in bad weather which was declared a friendly, then they played at Tynecastle in the Scottish Cup – also declared a friendly because of a frozen pitch. Then they played the first real Scottish Cup game at Tynecastle – a tactless 1-1 draw which did little to stop the rumours of 'fixes' and 'stitches up', before eventually on 22 February 1902, Celtic won through at Parkhead. Celtic had been at Rothesay for special training the previous midweek, and this may have helped. After an early reverse they took control of the game and Sandy McMahon scored twice to put Celtic into the semi-final. It was some revenge for last year's defeat in the final.

The semi-final on 22 March was against St Mirren for the second year in a row. Games between these two had a reputation for being tough affairs with not a little crowd trouble as well if the game were played in Paisley. This one was no exception. George Livingstone scored early on, Johnny Campbell added another and although the Saints had pulled one back before half-time, Tommy McDermott's third goal for Celtic was the vital one, and they were able to stave off St Mirren's late rally. On the same day Rangers, now league champions for four years in a row, went down to Hibs in the other semi-final and thus we had the 'Irish' cup final of Hibs v Celtic or as *The Dundee Courier* put it, 'Greek meeting Greek'.

If 1902 was disappointing, 1903 was a great deal worse. St Mirren featured again! An incredible total of six Saturdays were required before Celtic could get past St Mirren. There were two postponements, two draws and an abandonment before Celtic eventually did the business by beating them 4-0 on St Valentine's Day, the process having started on 10 January! There was every indication that the supporters were highly scunnered by the whole business (which did indeed line a few pockets, it has to be said!) and maybe this was reflected in the meagre attendance for the 2-0 win over Port Glasgow in the next round. The whole sorry business came to a shuddering halt on 28 February when Celtic played their worst game for many years to lose three first-half goals to Rangers before 40,000 bewildered fans at Celtic Park.

The good news about the Scottish Cup disaster of 1903 was that Celtic and Maley did learn. 'Before we can taste the fruits of victory, we must also sample the bitterness of defeat,' said Maley. It was the end of an era and time to rebuild. Barney Battles, Sandy McMahon and Johnny Campbell had served Celtic well and had to be disposed of (although a mistake was made in the case of Johnny Campbell who went on to become a success with Third Lanark), Watson, Murray and McDermott were possibly not really Celtic class, and although there was talent already there in the shape of Jimmy McMenemy and Jimmy Quinn, they were still raw. But the astute Willie Maley saw all that, and in a few years' time he had, in the words of the song, 'made them the greatest of them all'.

It was the Scottish Cup of 1904 which proved to be the launching pad. 1903/04 was different for many reasons. There was now a huge new stadium at Hampden built to challenge Celtic Park, Celtic started the season playing in green and white horizontal stripes, hoops, rather than the vertical ones – something that made them look leaner, fitter and faster – and Celtic now had on their books the man who was to change it all – James Young, 'Sunny Jim' – as the half-back line of Young, Loney and Hay came together.

The Scottish Cup saw a walkover in the first round when Stanley of Perthshire scratched, then a 4-0 victory over St Bernard's at the Gymnasium Ground in Edinburgh before three games were necessary to beat Dundee. The first two games were tight, but the third saw Celtic simply go up a gear and win 5-0. The semi-final against this year's league champions Third Lanark, with Johnny Campbell now in their ranks, attracted 36,000 to Celtic Park on a wet day, and they saw Celtic struggle and go one behind to a talented Third Lanark side, until Bobby Muir equalised and Jimmy Quinn scored the winner.

With Rangers having defeated Morton in the other semi-final, we now had the spectacle of Glasgow's two best-supported professional sides playing in the first Scottish Cup Final, on 16 April 1904, at the new and very impressive Hampden Park before what was described as a 'huge crowd' (as indeed it was for the times) of about 65,000. It was the first chance the press had to see this new, well-appointed stadium with its many turnstiles, good press facilities and 'conveniences' (as they are coyly described) for gentlemen, and even a 'rest room' for ladies.

Maley had had a problem with selection when his centre-forward Alec Bennett, a man from a Rangers-supporting background, had revealed a distinct reluctance to play. Maley decided not to force the issue, used words like 'ill', 'indisposed' and 'flu' to explain Bennett's absence and put Jimmy Quinn in the centre-forward position with Peter Somers at inside-left. It was one of his best-ever decisions.

But it did not look like that at the start, for a nervous Celtic defence, with goalkeeper Davie Adams looking particularly ill at ease, conceded two early goals. But enter Jimmy Quinn for what is possibly the most famous Scottish Cup Final of them all. Before half-time, Celtic were level, with Quinn having raced through two Rangers defenders to score the first, and then Quinn finished a Bobby Muir cross for the second. The second half was hard-fought and even, until well within the last ten minutes in what was almost a carbon copy of the first goal, the 'Croy Express' charged through two Rangers defenders once again to score before being 'nearly dismembered by the wild embrace of his mates'. Another report describes how a spectator watched him walk back to the centre line 'as cool as hell' when everyone else was going crazy round about him.

The half-back line of Young, Loney and Hay then closed down the game at the halfway line and Celtic's team of Adams, MacLeod and Orr; Young, Loney and Hay; Muir, McMenemy, Quinn, Somers and Hamilton saw Celtic home to win their fourth Scottish Cup to a great cacophony of 'bugles and other instruments, far from musical' of the Celtic support which 'came up from the slopes' as the *Dundee Evening Post* put it.

Quinn, modest, self-effacing and shy, was deservedly the hero of the hour and the talk of all Scotland – a status he would enjoy for the next ten years – but he was famous for other reasons as well, particularly the next year following the semi-final against Rangers on 25 March 1905. Dumfries (not Queen of the South as we know them now) put up some resistance in the first round, but Lochgelly United and Partick Thistle were swept aside with little bother to set up this semi-final clash against Rangers – and by now, the term 'Old Firm' had been coined and was freely used in token of their undeniable ability to make money. Neutral venues were not used for semi-finals until 1912, and this game was played at Celtic Park.

The game became a 'cause célèbre', as much talked about in Scotland as the Dreyfus Case in France a decade previously. There was certainly a whiff of injustice about it all, but there is no disputing that the riotous scenes were caused by Celtic supporters. In any case, Rangers were 2-0 up, and Celtic were down to ten men, Donnie MacLeod having been taken off injured. Rangers had just scored their second goal in the 80th minute, and a fightback, though not impossible from this fine Celtic team, was distinctly unlikely, especially as they had only ten men, shortly to be reduced to nine. Alec Craig, Rangers' full-back, slipped on the wet turf and to break his fall, grabbed Jimmy Quinn as he fell to the ground. Quinn shook his leg to get free of Craig's arm, the referee

Tom Robertson interpreted this as a kick and Quinn was sent off. Some idiots in the crowd invaded the field, the teams had to be taken off, the ground was temporarily cleared, the players came out again, another invasion followed and Celtic decided to concede the tie. They would have lost it in any case.

The press turned on Quinn, but significantly two Rangers players, Alec Craig and Jimmy Stark, did not. Craig, a decent man, wrote a letter to the SFA giving the truth of the incident and Stark told the press 'there was no kicking'. But Quinn was not allowed to call either Craig or Stark at his hearing and was suspended for a month (thereby depriving him of a Scotland cap against England in a game where England won 1-0 but might not have if Quinn had been there!) and his appeal was turned down. It was probably not correct to say that this was the birth of the Celtic paranoia and the conception that the world was against them (such feelings had already been around for a few years) but the Quinn case certainly stoked the fires. It was also true, however, that even with Jimmy Quinn on the park, Rangers would probably still have won the game.

Celtic had their revenge when they won the Scottish League (by a play-off) in early May 1905. It was the first time since 1898 and they would win the league again in 1906, 1907, 1908, 1909 and 1910 but the Scottish Cup campaign of 1906 was a disappointment. It had started well at a very crowded Dens Park (about 30,000 attended according to some reports) at the end of January where Celtic edged through 2-1 thanks to an own goal and then a late one from Jimmy Quinn (*The Dundee Courier* uses the word 'lucky' to describe Celtic, but then again it would, wouldn't it?). Bo'ness were then dispatched 3-0 without any bother to set up the tie of the round against Hearts at Parkhead.

The attendance was 50,000 and there were several injuries when a barricade collapsed under the pressure of the crowd. If Celtic had been lucky to beat Dundee, their luck deserted them against Hearts, for after leading at half-time through McMenemy, Celtic conceded a goal just after the restart and although the game swung to and fro, it was Menzies of Hearts who got the winner. Hearts went on to win the Scottish Cup that year, thus completing a remarkable sequence of winning it every five years in 1891, 1896, 1901 and 1906. It would be 50 years before they won it again, and people said that Scotland was a strange country where the Scottish Cup and the Scottish capital were not on speaking terms.

But Celtic would have better luck in 1907. No Scottish team had as yet won a 'double' of the Scottish League and Scottish Cup in the same season (both Aston Villa in 1897 and Preston North End in 1889 had done so in England, and Rangers had come close in Scotland in 1899). The superb Celtic team, now nearing the peak of their abilities but still young and fiercely committed, were well clear in the league, and there was thus some extra pressure on them to do well in the Scottish Cup, with Willie Maley losing no opportunity to talk up their chances and to tell them how good they were.

But early 1907 saw Celtic without the central backbone of their team. Willie Loney was out badly injured and Jimmy Quinn was serving a two-month suspension, once again as a result of a game against Rangers and once again with a feeling of injustice about it. Alec McNair stepped in to fill Loney's place without a great deal of bother, but the team without Quinn struggled to score goals. However, in the Scottish Cup Clyde were beaten 2-1, before three games were required in February to beat Morton until a Jimmy Hay header won the day.

But Quinn returned in early March. By supreme irony his first game back was against Rangers at Ibrox in the quarter-final of the Scottish Cup! Glasgow was whipped up into a frenzy about this game; 60,000 appeared in spite of intermittent snowstorms, but it was Celtic and Quinn's day. Rangers were so obsessed with marking Quinn that they forgot about the other Celtic forwards. Peter Somers scored early, Jimmy Hay just before half-time and Davie Hamilton soon after half-time to make it as complete a victory as one could have wished for. Not only that, but Jimmy Quinn recaptured the moral high ground. After a crunching tackle from Joe Hendry (the man at least partially responsible for his suspension), designed with no other intention than to provoke Quinn to retaliation, Jimmy got up and limped away. He did not need to do anything else. He had made his point.

There followed two dull games against Hibs in the semi-final, 0-0 in each case, the first at Celtic Park, the second at Easter Road. There were at least two odd things about this second game. One was that it was played on the same day that Scotland were playing England at Newcastle in a 1-1 draw, and the even more surprising thing was that not a single member of this fine Celtic side was chosen to play for Scotland! Less surprising were

the mutterings and raised eyebrows about the fact that a
third game was necessary, it being a common theme for
discussion among supporters in Edwardian Scotland that
cup ties between well-supported teams had a funny habit
of ending up as draws the first time round! When the
second game was also a draw, punters had a tendency to
lose patience, and the press tended to be a lot more direct
in the point they were making!

However all that may be, Celtic at last turned it
on against Hibs the next week, 13 April, with a 3-0
hammering at Celtic Park, leading to the press comment
that 'the beauty of the movements of the McMenemy,
Quinn and Somers trio is unsurpassed in football' – each
of these three players having scored in this rather one-
sided replay, which prevented the possibility of an all-
Edinburgh final, as indeed had happened in 1896.

And so to the Scottish Cup Final against the other
Edinburgh team, Hearts, a team that Celtic met often
in the cup in the Edwardian era. As always in those
days, Hearts were well supported with trains running all
morning to bring supporters to Glasgow, and the railway
companies having the good sense not to up their prices
too much. Severe traffic jams in Glasgow meant that
Hearts's goalkeeper Tommy Allan was caught up in it
all and the game was delayed by quarter of an hour –
the delay also allowing the police more time to pack the
crowd (sometimes given as 50,000 but in all probability
a lot more than that, even though rain continued to fall
steadily) into Hampden to see the cup holders take on the
league champions elect (Celtic would win the league on
the following Wednesday). Hearts were without their star

man Charlie Thomson, and Celtic, still without Willie
Loney, lined up as Adams, MacLeod and Orr; Young,
McNair and Hay; Bennett, McMenemy, Quinn, Somers
and Templeton.

The first half was even but bereft of goalmouth
incidents, and then early in the second half Jimmy Quinn
was tripped in the penalty box. The award of the penalty
was disputed (indeed, Hearts fans would dispute it for
the next 50 years!) but Willie Orr duly sank it, and then
Celtic took total control, scoring twice more, in both
cases, with Peter Somers tap-ins from Bennett crosses.
Once again Jimmy Quinn was marked out of the game
– but what a marvellous decoy he proved to be! – while
everything was totally controlled and set up by the genius
that was Jimmy 'Napoleon' McMenemy.

The game turned out to be a watershed in the history
of Hearts who would not now win another trophy
until the Scottish League Cup of 1954. They had fine
players and a huge support, but never a great team. Two
world wars and an awful lot else would happen before
Edinburgh saw another football triumph. By that time,
football in Edinburgh had lost out to rugby, especially
after Murrayfield was built in 1925.

If 1907 was good for Celtic, 1908 was even better as
they won all four competitions that they entered – the
Scottish League, the Scottish Cup, the Glasgow Cup and
the Glasgow Charity Cup. (In 1907, to the fury of Willie
Maley, they had missed out on the Glasgow Charity Cup!)
The first game in the 1908 Scottish Cup campaign was
against Peebles Rovers at Parkhead, and Celtic won at a
canter against the overawed Borderers. More demanding

was the next game against Rangers at Ibrox – again – and Celtic were without Jimmy Hay, who was recovering from a life-threatening (in 1908) appendicitis operation, and Jimmy Quinn, who had a septic toe. Rangers did themselves few favours by doubling the admission charge and were duly rewarded when only 23,000 turned up to see Celtic dump them out with a 2-1 victory, both goals coming from Quinn's deputy Willie Kivlichan.

Raith Rovers were next at Kirkcaldy, and all the plans to welcome Celtic with local bands playing 'Songs of Ireland' etc. came to naught as the weather was so foul. Celtic won 3-0 without much bother but then they were sent to Aberdeen to play at Pittodrie in the semi-final. Aberdeen were a new club, of course – they had only been founded in 1903 – but on 21 March they put up a great show, and Celtic, who had been staying at the Murtle Hydropathic Hotel for a few days, only scraped through with a late McMenemy header into the goal at the sea end. The *Aberdeen Press and Journal* was very impressed with the huge 20,000 crowd, the biggest yet seen at Pittodrie with lawyers, clergymen and doctors present and even a few ladies, 'some of them fashionably attired and wafting sweet perfumes around'.

There was a less wholesome aspect of the crowd as well, for missiles were thrown at the carriage of the referee and the charabanc of Celtic by some of the less well-educated of the Aberdeen support. The local press was horrified and called upon the magistrates 'not to stint' in their dealings with such low life. Whether there had been too much ale 'in the environs' or not, or whether it had all been the fault of the Glasgow 'ragamuffins' or some 'local ruffians', it did not matter. There was no place for such behaviour.

Celtic's opponents at Hampden on 18 April 1908 were St Mirren, playing their first final. The weather was bright and blustery, and a large 60,000 crowd appeared. Very few really expected a shock (although the Buddies had finished a respectable seventh in the league) and the game went as was expected with Adams, McNair and Weir; Young, Loney and Hay; Bennett, McMenemy, Quinn, Somers and Hamilton winning comfortably 5-1. Bennett scored twice, every other member of the forward line scored once apart from McMenemy who nevertheless was the best player on the field, showing the craft and guile which showed how he was worthy of the nickname of Napoleon. Celtic had now won the Scottish Cup six times.

The *Dundee Evening Telegraph*, now decidedly pro-Celtic, cannot really hide its joy. 'Was there ever such a consistent team as Celtic?' it asks, then goes on to explain that the secret is that the directors have kept this group of players together, they know each other, and they all love the club. Poor St Mirren were 'outclassed' and it talks of spectators leaving Hampden with a good half hour to go, such was the one-sided nature of the entertainment. Those who stayed sang Irish songs and even a few music hall favourites like 'Daisy, Daisy' and 'Goodbye Dolly Gray' and cheered on their team, without much doubt, in 1908, the best team in the world and the greatest show on earth.

The year 1909 was an infamous one in the history of the Scottish Cup. It was the year of the Hampden riot, and the one and only peacetime year since 1874 in which there was no winner of the Scottish Cup. This must not be confused, of course, with the other Hampden riot of 1980 which was entirely different. The Scottish Cup of 1909 was officially withheld by the SFA on the night of Monday, 19 April after riotous scenes on Saturday, 17 April at the Scottish Cup Final replay had more or less destroyed Hampden Park. Nor was it, in any sense, a sectarian riot – however, some later historians have tried to imply that it was.

Celtic's road to the final had seen a victory over Leith Athletic by 4-2 at Logie Green, Edinburgh thanks to a Jimmy Quinn hat-trick, and then competent home wins against Port Glasgow Athletic and Airdrie, before a more difficult struggle to beat the fast-improving Clyde side who held Celtic to a 0-0 draw in the first game at Parkhead before Celtic won 2-0 in the replay, also played, by arrangement, at Celtic Park. The fact that there was a replay here was possibly significant in the events that were about to unfold, for the perception was growing – indeed, it was now prevalent – that drawn cup ties involving large attendances between Glasgow teams were not necessarily what they seemed to be, and that some match-fixing was going on. The Glasgow Cup last autumn, for example, had seen a replay involving Celtic against Queen's Park, a replay against Rangers and two replays before an equally strange and inexplicable 0-4 defeat by Third Lanark.

The press could not, of course, say that games were being fixed, but they did hint at it, talking about 'another' boost to finances, or far more effectively, using the Ciceronian rhetorical device of 'praeteritio', to say something by claiming not to, and telling everyone how difficult it would be to 'fix' a football match. Such bogus denials in fact kept the pot boiling.

10 April 1909 saw the Scottish Cup Final between Celtic and Rangers, a repeat of the Scottish Cup Finals of 1894, 1899 and 1904. A crowd of 70,000 saw Jimmy Quinn score first, a lead held until the last quarter of an hour when Rangers scored twice through Tommy Gilchrist, then through ex-Celt Alec Bennett. Rangers thus looked likely winners until their goalkeeper Harry Rennie stepped aside to avoid a Jimmy Quinn shoulder charge and in so doing stepped over his line with the ball in his hands. Referee Stark gave a goal, correctly, but as it was an unorthodox goal which led to a draw, people wondered and tongues wagged. Nevertheless, this game was considered to have been a good game of football, and over the piece, a fair result. The replay was to be held next Saturday, 17 April.

Possibly aware of the undercurrents and certainly keen to start playing off his huge backlog of league fixtures (caused by the surfeit of cup replays!), Willie Maley suggested that extra time might be played in the event of another draw, or that the game might be played to a finish on what would be known a century later as the 'golden goal' after the regulation time was up. (No one had ever dreamed about a penalty shoot-out!) Neither Rangers nor the SFA showed any interest in his sensible suggestion, but it had at least opened up the possibility of extra time being played. Crucially and tragically, it meant that people came to the game without any clear knowledge of whether there would be extra time or not.

The replay attracted 60,000 (10,000 down on the first game but still a huge crowd) and it was another draw. Jimmy Gordon scored for Rangers in the first half and inevitably Jimmy Quinn for Celtic in the second, and the game finished 1-1. But would there be extra time? Some players, mainly the Celtic ones but a few Rangers ones as well, thought there would be and stayed on the pitch thereby encouraging the crowd to think so, but referee Mr Stark had disappeared with the ball and failed to return. Some younger members of the crowd came on to the field possibly just at this stage wanting to talk to Jimmy Quinn or another of their heroes, but then an uglier element came on throwing the cinders (at nobody in particular) which filled the terracing steps and the players beat a hasty retreat.

Mobs and rioters do not usually follow any rational pattern, and soon for a bit of a laugh (as there was to be no extra time, apparently) and with every pea-brain trying to outdo the others in bravado and folly, goalposts were set on fire, bits of the stand likewise and barriers were ripped out of the terracing, and within an hour or so, the new Hampden lay in ruins. There was no violence of fans to each other and the players were never in any danger. Alec Maley, the younger brother of Willie, rescued the Scottish Cup itself, and the fact that it was property that was destroyed, and the property of Queen's Park and the SFA, possibly tells us a great deal about the beliefs and perceptions of the day. Maybe Edwardian Scotland was not as socially cohesive as people like to think, and a small spark like no extra time in a cup final and the perception that fans were being taken for a ride by the rich and privileged was all that was needed for real violence. The middle classes were horrified at such ochlocracy or mob rule, but there was no Scottish Cup in 1909.

1910 saw the last of Celtic's six league championships in a row. It was also the first Scottish Cup Final that they had not contested since 1906. They had had an undistinguished, even lucky, passage to the semi-final – a narrow 2-1 win over Dumbarton at a frosty Boghead, then slightly more comfortable home wins over Third Lanark and Aberdeen, before they came up against Clyde at Shawfield in the semi-final. They were without the ill Davie Adams who had pneumonia, the suspended Sunny Jim and the crocked Jimmy McMenemy, who had been badly kicked by a Welshman when playing for Scotland the previous week. These were a mighty three to be without; the rest of the team clearly missed them and Celtic went down 1-3, the on-loan goalkeeper Leigh Roose (of Sunderland and Wales) at one point running out of his goal to congratulate a Clyde player who had just scored against him! Roose was a well-known eccentric. Sadly he was fated to die at the Somme in October 1916.

This result shocked Celtic and Scotland. Dundee actually won the cup that year after another two tactless draws in the first two games, but in 1911 Celtic, although now clearly past their best and losing the Scottish League to Rangers, bounced back to win the Scottish Cup in a campaign which, generally speaking, does not have a high reputation among Celtic historians. It is remarkable for the fact they never lost a goal and that they were never out of Glasgow – four games at Parkhead and two at Ibrox – but there the good news ends, for they did not score many goals either, and, generally speaking, they failed to scintillate.

2-0 v St Mirren was good enough, but then 1-0 v Galston heard the unaccustomed sound of boos reverberating round Parkhead. These were followed by hard-worked 1-0 wins over more potentially demanding opposition in Clyde and Aberdeen, and thus Celtic found themselves in the final against Hamilton Academical, playing their first-ever final after beating Dundee in the semi-final. The first game (a 0-0 draw at Ibrox on Saturday, 8 April) would have been a strong candidate for the most boring Scottish Cup Final of them all on a bright, windy day and a dry pitch, with a light ball, between an overawed Hamilton Academical and an underperforming Celtic. The 45,000 spectators were not happy.

The replay (a seemingly inevitable occurrence at that time in spite of the turbulent events of 1909) on 15 April 1911 was no better, although a shower of rain before the start had reduced some of the unpredictable bounce of the pitch. Celtic dropped John Hastie, whose shooting had been woeful in the first game, and rejigged their forward line to give a place to the promising young Andy McAtee. The 25,000 crowd were showing signs of impatience until Celtic decided to give up on their plans of walking the ball into the net, and decided to shoot from a distance instead, especially as they were now playing with a strong wind behind them.

Three Crojans (men of Croy) played in that final – Jimmy Quinn, Tommy McAteer and Andy McAtee – and two of them, Quinn and McAteer, shot from a distance and scored within the last ten minutes as Adams,

McNair and Hay; Young, McAteer and Dodds; McAtee, McMenemy, Quinn, Kivlichan and Hamilton delivered Celtic's seventh Scottish Cup, even though it was a 'none too memorable' final in the underwhelming words of the *Scottish Referee*. It was more than adequate compensation for the loss of the Scottish League after six glorious years.

1912 was the year of the first and last sailing of the *Titanic*, and the year when various people claimed to have reached the South Pole, but in Scottish football, things stayed the same in the sense that Rangers won the Scottish League again, but Celtic won once more what was considered in 1912 to be the greater honour – the Scottish Cup. It was not the easiest of times for Celtic in that Maley's first great side had broken up, and his new team had not yet emerged.

Dunfermline Athletic paid their first-ever competitive visit to Celtic Park on 27 January, and put up a good fight as they lost 0-1. Two weeks later, Celtic quietly beat East Stirlingshire 3-0 on a day when the headlines were occupied with the Clyde v Rangers game which Rangers were compelled to concede when their supporters invaded the park to get the game stopped. Celtic thus have no monopoly of supporters invading parks when things are not to their liking!

Celtic now had to travel to Pittodrie to play Aberdeen in the quarter-finals. It was a strange game in many ways, for the black and golds were two goals up soon after half-time and Andy McAtee had missed a penalty, upset apparently by the strange stance of goalkeeper Greig. Things looked grim for Celtic, but then they got another penalty. This time Jimmy Quinn took it, the goalkeeper parried, but the ball came back to Quinn again, and this time he scored. Then Andy McAtee equalised from a fine cross by John Brown to level the tie which really should have been won in the last minute when Peter Johnstone was clean through, but Greig saved brilliantly.

A fortnight later in the replay at Parkhead, Paddy Travers scored two goals to seal Celtic's place in the semi-final. It was not a brilliant performance but it was enough to set up a semi-final game against Hearts, a club that Celtic seemed to meet often in the Scottish Cup in that era. For the first time, semi-finals were at a neutral venue, so in this case Ibrox was the venue for one of Celtic's best games of this season as they beat Hearts 3-0. Andy McAtee was superb, but a rail strike made it difficult for fans to get there, especially those from Edinburgh.

As often seems to have been the case when the Scottish Cup Final was played at Ibrox (in 1900 and 1911, for example) a strong wind was blowing from the west for the game against Clyde. It was Clyde's second cup final in three years (they had lost to Dundee in the final of 1910 after they had beaten Celtic in the semi-final) but today Celtic, in the shape of Mulrooney, McNair and Dodds; Young, Loney and Johnstone; McAtee, Gallacher, Quinn, McMenemy and Brown, won comfortably, playing well both with the benefit of the wind and without. Both goals, however, came from goalkeeping errors, and they were scored by Jimmy McMenemy in the first half and Patsy Gallacher in the second, with 46,000 there to see Celtic winning the Scottish Cup for the eighth time. They were rapidly catching up on Queen's Park who had won the trophy ten times, and it did not now look as if the amateurs were going to win it very many more times.

A veil might, with advantage, be drawn over Celtic in season 1912/13. It was their silver jubilee and might have been a great season … but it wasn't. It was the first since 1902/03 that they didn't win either of the two major Scottish honours. There were reasons for this – McMenemy had a run of injuries, Quinn was not getting any younger, Gallacher was prodigiously talented but not yet experienced enough, there were goalkeeping problems – and the Scottish Cup was a major disappointment. Celtic had beaten Arbroath and Peebles Rovers, but they exited the tournament on a wonderfully warm and sunny day on 8 March at Celtic Park before a crowd given as 66,000 when the great Bobby Walker of Hearts (now commonly known as 'Houdini' because of his ability to give defenders the slip) scored the only goal of the game. It was revenge for Hearts after last year's defeat in the Scottish Cup semi-final, but it didn't do them a great deal of good, for they lost in 1913's semi-final to the eventual winners, Falkirk.

But this was only a temporary hiccup in the Scottish Cup. Next season, 1913/14, Celtic were back. The goalkeeping problem had been solved with the signing from Queens Park Rangers of Charlie Shaw, a man from Twechar who had played for Port Glasgow before he went to London. When they began their Scottish Cup campaign in February, they were in the middle of a long unbeaten run in which they had lost only one goal since early October! The run continued in the Scottish Cup with a 2-0 win over Clyde (after a somewhat disappointing 0-0 draw), then a famous trip to Forfar where they won

5-0, a 3-1 win at Motherwell in the quarter-final and a 2-0 win over Third Lanark in the semi-final at Ibrox.

The team was a joy to behold and even compared favourably with the teams of 1907 and 1908. Sunny Jim, Alec McNair and Napoleon McMenemy had straddled the two great sides, and others had joined, notably Patsy Gallacher and Charlie Shaw, who were certainly superior to their predecessors, while there were also Joe Dodds, Peter Johnstone, Andy McAtee, Johnny McMaster and Johnny Browning who were more than adequate. It was a supremely talented side. It was Maley the Magician once again who had found another magic wand.

Hibs were the opponents in the final at Ibrox on 11 April. It was the second 'Irish' cup final, and in 1914, this game was not without its political significance. Home Rule for Ireland, something that had been in the background for that past half-century, was now very much in the forefront of political thought, especially now that the House of Lords had been emasculated by the Liberals. The whole crowd sang 'God Save Ireland' and 'The Wearin' O' the Green' before the start of the first game, to the shock and embarrassment of the establishment, one feels, but the game itself was a huge disappointment and ended 0-0 with Hibs coming closer at the end than Celtic did.

It was a different story in the replay the following Thursday, 16 April. Celtic dropped the red-headed Englishman Ebenezer Owers in favour of Jimmy 'Sniper' McColl, and he scored twice in the first ten minutes as Celtic took complete control. Johnny Browning scored a third before half-time and a fourth after half-time as

Celtic won comfortably 4-1 with Patsy Gallacher now the complete player that he promised to be, and Napoleon still in charge of the midfield, distributing passes along the carpet and in the air to the eager Andy McAtee and Johnny Browning. Behind them all was the inspirational captain Sunny Jim Young who had now been with the club for 11 years, and still had a long way to go. The men who won Celtic's ninth Scottish Cup were Shaw, McNair and Dodds; Young, Johnstone and McMaster; McAtee, Gallacher, McColl, McMenemy and Browning. Young and McMenemy had now won the Scottish Cup six times each!

But, as the Celtic fans made their way back across the city in triumph that night (they would win the Scottish League as well on Saturday, also, funnily enough by beating Hibs) no one could possibly guess what the latter part of 1914 was going to bring. If the future was talked about at all, it would have been in the context of Celtic going on a trip to Germany and central Europe in May, or whether a deal could be reached between the mild and moderate Redmond and the obdurate Carson to deliver the much longed for Home Rule for Ireland. No one possibly guessed that the next Scottish Cup would not be until 1920, and that Europe would be devastated, Ireland would be totally different, women would have the vote and the male population would be much reduced!

Season 1899/1900: Winners

13/01/1900	Bo'ness	home	7-1	McMahon 2, Somers 2, Orr, Divers, Bell
27/01/1900	Port Glasgow	away	5-1	Campbell 3, Gilhooly 2
17/02/1900	Kilmarnock	home	4-0	Gilhooly, Bell, McMahon, Divers

24/02/1900	Rangers	away	2-2	Campbell, Bell
10/03/1900	Rangers	home	4-0	McMahon 2, Hodge, Bell
14/04/1900	Queen's Park	Ibrox	4-3	Divers 2, McMahon, Bell

Season 1900/01: Finalists

12/01/1901	Rangers	home	1-0	McOustra
09/02/1901	Kilmarnock	home	6-0	Campbell 2, Divers, McOustra, McMahon, Findlay
16/02/1901	Dundee	away	1-0	Findlay
23/03/1901	St Mirren	home	1-0	Campbell
06/04/1901	Hearts	Ibrox	3-4	McOustra, Quinn, McMahon

Season 1901/02: Finalists

11/01/1902	Thornliebank	home	3-0	Livingstone 2, Campbell
25/01/1902	Arbroath	away	3-2	Campbell, Marshall, Orr
08/01/1902	Hearts	away	1-1	untraced

Game played as a friendly because of snowstorm

15/02/1902	Hearts	away	1-1	Quinn
22/02/1902	Hearts	home	2-1	McMahon 2
22/03/1902	St Mirren	away	3-2	Livingstone, McDermott, Campbell
26/04/1902	Hibs	home	0-1	

Season 1902/03: Quarter-Finals

24/01/1903	St Mirren	home	0-0	
31/01/1903	St Mirren	away	1-1	McDermott
07/02/1903	St Mirren	Ibrox	1-0	untraced

Game abandoned because of wind and rain

14/02/1903	St Mirren	home	4-0	Campbell, Murray, McMahon, Watson
21/02/1903	Port Glasgow	home	2-0	Campbell, McDermott
28/02/1903	Rangers	home	0-3	

Season 1903/04: Winners

13/02/1904	St Bernard's	away	4-0	McMenemy 2, Orr 2
20/02/1904	Dundee	home	1-1	Hamilton
27/02/1904	Dundee	away	0-0	
05/03/1904	Dundee	home	5-0	McMenemy 2, Bennett, Quinn, Muir

81

| 19/03/1904 | Third Lanark | home | 2-1 | Quinn, Muir |
| 16/04/1904 | Rangers | Hampden | 3-0 | Quinn 3 |

Season 1904/05: Semi-Finalists

28/01/1905	Dumfries	away	2-1	Quinn, Bennett
11/02/1905	Lochgelly Utd	home	3-0	Somers, Orr (pen), Quinn
25/02/1905	Partick Thistle	home	3-0	Somers, Orr (pen), Bennett
25/03/1905	Rangers	home	0-2	

Season 1905/06: Quarter-Finals

27/01/1906	Dundee	away	2-1	Somers, og
10/02/1906	Bo'ness	home	3-0	McMenemy, Loney, Quinn
24/02/1906	Hearts	home	1-2	McMenemy

Season 1906/07: Winners

02/02/1907	Clyde	home	2-1	Hamilton, Bennett
09/02/1907	Morton	away	0-0	
16/02/1907	Morton	home	1-1	McMenemy
23/02/1907	Morton	home	2-1	McMenemy, Hay
09/03/1907	Rangers	away	3-0	Hamilton, Hay, Somers
30/03/1907	Hibs	home	0-0	
06/04/1907	Hibs	away	0-0	
13/04/1907	Hibs	home	3-0	Somers, Quinn, McMenemy
20/04/1907	Hearts	Hampden	3-0	Somers 2, Orr (pen)

Season 1907/08: Winners

25/01/1908	Peebles Rovers	home	4-0	Kivlichan 2, Hamilton, Somers
08/02/1908	Rangers	away	2-1	Kivlichan 2
22/02/1908	Raith Rovers	away	3-0	McMenemy 2, Kivlichan
21/03/1908	Aberdeen	away	1-0	McMenemy
18/04/1908	St Mirren	Hampden	5-1	Bennett 2, Hamilton, Somers, Quinn

Season 1908/09: Finalists

23/01/1909	Leith Athletic	away	4-2	Quinn 3, Hay
06/02/1909	Port Glasgow	home	4-0	Hay 2, Quinn, Hamilton
20/02/1909	Airdrie	home	3-1	McMenemy 2, Hamilton
20/03/1909	Clyde	home	0-0	
27/03/1909	Clyde	home	2-0	Quinn, Somers

10/04/1909	Rangers	Hampden	2-2	Quinn, Munro
17/04/1909	Rangers	Hampden	1-1	Quinn

Scottish Cup withheld following riot

Season 1909/10: Semi-Finalists

22/01/1910	Dumbarton	away	2-1	Loney, McMenemy
12/02/1910	Third Lanark	home	3-1	Quinn 3
19/02/1910	Aberdeen	home	2-1	Quinn, McMenemy
12/03/1910	Clyde	away	1-3	Kivlichan

Season 1910/11: Winners

28/01/1911	St Mirren	home	2-0	McMenemy, Hastie
11/02/1911	Galston	home	1-0	Quinn
25/02/1911	Clyde	home	1-0	McMenemy
11/03/1911	Aberdeen	home	1-0	Quinn
08/04/1911	Hamilton	Ibrox	0-0	
11/04/1911	Hamilton	Ibrox	2-0	Quinn, McAteer

Season 1911/12: Winners

27/01/1912	Dunfermline A	home	1-0	Brown
10/02/1912	East Stirlingshire	home	3-0	Quinn 2, Travers
24/02/1912	Aberdeen	away	2-2	Quinn, McAtee
09/03/1912	Aberdeen	home	2-0	Travers
30/03/1912	Hearts	Ibrox	3-0	McMenemy 2, Brown
06/04/1912	Clyde	Ibrox	2-0	McMenemy, Gallacher

Season 1912/13: Quarter-Finals

08/02/1913	Arbroath	home	4-0	Johnstone 2, Gallacher, Brown
22/02/1913	Peebles Rovers	home	3-0	McMenemy 2, Quinn
08/03/1913	Hearts	home	0-1	

Season 1913/14: Winners

07/02/1914	Clyde	away	0-0	
10/02/1914	Clyde	home	2-0	Gallacher 2
21/02/1914	Forfar Athletic	away	5-0	McColl 3, Dodds, McMenemy
07/03/1914	Motherwell	away	3-1	Gallacher, McColl, McAtee
28/03/1914	Third Lanark	Ibrox	2-0	McAtee, Owers
11/04/1914	Hibs	Ibrox	0-0	
16/04/1914	Hibs	Ibrox	4-1	McColl 2, Browning 2

CHAPTER THREE

BETWEEN THE WARS
1920–1939

THE BIGGEST cliché of Great Britain in the 1920s was 'the war changed that'. It was obviously true. Massive changes came about in social structures, the role of women, industrial relations, Ireland and Britain's role in the world. Even the Scottish Cup saw a huge change with three new names in Kilmarnock, Partick Thistle and Morton appearing on the Scottish Cup in the first three years after the war. Celtic, who had won the trophy five times out of eight in the years immediately before the war, were eliminated in the quarter-finals each year, but their travails were nothing as compared with Rangers who had not won the Scottish Cup since 1903, and would continue to fail until 1928, as the jokes continued at their expense.

There was no Scottish Cup in season 1918/19, as the war had only finished in November 1918. There was a hastily arranged Victory Cup won by St Mirren in 1919, but the first Scottish Cup after the conflict was in 1919/20. Celtic's first Scottish Cup tie in 1920 was at Dens Park, Dundee on 7 February. With Dundee having defeated Celtic in the league the week before, a huge crowd of 34,786 thronged Dens Park, a new element being the amount of motorised 'autobuses' and charabancs bringing the Celtic hordes from Glasgow, although more still came by train. The Green and White Brigades were rewarded when Adam McLean scored in the first minute of the game, Tommy McInally did likewise in the first minute of the second half and centre-half Willie Cringan, who had a magnificent game, scored halfway through the second half, as Celtic won impressively 3-1.

In spite of the obvious problems of poverty, unemployment and the continuing labour unrest (not to mention the ongoing problem of Ireland, now in perpetual political uncertainty with words like 'anarchy' and 'civil war' being bandied about and which struck a particular chord with Celtic fans) there was nonetheless a certain optimism in the air. Everyone was at least alive. Very few families had emerged from the conflict totally unscathed, but the relief that it was all over did at least give a certain amount of optimism. And the war had not been all bad for everyone. Many people had had a chance to travel and see other things and other parts of the world. In some strange way, it had been a liberating experience for some. Clearly, however, not for the widows, the orphans, the disabled, the blind and the traumatised.

Two weeks after Dundee, over 60,000 were at Celtic Park to see Celtic beat Partick Thistle 2-0 with goals from Tommy McInally and Willie McStay, and Celtic won plaudits for their ability to accommodate large numbers of disabled soldiers. Andy Aitken, 'the Daddler', one time of Newcastle United and Scotland, and now a freelance journalist, lost no opportunity to express his admiration of Willie Maley in this respect. The victory over Partick Thistle brought about the first of several meetings with Rangers in the Scottish Cup in the 1920s, but this one at Ibrox before an astonishing 85,000 was an unhappy one with the experiment of playing Patsy Gallacher at centre-forward instead of Tommy McInally, commonly known as 'the boy wonder', no great success. Patsy, great player though he was, was no centre-forward, and Tommy, although prone to off days and the occasional manifestation of some strange behaviour, was a great goalscorer. Rangers, a noticeably more physical side than Celtic, won 1-0, although the consensus of the press was that Celtic deserved another chance.

1921 saw similar disappointment. A 3-0 win at Vale of Leven was a fine nostalgic trip to the Dunbartonshire town of Alexandria, correctly believed to be one of the cradles of Scottish football. Today, however, saw Celtic easily dispose of the club which had won the Scottish Cup in 1877, 1878 and 1879 (the last year being the time that Rangers failed to turn up for the final replay!) with two goals from Joe Cassidy and one from Adam McLean. Then Celtic made their first-ever trip on competitive business to Methil to play East Fife, a team which had been born in 1903 and which had started their life playing in green and white! Great local excitement was engendered, but Celtic won comfortably 3-1 with two goals from McInally and one from Gallacher, even though East Fife scored first through a McTavish penalty.

But Celtic's luck ran out against Hearts on a rainy day at Celtic Park on 5 March. Patsy Gallacher scored first from a McInally pass, then Hearts, taking advantage of hesitancy in the Celtic defence that lacked McNair and Cringan, equalised, then took the lead. Although Celtic then peppered the Hearts goal for an equaliser, it never came and Celtic were once again out of the Scottish Cup. Tommy McInally hit the underside of the bar in the last minute, and sandwich board men walked around Glasgow that night advertising the *Evening Times*. On one side of the board was the momentous and important 'Kirkcaldy By-Election Triumph for Labour' and on the other the laconic and epigrammatic 'Celts Out As Tom Hits Bar'.

Yet there was a little recompense for Celtic supporters in 1921. In the same way as Celtic supporters of a future generation roared on Hibs in the Scottish Cup Final of 2016, so too did they lend their willing encouragement to Partick Thistle in 1921's Scottish Cup Final. The game was at Celtic Park, but there was another Celtic connection in that Jimmy McMenemy was now playing for the Jags. Now in his 40s and ageing, he was still, nevertheless, able to mastermind the Thistle team to their one and only Scottish Cup victory on 16 April, the only goal of the game coming from John Blair. Celtic fans probably did not go to the game that day, however, for the SFA had raised the admission price to the extortionate two shillings! Not only that, but the country was, not for the first or last time in the era, suffering from a miners' strike, and the railway workers were sympathetic. But it now meant that Napoleon had a record seven Scottish Cup winners' medals!

There was sympathy for the wayward Tommy McInally in 1921, but a lot less for him in 1922 when Celtic went out of the Scottish Cup, again at the quarter-final stage. This time, however, it was the shock result of the day when the team went down 1-3 to Hamilton Accies at Celtic Park, and even then, Celtic's only goal came from a Joe Dodds penalty in the 87th minute when most of the crowd had departed, muttering curses about McInally's clowning and apparent inability to be upset about the team losing. There were also the usual moans about associations with bookmakers and general puzzlement at the team's lacklustre performance, but that did less than justice to a grand performance from Hamilton Accies. McInally disappeared from the first team soon afterwards and Celtic went on to win the league without him. McInally was transferred to Alec Bennett's Third Lanark in the summer. But … he would be back!

Earlier Celtic had easily accounted for Montrose, a club making their first trip to Parkhead, but had more of a problem with Third Lanark, Andy McAtee scoring a controversial goal direct from a corner kick, which was illegal in 1922. But Celtic and referee Tom Dougray thought that the ball was headed in by Adam McLean before it crossed the line, whereas Thirds thought that Adam touched it when it was already over the line. It was a point that was much disputed in the pubs and dance halls of Glasgow that night.

The defeat from Hamilton Accies in 1922 was too bad for the mighty Celts, but the wheel turned in 1923. In truth, it wasn't the greatest Celtic team of all time, but they had unearthed a great goalscoring machine in Joe Cassidy. It began at Lochgelly United in January – one of the few early Celtic games recorded on film – and a very tight game against the Fifers who held Celtic at 2-2 until late in the game when Cassidy got the winner and his own hat-trick (although some newspapers say it was Fifer 'Jean' McFarlane who scored the winner). Hurlford caused less bother in the next round, Cassidy scoring all four and even managing to miss a penalty and its retake as well!

Two Fife teams now came to Celtic Park in the next two rounds. Without playing brilliantly, Celtic beat East Fife 2-1 and Raith Rovers 1-0. Cassidy scored twice against East Fife, but failed to do so against Raith Rovers' Dave Morris, who would one day captain Scotland. It was Adam McLean who scored the only goal of this very tight game which the Kirkcaldy team might just have won, had Adam's shot not been deflected by a defender into the Rovers net. This was the only game in this Scottish Cup campaign in which Cassidy did not score.

The semi-final was against Motherwell at Ibrox on 10 March 1923, and within a minute, Cassidy had taken advantage of a miskick to put Celtic 1-0 up, and Celtic never really looked back after that with Andy McAtee scoring direct from a free kick (now legal) and Cassidy missing a penalty which would have made it 3-0.

71,506 were at that game, and about 82,000 attended the Scottish Cup Final at Hampden about three weeks later on the early date of 31 March. The opponents were Hibs, whom Celtic had last met in a Scottish Cup Final only nine years previously but in a totally different world.

It was generally agreed to have been, entertainment-wise, one of the poorest cup finals of them all, but Celtic were not bothered about that because not only did this cup final break their 'duck' since the war, but it also meant that they had now equalled the record of Queen's Park in winning the trophy ten times.

Joe Cassidy was once again the hero of the hour, scoring the only goal of the game with a header of a bouncing ball from Paddy Connolly which eluded the rest of the defence as Joe placed it past goalkeeper Harper. This happened in the 65th minute at the Mount Florida end of the ground, and Celtic thereafter retained control of the game with veteran full-back Alec McNair outstanding. 'Eck' had now given the club a good 20 years and had won six Scottish Cup medals. The team was Shaw, McNair and W. McStay; J. McStay, Cringan and McFarlane; McAtee, Gallacher, Cassidy, McLean and Connolly.

Those who attended this game gave eloquent accounts of the beggars that they saw outside the ground. War-wounded men with one leg begging for money, their cap being held by a snotty-nosed ill-clad little girl, a few plaintive singers trying their best at romantic Scottish and Irish songs – 'Mary, My Scots Blue Bell', 'Slievenamon' and 'The Old Rustic Bridge By the Mill' mingled with a few of the Great War ditties that had inspired everyone just a few years ago – young women (and a few older ones) indicating with a knowing smile and a wink how they were trying to earn their money – no, Mr Lloyd George, this was emphatically not 'a land for heroes to live in'.

Season 1923/24 was a bad one with perpetual complaints about Celtic not having enough money, and Maley, himself not a well man who may even have been suffering from depression, was clearly unable to cope with some of the post-war generation of players. Cringan joined Dodds, Gilchrist and McInally in the crowd of men who might have been of benefit to Celtic but who were now playing elsewhere. Celtic's Scottish Cup campaign lasted one game. Ironically, just a matter of days after Ramsay MacDonald became the first-ever Labour Prime Minister of Great Britain – a hint that general improvement was possible – Celtic went to Kilmarnock and deservedly lost 0-2, a lowlight in what was already a desperately awful season.

Celtic remained down and demoralised throughout the rest of 1924, and when 1925 dawned they were already more or less out of the Scottish League race even before the 4-1 drubbing on New Year's Day at the hands of Rangers. The first Scottish Cup game, however, played during a partial eclipse of the sun on 24 January, saw an impressive 5-1 beating of Third Lanark at Cathkin and a youngster called Jimmy McGrory scoring four goals.

Alloa came next and fought back well to reduce the leeway to 2-1, after McGrory had scored twice. After them came Solway Star, paying their one and only visit to Celtic Park to lose 2-0. McGrory had now scored in all these three cup ties. Now came a prolonged (and controversial) struggle to beat St Mirren, a club with whom Celtic were destined to have quite a few tussles in the Scottish Cup.

In spite of everything, Celtic's support stayed with them – and in great numbers. A goalless draw at a packed Love Street before a barely credible 47,428 was followed by 1-1 at Parkhead on the following Tuesday before an equally impressive 36,000 (on a working-day afternoon!) and the tie was finally resolved in bizarre circumstances on the following Monday at neutral Ibrox, again before a huge crowd of 47,492.

It was not a good game on a bumpy pitch, and although St Mirren had had more of the play, Celtic were winning 1-0 through a McGrory header late in the game when Gillies of St Mirren went down on the edge of the box after a tackle from 'Jean' McFarlane. St Mirren claimed a penalty but referee Peter Craigmyle of Aberdeen insisted that it was outside the box. St Mirren then did an extraordinary thing. They refused to take the kick, still claiming a penalty. For about a minute Craigmyle and the St Mirren players stared at each other, while the Celtic players duly lined up to deal with the free kick. It was quite reminiscent of a stand-off or even an industrial strike of the kind that were all too frequent in 1920s Britain. Eventually, referee Craigmyle, ever the showman and clearly relishing and enjoying the situation, looked ostentatiously at his watch, picked up the ball, pointed to the pavilion and walked off! St Mirren were furious, but they had only themselves to blame for such pig-headed and self-defeating childishness.

All this meant that Celtic now, in five days' time, were taking on Rangers in the Scottish Cup semi-final. 101,714, Hampden's first six-figure crowd for a domestic game, turned up to watch. It had the makings of being an embarrassingly one sided encounter, as Rangers were so far ahead of Celtic in the league and had defeated them decisively in the Glasgow Cup. So it was indeed one-sided, but not in the way that everyone expected, for it was Celtic who won 5-0 with two goals from Jimmy McGrory, two from Adam McLean and one from Alec Thomson. Celtic had started off playing a totally defensive game, but gradually Patsy Gallacher took control, bringing into play men like Peter Wilson and Alec Thomson and particularly 'the greyhound', the grossly underestimated and consumptive-looking Paddy Connolly. In the context of the rest of Celtic's form that season, it was barely believable ... but it became one of Celtic's greatest-ever victories over Rangers, and much celebrated for many years, with those who now disapprove of the 'Hello! Hello!' song apparently unaware that Celtic supporters had it first and sang it to remind Rangers supporters of this game!

'Hello, hello, we are the Tim Malloys,
Hello, hello, you'll know us by the noise
We f***ed the Rangers in the cup,
Twas great to be alive,
Not one, not two, not three, not four but five!'

Rangers' Scottish Cup nightmare thus intensified, but the 1925 Scottish Cup Final is widely known (and with cause) as the Patsy Gallacher Cup Final. The first half against a competent and well-supported Dundee had been a disappointment, and Celtic went in 0-1 down, the Dundee goal having been scored by Davie McLean whom Celtic had bought from Forfar Athletic in 1907 and transferred to Preston North End in 1909, now some 16 years ago! The talismanic Patsy Gallacher had been having a poor game playing into the strong sunshine, the game simply passing him by, and supporters were depressed.

But it was a transformation in the second half! One of the great things about Patsy Gallacher, apart from his huge natural talent, was his ability to bring out the best in other players. As in the semi-final and as if they were well-trained circus animals, Peter Wilson, Alec Thomson and Paddy Connolly all now sprang into action, as Celtic took control, and Dundee made the fatal mistake of lying back. The famous Patsy Gallacher goal is something that we wish we could see on video. What seems to have happened is that Patsy wriggled through several players and somersaulted into the net with the ball wedged between his knees. Whatever happened, it was remarkable, and from now on there was no stopping Celtic and the winner came from a 'Jean' McFarlane free kick which sailed over all defenders until the green and white figure of young McGrory catapulted forth to head home a glorious winner.

This was certainly Celtic's most dramatic cup final to date, and remains so, even perhaps eclipsing 1965, 1985, 1988 and 2019 for great comebacks, and full marks to Shevlin, W. McStay and Hilley; Wilson, J. McStay and McFarlane; Connolly, Gallacher, McGrory, Thomson and McLean for landing Celtic their 11th Scottish Cup, a victory which edged them ahead of Queen's Park in the list of Scottish Cup winners.

It was completely different in 1926, and the Scottish Cup Final of that year was one of Celtic's big disappointments. Celtic won the Scottish League without any major bother and it was the great year of the return of Tommy McInally, who fitted in seamlessly to the role vacated by the injured and increasingly out of favour Patsy Gallacher. McGrory was on song that season as well, and the path to the Scottish Cup Final was comparatively easy as they beat Kilmarnock 5-0 at Rugby Park, Hamilton Accies 4-0 at Celtic Park, then Hearts 4-0 at a grossly and dangerously overcrowded Tynecastle in front of 50,500 spectators. *The Sunday Post* gives a vivid account of the crushing, and it was a wonder that no one got killed. It also, however, tells funny stories of Glasgow supporters 'buying' the front room from people in Gorgie whose house overlooked Tynecastle! Celtic then beat Dumbarton 6-1 at Celtic Park with words like 'invincible' freely used in the press to describe the goalscoring of Jimmy McGrory, the speed of Adam McLean and the wizardry of Tommy McInally.

Celtic did at last get a hard game when they returned to Tynecastle to play Aberdeen in the semi-final. The crowd was still large at 35,000 but not nearly as much as their last visit to Tynecastle, and this time the win was narrow with Aberdeen convinced that they had been robbed. McInally had scored a wonderful goal for Celtic and Hutton had equalised for Aberdeen with a penalty. Then came Celtic's controversial winner.

Some sources say that it was Tommy McInally who was the person involved but more likely it was Celtic's inexperienced reserve left-winger Willie Malloy (playing for the injured Adam McLean) who chased a ball to the byline and may have brought it back into play with a hand. The linesman flagged, either for a foul or for the ball being out of play, but Malloy then crossed for McGrory to score – and referee Mr Dougray gave the goal! This was a decision that caused a great deal of consternation in the Granite City until well after the Second World War, and did little to discourage the incipient Aberdeen paranoia that all Glasgow was against them! (Celtic are far from the only club whose supporters believe that the world is against them!)

But it was Celtic v St Mirren in the Scottish Cup Final on 10 April, the Saints having surprisingly beaten Rangers at Parkhead that same day in the other semi-final. Hardly anyone gave St Mirren a chance against this excellent Celtic side, particularly as Celtic had beaten them 6-1 in a league match a month before. But Celtic were still without Adam McLean and both McGrory and McInally had an off day. Celtic were wearing white jerseys with a green shamrock, and as often happened when they didn't look like Celtic, they didn't play like Celtic either. They lost a goal in the second minute, and another on the half-hour mark, and never really got going. It was puzzling, but the allegations of collusion with bookmakers, a common theme in the 1920s when Celtic lost, are unfair. This was a good St Mirren side, whose day this was and who had also, of course, beaten Rangers as well. But it may be that Celtic, who had been league champions for several weeks, simply approached the game too casually. In particular, they may have been 'ambushed' by their 6-1 win in the league match. (That certainly happened with the same two sides in 1962, and may have happened here as well.)

Celtic's campaign of 1927 was a most significant and unusual one in the club's history. The team had the opportunity to visit different grounds like Palmerston Park, Dumfries, Glebe Park, Brechin and Newton Park, Bo'ness, they unearthed a new star, said goodbye to an old one, played a game while a part of their stand had been blown off by a gale and ended up winning their 12th Scottish Cup against a heroic Second Division team in front of a new medium of communication called a radio or a wireless! And it was also the year of Tommy McInally!

Their first game was in Dumfries against Queen of the South on 22 January, and the 0-0 draw (which could well have ended up in favour of the home side) was a major disappointment to the local Celtic support on a day of snow and ice, but the replay at Parkhead saw an easy 4-1 victory with McInally outstanding. It was another vicious day. The snow had gone, but wind and rain dominated and a chunk of the Grant Stand (where the Main South Stand is now) was blown off, but fortunately without any injury to any spectator. It was, however, the beginning of the end of the Grant Stand which had never been the greatest success at the best of times.

Better weather was forthcoming when the team travelled to Glebe Park, Brechin, where the local Celtic support enjoyed a fine 6-3 win. But it was the three goals lost (all scored by a star-struck, Celtic-daft local boy called Wattie Gentles) that caused concern to Willie Maley. Goalkeeper Peter Shevlin was blamed for this, and in came a young man from Fife called John Thomson for his debut in a league game against Dundee. In the next round Celtic returned to Angus to play Dundee in the Scottish Cup and Thomson was superb in goal, keeping out former Celt, the much-loved Joe Cassidy, as Celtic won 4-2. In affectionate tribute to the now veteran Cassidy, Celtic fans sang the Negro slave song 'Poor Old Joe'.

Bo'ness, who had had a good season, provided very little opposition in the quarter-final, going down 0-5 before pulling two consolation goals back, but the next round was the semi-final at Ibrox against Falkirk, now with Patsy Gallacher on board. The Bairns had put out Rangers in the previous round – once again Patsy Gallacher thwarting Rangers' Scottish Cup hopes. Gallacher had played only a couple of times for Celtic after his great Scottish Cup Final of 1925. He had then been offloaded by Celtic who now had Tommy McInally back to replace him. He had found his way to Falkirk where he was enjoying an Indian summer. Some Celtic fans felt that Celtic had been too hasty to release Patsy, and before the start of the game, the Jacobite anthem 'Will You No' Come Back Again' was belted out by the 73,000 crowd as a token of love and respect for the beloved Patsy.

In the game, however, the ageing Patsy (he was now 36) came off second-best to Tommy McInally, but it was a tight game nevertheless, with only an Adam McLean goal to separate the teams. Celtic were now in their 17th Scottish Cup Final, and this time their opponents were the surprise packet of Second Division East Fife. Their achievement in reaching the final is a story in itself given the recent history of the general strike, the miners' strike and its vicious aftermath. How they reached that final to give their beleaguered community some self-respect is a great tale, as is the decision of the infant BBC to broadcast a commentary on the game. Not everyone had a radio or wireless, as it was called, in 1927, but some enterprising café owners in Glasgow, Methil and elsewhere rigged up wirelesses for their customers. It was the forerunner of pubs showing football matches on satellite TV some 70 years later!

It was, however, a very one-sided final on 16 April, even though Jock Wood scored first for the Fifers. Celtic hit back (with an own goal!) and even without the injured McGrory took command, scored goals through McLean and Connolly and in the second half, with the Fifers barely able to get the ball over the halfway line, McInally deliberately missed chances, 'delighting the now happy Celtic choristers with a few of the balloon variety' (as *The Dundee Evening Telegraph* put it) perhaps through general clowning, but perhaps having no desire to further humiliate the decent men from Fife. 3-1 it finished, and the team who won Celtic's 12th Scottish Cup was J. Thomson, W. McStay and Hilley; Wilson, J. McStay and McFarlane; Connolly, McMenemy, McInally, A. Thomson and McLean.

Willie Maley was perpetually mercurial during the 1920s – sometimes well on top of things, other times less so. He was clearly on song in April 1927. The players felt that they should get a bonus if they won this final, and captain Jimmy McStay was appointed by the players to beard the lion in its den, and to ask the question. Plucking up all the courage he could find, he approached Maley. 'What? An extra bonus for beating a team of miners from Fife? A Second Division team! Get out and bring me back that cup!' Yet, apparently, he did make a slight adjustment to the pay packets after the game!

The other story concerned John McMenemy, the son of Napoleon. McGrory being injured, McInally played in the centre-forward position, and the young John was brought in at inside-right. He was only 19 and struggling to cope at Celtic Park, being frequently compared unfavourably with his illustrious sire. Naturally nervous before a cup final, John was visibly shaking and not really coping with the banter of McInally. The kindly Alec Thomson was trying to cheer him and the other youngster, goalkeeper John Thomson, up when in walked Maley. He made a beeline for McMenemy and said 'John, what are you shaking at? It's the guys who are facing you that should be shaking! It's an honour and a privilege to wear that green and white jersey! Your father did it often enough! Go out and do likewise!' A couple of hours later, as John McMenemy collected his winners' medal, his father Jimmy reckoned that there were now eight Scottish Cup winners' medals in the family!

1928 was all about Rangers. As they were themselves too well aware, they had not won the Scottish Cup since 1903 some 25 years earlier, and they were fed up of all the music hall jokes about the man who had lost his memory in the Great War and could not remember Rangers winning the Scottish Cup. So he asked all his friends – and they couldn't remember either! During this 25-year period, Celtic had been triumphant in 1904, 1907, 1908,

1911, 1912, 1914, 1923, 1925 and 1927 – and that hurt just as much as Celtic's European Cup of 1967 hurt their descendants.

If 1927 saw the better side of Tommy McInally, 1928 saw the downside of him. Repeatedly he was in trouble, and repeatedly Maley, who did not usually suffer fools gladly, made excuses for him even when his behaviour was outrageous. There was also the undeniable fact that however much the supporters loved Tommy, his team-mates didn't – and the team certainly played better when he was out suffering from an injury or from one of his psychological disorders.

For example, after Celtic had defeated Bathgate in the first round, they were drawn away to Keith in early February. Kynoch Park saw a great Celtic 6-1 win with McInally outstanding. But he had annoyed and upset his team-mates by cooperating with the opposition, so that they could get a goal, particularly when he heard that a local draper was offering a free suit to anyone who scored a goal against Celtic. This did not go down at all well with his team-mates, and words were exchanged.

McInally then suddenly disappeared, failed to return to Glasgow with the rest of the team and turned up a few days later wondering what all the fuss was about. It did not take a huge leap of faith to work out that there may have been a Highland lady involved here, but apparently Tommy apologised and was welcomed back. He then played in the next round, a mundane 2-0 defeat of Alloa, but then before Celtic played Motherwell in the quarter-final on 3 March, McInally was suspended. He had walked out of training at Seamill Hydro because some team-mates had played a prank on him by phoning him and pretending to be a journalist. Tommy's sense of humour was conspicuously absent when he himself was the victim of a prank. He had to be punished for going AWOL. In his absence, Celtic beat Motherwell 2-0, McInally's deputy Frank Doyle scoring one of the goals.

McInally was still out for the semi-final on 24 March against Queen's Park at Ibrox. Celtic won 2-1 but it was tight and they had to survive some heavy Queen's Park pressure in the second half. Rangers on the other hand beat Hibs 3-0 in the other semi-final to set up the first Old Firm final since the riot final of 1909.

It was now that Maley made a crucial mistake which gave Rangers the Scottish Cup far more directly than Meiklejohn's penalty did. He reinstated McInally. McInally had returned contrite and full of apologies. Maley took him back, adding in later years, 'I always had a soft spot for the boy.' Celtic, with McInally on board, then lost a couple of league matches in Lanarkshire to Motherwell and Airdrie, thus effectively losing them the league, and even then when the danger signal was up, Maley still played him in the cup final on 14 April. Celtic had a great chance in the first half but McInally's shot was saved by goalkeeper Hamilton. Meiklejohn scored a famous penalty for Rangers halfway through the second half, and Celtic then collapsed as Rangers won 4-0. McInally was a reluctant and ill-willy passenger and the rest of the team played with a lethargic acceptance of their fate.

More Celtic self-destruction followed next year. The obsession was the demolition of the Grant Stand

and the building of a new one, and for financial reasons Tommy McInally and Adam McLean were allowed to go to Sunderland and despicable attempts were made to sell Jimmy McGrory and John Thomson to Arsenal as well – but neither wanted to go! – and all the time, team building was neglected as the club still lived under the shadow of depression following last season's 4-0 defeat by Rangers. Beneath all the claptrap of 'It's a good thing for Scottish football that Rangers have at last won the Scottish Cup' and 'We have always been friends of Rangers' that Maley and the directors spouted from time to time, the whole club was really quite demoralised, and the support became dangerously alienated.

After tolerably good performances against mediocre opposition in old friends Arthurlie, then East Stirlingshire, then Arbroath, and a 2-1 win over Motherwell in a replay which temporarily raised hopes and built up spirits, the semi-final at Ibrox on 23 March saw a dismal collapse to a strong Kilmarnock team which thoroughly deserved their 1-0 win and went on to win the cup that year by beating Rangers in the final.

The depression continued into the following season, not helped by the arrival from early 1930 onwards of another sort of depression, the economic one which threw so many millions on to the scrapheap. Celtic did beat Inverness Caledonian 6-0 at Telford Street, then Arbroath 5-0 at Celtic Park, but the first sight of meaningful opposition in St Mirren saw a pitiful 1-3 defeat before a subdued and unhappy Celtic Park crowd of 32,000. There was now a fine stand in place at Celtic Park. Sadly, so few of the Celtic supporters had the financial ability to enjoy its facilities and in any case, supporters come to see a good team, not a beautiful stand.

1931, however, is rightly considered to be one of the most famous seasons for Celtic in the Scottish Cup with its epic final in which the first drawn game is more famous than the victorious replay! A straw in the wind came in autumn 1930 when Celtic won the Glasgow Cup. Were things changing? Well, yes, at least in the Scottish Cup where in early 1931 the form gradually improved and the crowds gradually increased, unemployment or no unemployment, to show the appetite that there still was for Celtic success. Some key players had come in – Charlie Geatons, Bertie Thomson, Peter Scarff, Charlie Napier and a few others and there was still Jimmy McGrory!

The first game in the Scottish Cup was at Methil against East Fife and it was tight with East Fife one up at half-time and the pressure on Celtic tightening, until the new left wing came to the rescue with Charlie Napier equalising and Peter Scarff getting the winner inside the last five minutes. The next round's game at Dundee United on 31 January was snowed off, but replayed a few days later on the Wednesday afternoon before a creditable attendance of 13,000.

One of the benefits of unemployment is that there is no problem getting off your work! Wise football clubs (Celtic included at this time) realised this, and offered lower admission through an 'unemployed' gate. There was still snow about at the primitive Tannadice Park, but the pitch was playable and once again Celtic squeezed through thanks again to the left-wing combination.

United were twice in front but Peter Scarff equalised twice and Charlie Napier got the winner.

Tough going so far, but then Celtic went to Greenock and hammered Morton 4-1, McGrory scoring a hat-trick, and then on the last day of February with the weather and the standard of play steadily improving, 64,699 were at Celtic Park to see a Bertie Thomson hat-trick and the almost inevitable goal from Jimmy McGrory as the strong-going Aberdeen were put to the sword 4-0.

The semi-final was a repeat of two years ago against Kilmarnock, but this time there was no fecklessness from Celtic as they beat Killie 3-0 with goals coming from Charlie Napier, Willie Hughes and, of course, Jimmy McGrory. So thus it was Celtic v Motherwell in the final in 1931. It was Motherwell's first final, and Celtic were going for their 13th Scottish Cup. History certainly favoured Celtic, but this was a bright Motherwell side managed by John 'Sailor' Hunter, who had won a Scottish Cup medal with Dundee in 1910. 'The Well' teemed with good players, including John McMenemy, the son of Napoleon, who had won a Scottish Cup medal with Celtic in 1927 but had now found a new lease of life at the less-pressurised Fir Park. There was also a strong and famous left wing in Stevenson and Ferrier. They would indeed win the Scottish League next year, but their time had not yet come.

There was at Hampden Park on the main South Stand in 1931 a clock. The second half had kicked off about 3.55pm with Motherwell two ahead, one of them having come from John McMenemy, to the mixed feelings, one suspects, of his father. The second-half Celtic blitz did not materialise, and although Celtic were ahead on pressure and although Motherwell were 'prodigal of fouls', the big hand of the clock at Hampden had reached the perpendicular and was beginning to head upwards to 4.40pm when the game was due to end. Celtic fans on the north terracing opposite watched the progress of the clock and despaired.

Some of Celtic's weaker brethren were beginning to go home to avoid the crush of the 104,803 crowd. Celtic won a free kick about 25 yards from goal, more or less at the same spot that McFarlane had taken his free kick in the famous 1925 Scottish Cup Final. Napier took it. The defence expected a shot at goal or an attempt to find McGrory's head. It was neither. It was a gentle lob over the heads of everyone, and McGrory was able to run forward and toe-poke the ball into the net.

Celtic had a reprieve, but McGrory was seen to shake off the congratulations of his team-mates and run back to the centre circle, clearly pointing to the clock which was now only five minutes from full time. 'Well, well, well', as the saying went, 'the clock was ticking well for Motherwell, well, well' and their fans on the Mount Florida end which had some supporters holding up letters M,O,T,H, etc. to make up 'Motherwell' with their piercing chant of 'Give us an M, give us an O' etc. Sadly, but predictably, the Mount Florida end also contained a few Union Jacks and Rangers colours.

But now, a goal having been scored at last, the Celtic crowd was animated and alive. Some who had left the ground came back. Was there something to see here? Wing-halves Peter Wilson and Charlie Geatons powered forward. Bertie Thomson on the stand side at the King's Park end had the ball. He was well policed though, and saw no clear way through. So for want of anything else, he tried a hopeful punt hoping to find the head of McGrory. There seemed no danger, however, as Alan Craig, Motherwell's centre-half, rose confidently to clear, until to his horror the ball skidded off his head past his unsighted goalkeeper. A split second or two passed before everyone realised what had happened, but the Celtic end erupted in joyful noise and the realisation that the team had been saved.

More than 60 years later, a veteran supporter would recall the scene of everyone in green and white dancing with joy, the supporters in the stand on their feet, McGrory skipping with delight and the luckless Alan Craig lying on the ground thumping his fists in anguish on the turf. The final whistle had now gone, and the ever-gentlemanly Jimmy McGrory and referee Peter Craigmyle helped Craig to his feet as the Motherwell team walked off in a catatonic trance, and Willie Maley shook the hand of his old friend 'Sailor' Hunter.

The replay on Wednesday, 15 April attracted only a few less than 100,000, but this time Celtic were always in command – not totally though, and it was not until McGrory scored in the 89th minute to change it from 3-2 to 4-2 that Celtic felt in any way secure. It was McGrory's second goal, and Bertie Thomson had scored the other two. One had to feel sorry for Motherwell, but it was a great triumph for Celtic, who had now banished the pain of the last few years and had won the cup for the 13th time. This team of Celtic immortals was J. Thomson,

Cook and McGonagle; Wilson, McStay and Geatons; R. Thomson, A. Thomson, McGrory, Scarff and Napier.

Motherwell got their revenge in 1932. It was a poor season for Celtic who never really recovered (and how could they?) from the John Thomson tragedy of 5 September 1931. Indeed, there was more. By early January 1932 it was reported that Peter Scarff was ill. He would have a few brief remissions but would eventually die in the Bridge of Weir sanatorium with pulmonary tuberculosis in December 1933. In the Scottish Cup, Celtic struggled to beat Falkirk in the middle of January, then paid a rare visit to Muirton Park, Perth to beat St Johnstone 4-2 on a day of relentless biblical rain which caused the crowd (a record one of 19,185) to depart more or less en masse when Alec Thomson scored Celtic's fourth, and thus St Johnstone's two late consolation goals were scored in front of a virtually empty stadium!

But Celtic then met their match at Fir Park, Motherwell on 13 February. Motherwell scored first, then immediately after that, McGrory had to limp off with a wrenched knee and Celtic never recovered from these two blows, the competent Motherwell team running out 2-0 winners. It was revenge for last year, and Motherwell deservedly won the league that year, although they lost to Rangers in the next round of the Scottish Cup.

Motherwell were once again involved with Celtic in the Scottish Cup of 1933. Again, like 1931, it was the final as Kennaway, Hogg and McGonagle; Wilson, McStay and Geatons; R. Thomson, A. Thomson, McGrory, Napier and O'Donnell won Celtic their 14th Scottish

Cup in a very poor cup final on a dull day, the game being decided by a simple McGrory tap-in, reputedly McGrory's simplest goal of his life. Sir Harry Lauder sang a silly song at this time called 'Ah'm the saftest o' the familie', and it was said that this was McGrory's 'saftest' of them all.

En route, with McGrory scoring a hat-trick, Celtic had beaten Dunfermline 7-1 on a heavy pitch at East End Park, then Falkirk at Celtic Park in a low-key game where McGrory scored both goals in a 2-0 victory. They had a tougher game against Partick Thistle in mid-February at Celtic Park when McGrory and Bertie Thomson got the goals as Celtic came from behind to win. In the quarter-final at Albion Rovers, stern resistance was shown by the Coatbridge men in a 1-1 draw after both teams had met Sir Harry Lauder before the game. Celtic then won the replay at Parkhead 3-1.

Hearts, a sadly underperforming unit in the 1930s, in spite of having some great players (Jack Harkness, Alec Massie and Barney Battles Jr) and attracting consistently larger crowds than Celtic did, were the opponents in the Hampden semi-final in front of a crowd of 87,000. They were all disappointed at a 0-0 draw, but 63,756 of them came back to see the replay on Wednesday afternoon where McGrory scored before half-time, Alec Thomson did so in the second half, and the defence were good enough to hold out when Hearts pulled one back late in the game.

So, 1933 was another Scottish Cup triumph, but the next three years were not happy ones. 1933/34 was as poor a year as Celtic have ever had with manager Willie

Maley possibly even suffering from clinical depression (Peter Scarff died of tuberculosis in December 1933 to add to the list of tragedies of Sunny Jim in 1922 and John Thomson in 1931 which he never really got over) and clearly not coping. Attendances fell and it was not a happy time with Maley not helping matters by banging his drum relentlessly about 'the Celts of old' and comparing them favourably with the present day wearers of the green. Such comparisons were understandable, but they did not help.

But there were good days as well. On 20 January 1934, in 'crisp but congenial weather' Celtic travelled to Maidenholm in the south of Scotland to play Dalbeattie Star and to win 6-0 in the first round of the Scottish Cup. Next followed a hard-fought game at Ayr United when Celtic were twice behind but fought back to win with a McGonagle penalty and a goal from each of the O'Donnell brothers, Frank and Hugh. Two weeks later Falkirk came to Celtic Park and before a huge crowd of 43,000 served up a great game of football which might have been a lot different if Canadian goalkeeper Joe Kennaway hadn't saved a penalty kick when Celtic were only 2-1 up. As it was, Celtic won 3-1 with a goal from McGrory and two from Frank O'Donnell.

But then Celtic met their Scottish Cup nemesis of this time in St Mirren. In early March before a crowd of 33,434 at a packed Love Street, Celtic exited the 1934 Scottish Cup in a game that was full of incidents, but also full of disappointments. Celtic missed two penalties (one by Peter Wilson and one by Peter McGonagle) and generally failed to get going. St Mirren, who also missed a penalty, scored one goal in each half in what was a miserable experience for Celtic, who had now exited the Scottish Cup to the Buddies in 1926, 1930 and 1934.

1935 was in every sense better, the club benefitting from the return of Jimmy McMenemy as trainer in October 1934, and the emergence of a young man called Jimmy Delaney. But there was still disappointment in the Scottish Cup. Montrose were beaten 4-0 at Celtic Park, then in a replay, Celtic got the better of Partick Thistle after a tight 1-1 first game at Firhill, a game which attracted 54,180 to a dangerously overcrowded ground. Hugh O'Donnell scored Celtic's equaliser that day, and it was the same man who scored twice in the replay as Celtic won 3-1.

But things came to a shuddering halt at Pittodrie, a ground where Celtic seldom did well in those days. The crowd was a huge 40,105, by some distance Aberdeen's record attendance. It now being generally agreed by economists that the worst of the recession was over, crowds began to flock back to football. Pittodrie that day and contained a large number of Celtic fans who had travelled up by train and even by bus overnight (with inhabitants of douce towns like Forfar, Brechin and Laurencekirk wondering on Saturday morning where all their bottles of milk and bags of rolls had disappeared to), but it was a great day for the black and golds, particularly their legends Matt Armstrong and Willie Mills. Armstrong scored two penalties, Mills scored Aberdeen's other goal, and Celtic were a beaten side long before Jimmy McGrory pulled one back for them at the end. Pittodrie was far from a happy hunting ground for Celtic in the 1930s.

It was 1936 when Celtic at last fought back – but not yet in the Scottish Cup. The league was won by some distance, McGrory scored 50 goals and things were a lot brighter at Celtic Park than they had been for a long, long time. But the Scottish Cup exit was baffling. Celtic had been due to play Berwick Rangers on 25 January but a waterlogged pitch put the game off, and the men from Berwick then scratched because the part-timers did not think they could raise a team for a midweek game in Glasgow! Celtic then lost a rare league game at Tynecastle 0-1 and clearly were still carrying luggage from that one when St Johnstone came to Parkhead for the Scottish Cup second-round tie. The pitch was hard, but that was no real excuse as St Johnstone amazed themselves by winning 2-1 – and deserving to do so, as too many Celts simply had an off day.

So Celtic were out of the Scottish Cup again. Words like 'hoodoo' were beginning to appear (after only three years!) in the supporters' conversations, and, of course, things were not helped by Rangers winning the cup every one of these three years. But then again, 'When the cat's away, the mice will play!' and Celtic supporters realised, not for the first or last time, that if Celtic don't stand up to Rangers, no one else will either.

But Celtic were now league champions and 1937 saw the return of the Scottish Cup. And yet that epic cup final against Aberdeen with the massive record crowd almost never happened. Celtic nearly went out at the first time of asking at, of all places, Stenhousemuir. There was snow about, and Delaney was out injured. McGrory scored, but then Stenny equalised and in the

89th minute, referee Peter Craigmyle refused Stenny a penalty kick for what looked like a handball offence to all the visiting journalists. Had that been given, who knows what might have happened? As it was, Celtic won the replay 2-0, although hardly convincingly. On the same day that Celtic nearly came a cropper at Ochilview, Rangers actually did come a cropper by losing to Queen of the South at Palmerston.

There followed another lively game against Albion Rovers – an even first half but full-time training told in the second as Celtic won 5-2. Then came a rather easier trip to Methil to beat the home side 3-0, before an epic battle against old Scottish Cup foes Motherwell in the quarter-final. The first attempt was snowed off. Then Celtic came back from being 2-4 down soon after half-time at Parkhead to draw 4-4. It being a Wednesday afternoon, only 36,259 were there but they would remember it! Then the replay on Wednesday, 24 March 1937 at Fir Park saw gates closed, swaying crowds, spectators climbing trees outside the ground to look in and youngsters five-deep sitting along the touchline as Celtic once again came from behind with goals from Jimmy McGrory and Willie Buchan to win 2-1. Many of the 36,500 crowd claimed to have walked all the way from Glasgow and walked back again.

Crowds in 1937 were huge – it may have had something to do with the obviously worsening international situation, making everyone enjoy life as much as they could – and 76,000 were at Ibrox for the semi-final to see Celtic beat Clyde in a Glasgow derby. Once again the game was tight but McGrory scored twice, once in each half (the second a deflection), to see Celtic into the final to play this time the black and golds of Aberdeen, whose first Scottish Cup Final this was.

A huge crowd was expected, but not quite as many as 146,433, only a shade fewer than the Scotland v England international of the previous week. (Both figures are disputed, and in each case, there were many 'wall climbers' – such was the passion for football in those days!) The Granite City had more or less emptied itself to come to Glasgow that day, and most people are prepared to admit that there were as many Aberdeen supporters as Celtic ones. And those who were at both games insisted that there were more at the cup final than there were at the international, on both occasions, the road from Mount Florida station to Hampden Park full of placard holders – the usual religious ones about 'Meeting Thy Doom' outnumbered this year by those who were urging young men to go to Spain and fight with the International Brigades.

One man played in both games – Jimmy Delaney – and in each case Jimmy was on the winning side of a 2-1 victory. The cup final was not one of the best, and there was a disappointment that McGrory in his last cup final did not score (he had done so in 1925, 1931 and 1933). Johnny Crum scored first. It was immediately countered by Matt Armstrong, but it was Willie Buchan who scored the second goal in the second half after charging through the Aberdeen defence. Full time brought Celtic's 15th Scottish Cup and a triumph for Kennaway, Hogg and Morrison; Geatons, Lyon and Paterson; Delaney, Buchan, McGrory, Crum and Murphy.

It would be Celtic's last Scottish Cup for some considerable time, longer in fact that anyone could possibly imagine. 1938 was a great year for Celtic in other tournaments but not in the Scottish Cup. Celtic continued their tradition of setting ground records in Scottish Cup ties when 43,877 appeared at Cathkin Park to see the game against Third Lanark in which Johnny Crum scored two early goals, and although the Thirds pulled one back, Celtic held on. That was in late January, and in February, they beat Nithsdale Wanderers 5-0 thanks mainly to a Frank Murphy hat-trick.

All this was done without Jimmy McGrory, who had retired from the playing side of things in autumn 1937 to become manager of Kilmarnock. His first game in his new role was funnily enough on Christmas Day against Celtic at Parkhead in the Scottish League, and it was an 8-0 doing from his old side. Now, quirkily, the Scottish Cup draw brought Kilmarnock to Celtic Park again and 39,528 turned up expecting to see a similar massacre. Not a bit of it. McGrory, with his inside knowledge of Celtic players, got his tactics right against his old club, Kilmarnock raised their game, Celtic complacently let theirs drop, and the Ayrshiremen ran out 2-1 winners, having scored twice in the first half. Celtic did pull one back through Malky McDonald, but Kilmarnock were the better side, and the confused Jimmy McGrory found himself shunned and ignored by Willie Maley, in one of his more boorish and misanthropical of moods, after the game! East Fife from the Second Division won the Scottish Cup that year, beating McGrory's Kilmarnock in a replayed final.

And then in 1939, with everyone hoping against hope that a war could be avoided, Celtic suffered another failure, this time the cup being won by Clyde. First of all there was a trip to Fife for a very easy 8-3 beating of Burntisland on 21 January, then a 7-1 win at Montrose in early February. No problems there, but then Hearts and Celtic enticed a total of over 130,000 people in four days to see them. Over 50,000 saw Celtic score twice in the first five minutes at Tynecastle (which was, as always, dangerously overcrowded when Celtic were the visitors), but the Edinburgh men fought back to equalise, and to take the tie to Celtic Park where an astonishing 80,840 (a record for a midweek cup tie other than a final) saw the game go to extra time before John Divers II scored the deciding goal.

It seemed that the likelihood, nay the inevitability, of war was encouraging more and more people to go to football matches, and the wise precaution was taken to make the quarter-final at Motherwell all-ticket. Motherwell and Celtic had crossed swords four times in the Scottish Cup in recent years, with Celtic winning every time except for 1932, but today on 4 March 1939 Motherwell deservedly won 3-1 with Jimmy Delaney scoring Celtic's only goal. Motherwell would go on to lose to Clyde in the final and Celtic would not play another Scottish Cup tie until 25 January 1947.

The inter-war years had seen six Scottish Cup triumphs in 1923, 1925, 1927, 1931, 1933 and 1937. It had been a curious era in Celtic history, full of romantic figures and passionate games, but also with a certain amount of disappointment that such a talented group of players, supported by a huge and committed following, did not do a great deal better.

Season 1919/20: Quarter-Finals

07/02/1920	Dundee	away	3-1	McInally, McLean, Cringan
21/02/1920	Partick Thistle	home	2-0	McInally, W. McStay
06/03/1920	Rangers	home	0-1	

Season 1920/21: Quarter-Finals

05/02/1921	Vale of Leven	away	3-0	Cassidy 2, McLean
19/02/1921	East Fife	away	3-1	McInally 2, Gallacher
05/03/1921	Hearts	home	1-2	Gallacher

Season 1921/22: Quarter-Finals

28/01/1922	Montrose	home	4-0	McFarlane 2, McInally, McLean
11/02/1922	Third Lanark	away	1-0	McLean
25/02/1922	Hamilton Accies	home	1-2	Dodds (pen)

Season 1922/23: Winners

13/01/1923	Lochgelly United	away	3-2	Cassidy 3
27/01/1923	Hurlford	home	4-0	Cassidy 4
10/02/1923	East Fife	home	2-1	Cassidy 2
24/02/1923	Raith Rovers	home	1-0	McLean
10/03/1923	Motherwell	Ibrox	2-0	Cassidy, McAtee
31/03/1923	Hibs	Hampden	1-0	Cassidy

Season 1923/24: First Round

26/01/1924	Kilmarnock	away	0-2	

Season 1924/25: Winners

24/01/1925	Third Lanark	away	5-1	McGrory 3, Gallacher, Thomson
07/02/1925	Alloa	home	2-1	McGrory 2
21/02/1925	Solway Star	home	2-0	McGrory, Thomson
07/03/1925	St Mirren	away	0-0	
10/03/1925	St Mirren	home	1-1	McGrory
16/03/1925	St Mirren	Ibrox	1-0	McGrory
21/03/1925	Rangers	Hampden	5-0	McGrory 2, McLean 2, Thomson
11/04/1925	Dundee	Hampden	2-1	Gallacher, McGrory

Season 1925/26: Finalists

23/01/1926	Kilmarnock	away	5-0	Thomson 2, McLean, McInally, McGrory
06/02/1926	Hamilton Accies	home	4-0	Thomson, McLean, McInally, McGrory
20/02/1926	Hearts	away	4-0	McInally 2, McGrory, Connolly
06/03/1926	Dumbarton	home	6-1	McGrory 2, McLean 2, Thomson, W. McStay (pen)
20/03/1926	Aberdeen	Tynecastle	2-1	McGrory, McInally
10/04/1926	St Mirren	Hampden	0-2	

Season 1926/27: Winners

22/01/1927	Queen of the South	away	0-0	
26/01/1927	Queen of the South	home	4-1	McGrory 2, McLean, Thomson
05/02/1927	Brechin City	away	6-3	McGrory 4, McLean, Thomson
19/02/1927	Dundee	away	4-2	McGrory, McLean, Connolly, W. McStay (pen)
05/03/1927	Bo'ness	away	5-2	McGrory 2, McLean, Thomson, McInally
26/03/1927	Falkirk	Ibrox	1-0	McLean
16/04/1927	East Fife	Hampden	3-1	McLean, Connolly, og

Season 1927/28: Finalists

21/02/1928	Bathgate	home	3-1	McGrory, McInally, McLean
04/02/1928	Keith	away	6-1	McGrory 3, McInally 3
18/02/1928	Alloa	home	2-0	McGrory, Connolly
03/03/1928	Motherwell	away	2-0	McGrory, Doyle
24/03/1928	Queen's Park	Ibrox	2-1	McGrory, McLean
14/04/1928	Rangers	Hampden	0-4	

Season 1928/29: Semi-Finalists

19/01/1929	Arthurlie	home	5-1	McGrory 3, Connolly, J. McStay
02/02/1929	East Stirlingshire	home	3-0	McGrory 2, J. McStay
16/02/1929	Arbroath	home	4-1	McGrory 4

06/03/1929	Motherwell	home	0-0	
13/03/1929	Motherwell	away	2-1	McGrory, Connolly
23/03/1929	Kilmarnock	Ibrox	0-1	

Season 1929/30: Quarter-Finals

18/01/1930	Inverness Caley	away	6-0	McGrory 3, Wilson, Connolly, Napier
01/02/1930	Arbroath	home	5-0	McGrory 2, A. Thomson, R. Thomson, Scarff
15/02/1930	St Mirren	home	1-3	A. Thomson

Season 1930/31: Winners

17/01/1931	East Fife	away	2-1	Scarff, Napier
04/02/1931	Dundee United	away	3-2	Scarff 2, Napier
14/02/1931	Morton	away	4-1	McGrory 3, Napier
28/02/1931	Aberdeen	home	4-0	R. Thomson 3, McGrory
14/03/1931	Kilmarnock	Hampden	3-0	Napier, McGrory, Hughes
11/04/1931	Motherwell	Hampden	2-2	McGrory, og
15/04/1931	Motherwell	Hampden	4-2	McGrory 2, R. Thomson 2

Season 1931/32: Third Round

16/01/1932	Falkirk	home	3-2	Napier 2, R. Thomson
30/01/1932	St Johnstone	away	4-2	Napier 3, A. Thomson
13/02/1932	Motherwell	away	0-2	

Season 1932/33: Winners

21/01/1933	Dunfermline Athletic	away	7-1	McGrory 3, H. O'Donnell 3, R. Thomson
04/02/1933	Falkirk	home	2-0	McGrory 2
18/02/1933	Partick Thistle	home	2-1	McGrory, R. Thomson
04/03/1933	Albion Rovers	away	1-1	Napier
08/03/1933	Albion Rovers	home	3-1	Napier 2, A. Thomson
18/03/1933	Hearts	Hampden	0-0	
22/03/1933	Hearts	Hampden	2-1	McGrory, A. Thomson
15/04/1933	Motherwell	Hampden	1-0	McGrory

Season 1933/34: Quarter-Finals

20/01/1934	Dalbeattie Star	away	6-0	Crum 4, F. O'Donnell 2
03/02/1934	Ayr United	away	3-2	F. O'Donnell, H. O'Donnell, McGonagle

| 17/02/1934 | Falkirk | home | 3-1 | F. O'Donnell 2, McGrory |
| 03/03/1934 | St Mirren | away | 0-2 | |

Season 1934/35: Quarter-Finals

26/01/1935	Montrose	home	4-1	F. O'Donnell 2, Paterson, Buchan
09/02/1935	Partick Thistle	home	1-1	H. O'Donnell
13/02/1935	Partick Thistle	away	3-1	H. O'Donnell 2, McGrory
03/03/1935	Aberdeen	away	1-3	McGrory

Season 1935/36: Second Round

Berwick Rangers scratched

| 08/02/1936 | St Johnstone | home | 1-2 | Buchan |

Season 1936/37: Winners

30/01/1937	Stenhousemuir	away	1-1	McGrory
03/02/1937	Stenhousemuir	home	2-0	McGrory 2
13/02/1937	Albion Rovers	away	5-3	McGrory 2, Buchan 2, Delaney
27/02/1937	East Fife	away	3-0	McGrory 2, Buchan
17/03/1937	Motherwell	home	4-4	Crum 2, Lyon, Buchan
24/03/1937	Motherwell	away	2-1	McGrory, Buchan
03/04/1937	Clyde	Ibrox	2-0	McGrory, og
24/04/1937	Aberdeen	Hampden	2-1	Crum, Buchan

Season 1937/38: Third Round

22/01/1938	Third Lanark	away	2-1	Crum 2
12/02/1938	Nithsdale Wanderers	home	5-0	Murphy 3, Carruth 2
05/03/1938	Kilmarnock	home	1-2	MacDonald

Season 1938/39: Quarter-Finals

| 21/01/1939 | Burntisland | away | 8-3 | MacDonald 3, Crum 2, Watters, Murphy, Delaney |
| 04/02/1939 | Montrose | away | 7-1 | Crum 3, Divers 2, Delaney, MacDonald |

18/02/1939	Hearts	away	2-2	Delaney, MacDonald
22/02/1939	Hearts	home	2-1	Divers 2
04/03/1939	Motherwell	away	1-3	Delaney

CHAPTER FOUR

THE LEAN YEARS
1947–1964

IT IS possibly a good thing that the Second World War years are not generally well chronicled by Celtic historians. The performances were dire and seldom did much to cheer up their many supporters serving overseas or working hard in the munitions industries (facing danger every day in both cases), but the saving grace was that the times were unreal and not really conducive for football. The veil that has been drawn over so much of Celtic in the Second World War is perhaps justified. There was, in any case, no Scottish Cup, and thus Clyde, who won the trophy in 1939, can claim that they were the Scottish Cup holders until Aberdeen took it off them in 1947! Portsmouth can make a similar claim in England!

In a Celtic context, however, it is less easy to be insouciant about the years immediately after the war. There is no real excuse. Those who had served abroad were back, a vigorous Labour government was in power doing all sorts of good things for everyone (not least in the production of healthy babies and children), industry was booming in an era of full employment, everyone had a job and football, like all other sports and the entertainment industry, shared in this growth. So why did Celtic not rise to challenge Rangers? It comes down to poor management and nothing else.

There was a manager who was no manager at all. He may have been the greatest goalscorer of all time, and we should still be proud of him, but a manager Jimmy McGrory was not. There was a chairman and a board of directors who said all the right things about the club, but failed to do any of the things that needed to be done. Performances remained dire on the field, yet paradoxically the support remained astonishingly loyal. They might well have been tempted to defect eastwards to a club that was making some sort of effort to challenge Rangers, namely Hibs, but they stayed with Celtic. There could be no possible excuse about Celtic not having the money.

Supporters were ill-rewarded. They may well have looked to the Scottish Cup to cheer them up. After all, Celtic were the record holders with 15 wins, as distinct from the ten each of Rangers and Queen's Park, and the epic days of 1904, 1925, 1931 and 1937 were much recalled by the faithful in their desperate attempts to cheer themselves up. But even here, in Celtic's favourite trophy, there was little happiness.

Celtic's first Scottish Cup tie after the war was at Dens Park, Dundee on 25 January 1947. Dundee were a Division 'B' side in 1946/47 but proved their credentials for Division 'A' by comfortably beating Celtic 2-1, and Celtic were well beaten long before a late goal scored by a fellow by the unlikely name of Gerald Padua McAloon gave them a lifeline which they could not take advantage of. It was technically a giant-killing of the 'Arthurlie 1897' stamp. The famously bad winter which arrived in February 1947 must have been doubly bad for Celtic supporters with no spring to look forward to. Aberdeen won the Scottish Cup in that first proper post-war season.

1948 was a shocking league season with the club narrowly escaping relegation through the cooperation of one or two 'old friends' (one in particular – Dundee) who feared the loss of big gates if Celtic were relegated, but there was also a reasonable run in the Scottish Cup which did resurrect some sort of pride in the club and a hope that they might yet again experience some success in their favourite trophy.

Celtic were lucky enough to have three home draws. It was no surprise when they beat Cowdenbeath 3-0 on 7 February with two goals from John McPhail and one from Willie Gallacher, son of the illustrious Patsy. More difficult visitors came to Parkhead in Motherwell two weeks later. The pre-war battles between these two were legendary, and this one lived up to the tradition. Celtic, with Jock Weir outstanding, in front of a 55,231 crowd, just edged it 1-0 thanks to a goal scored by Johnny Paton which looked dubious to every Motherwell player and supporter. They claimed that there were two Celts offside. But Mr Mitchell of Falkirk judged that they were not 'interfering with play', the goal was given and Celtic just deserved their victory.

By the time that Montrose arrived for the quarter-final on 6 March, Celtic supporters were convinced that a Scottish Cup triumph was a possibility. 38,678 (the biggest crowd that Montrose had ever played in front of) saw the brave Angus men hold Celtic for about half an hour until John McPhail (legally) shoulder-charged goalkeeper Norman Cook for the first goal, and then further goals followed from McPhail (again), Johnny Paton and Jock Weir.

The semi-final draw decreed that Celtic would play Morton. This seemed to be the best draw for Celtic as the other two teams were Hibs and Rangers. Both games were played in Glasgow that day of 27 March 1948 with more than 80,000 at Ibrox to see a Scottish Cup semi-final that might easily have been won by Celtic in the 90 minutes. But it went to extra time, Jock Weir missed an absolute sitter, but Eddie Murphy of Morton didn't, and there was to be no Scottish Cup for Celtic that year.

1949 was an absolute disgrace. Late 1948 had seen an improvement of sorts, thanks to the arrival of the new talismanic Irishman called Charlie Tully, but in early 1949 Celtic were drawn away to Dundee United at their then rudimentary Tannadice Park stadium. Dundee United were a poor Division 'B' side, rated far below their neighbours Dundee who were now flying high in Division 'A', but this was their day. An all-ticket crowd of 25,000 saw a game which ended 4-3 for United, but that is misleading, for Celtic's defence was barely existent on occasion, and in fact they were lucky to get off with losing only four goals. Only goalkeeper Willie Miller did anything to be proud about that day, and the game was also characterised by hooliganism with bottles landing on the park from time to time. In the long term, this was possibly a game which alienated a great many of Celtic's huge support in the city of Dundee itself. They began to look elsewhere.

Next year, 1950, was the halfway point of the century but still the Scottish Cup eluded Celtic. The campaign opened at Glebe Park, Brechin, where enterprising businessmen brought lorries into the ground and charged sixpence for spectators to stand on them and get a better view. They saw an easy 3-0 win for Celtic with two goals from Jock Weir and one from Billy McPhail.

Two weeks later, riotous scenes accompanied the Third Lanark v Celtic game at Cathkin when the game was called off because of snow after the crowd had been allowed in and had paid their money. Things were not helped when the clubs tried to play a friendly (which they used to do in these circumstances long ago) but the crowd wouldn't have it and invaded the field. It was astonishingly bad public relations, and things were not really helped when the game was played on the following Wednesday and it ended in a tactless draw, even though efforts had been made to reimburse fans who had paid up their money for the first game. Eventually, at the third attempt at a dry Parkhead on Monday, 20 February, a John McPhail hat-trick saw Celtic into the quarter-finals to play Aberdeen at Parkhead.

65,112 saw a good day weather-wise, but that was all that was good about it. It was a dour, tough struggle at a crowded Celtic Park where the spectators never failed to give Celtic encouragement. Celtic scored first after about eight minutes but it was correctly ruled out for offside, and then on about the half-hour mark, Chris

Anderson, who would become a very able administrator for Aberdeen in their glorious Alex Ferguson era 30 years later, scored the only goal of the game for the Dons. For Celtic fans, the post-war period continued to be a never-ending nightmare.

But 1951 at last brought relief. Not only was it a very successful campaign, it was also a very interesting (and indeed difficult) one with some good games and some players proving their mettle against the odds. The first round sent Celtic to East Fife on 27 January, by no means an easy task because East Fife had already won the League Cup twice and had many fine players at this time. It was a thrilling game which ended up 2-2 on a hard pitch and Celtic very much indebted to Bobby Collins for a late equaliser. The replay at Parkhead was a funny one with Celtic delighting their fans by going 4-0 up, but then giving them palpitations by losing two near the end for the game to finish 4-2.

Duns presented very few problems for Celtic in the next round, but then there was an epic trip to Tynecastle on 24 February. Not for the first or last time, Tynecastle found itself unable to cope with the large crowd that Celtic brought, and frequent crowd encroachments saw the game in serious danger of being abandoned. At one point George 'Sonny' Hunter, who had only recently made his debut appearance in the Celtic goal, found himself keeping out the Hearts forwards, their famous inside trio of Conn, Bauld and Wardhaugh, with spectators sitting on the grass behind his goal and even sitting on the goal net! Sonny had a brilliant game that day before a crowd given as 47,000 but in fact it was a lot more than that.

John McPhail and Jock Weir scored Celtic's goals in a 2-1 win.

Then in the quarter-final Celtic got ample revenge over Aberdeen for last year's defeat when they beat them 3-0. This time it was Celtic Park which struggled to contain the crowd, and boys had to be allowed to sit on the running track, such was the dangerous swaying of the crowd of over 75,000. Celtic were well on top with goals from John McPhail, Charlie Tully and John McPhail again, and Celtic were now in the semi-final.

Raith Rovers were in the semi-final for only the second time in their existence. 84,237, by some distance the largest crowd that Raith Rovers had ever played in front of, were at Hampden on 31 March to see a hard-fought game in which Charlie Tully was possibly the key factor. It was he who scored the late decisive goal after Raith had levelled twice. Celtic were now into their first post-war final and the excitement in Glasgow was almost tangible, with even the aged Willie Maley, still writing or ghosting the occasional column in the *Evening Times*, showing clear signs of getting carried away with it all, comparing some members (but by no means all) of the 1951 side with some of his great sides.

The opponents in the Scottish Cup Final on 21 April 1951 were those old rivals of Celtic, Motherwell, a team replete with great players. The crowd was a capacity 134,000 and they saw a game which was not the best there had ever been, but one which meant so much to Celtic whose fans made up about 80 per cent of the crowd, all desperate to see the return of a major trophy which had not been won for 14 years. The weather was sunny

The Celtic team who won the Scottish Cup for the first time in 1892

An artist's impression of the Scottish Cup Final of 1892 at Ibrox

Scottish Cup winners in 1899, having defeated Rangers 2-0 in the final

Sandy McMahon, three times winner of a Scottish Cup medal in 1892, 1899 and 1900

Jimmy Quinn, the famous hat-trick hero of the 1904 Scottish Cup Final

The Celtic Scottish Cup winning team of 1912

On the brink of war. Celtic with the Scottish Cup in April 1914. On the day that this photograph was taken, they won the Scottish League as well!

The programme for the 1925 Scottish Cup Final

Patsy Gallacher, the hero of 1925

The Scottish Cup in the USA, being held by Jimmy McGrory, in 1931

*Jimmy McGrory
in his prime in
1933*

Jimmy McGrory wheels away after scoring the only goal in the 1933 Scottish Cup Final

Willie Maley, who as player and manager won the Scottish Cup 15 times between 1892 and 1937

The two goalscorers in the final of the Scottish Cup of 1937, Willie Buchan and Johnny Crum, hold the Scottish Cup

John McPhail with the Scottish Cup in 1951

A selection of Scottish Cup semi-final and final programmes from the 1970s

'The Bhoys of the Old Brigade'. Dixie Deans (hat-trick hero of 1972) on right alongside assistant manager Sean Fallon and Willie Henderson of Rangers

Celtic with the Scottish Cup in 1985 after beating Dundee United 2-1

*Roy Aitken
in 1985*

Tommy Burns and Fergus McCann with the Scottish Cup in 1995

'I know there's three of you, but hands off me!' says Henrik Larsson to three Hibs players in the 2001 Scottish Cup Final

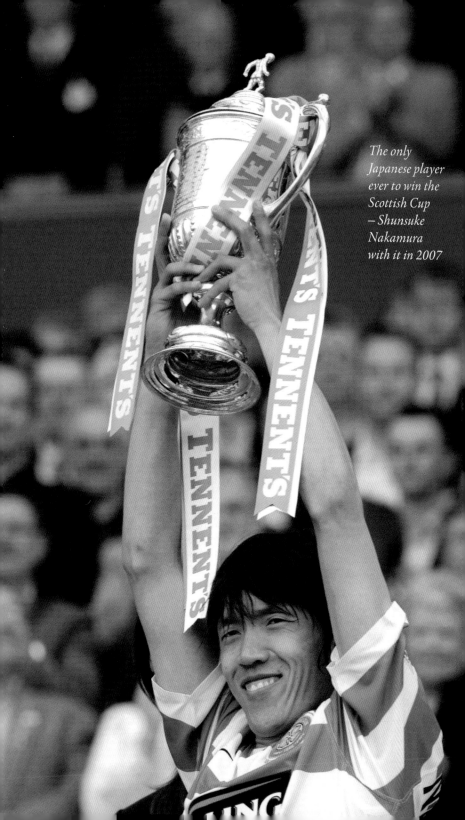

The only Japanese player ever to win the Scottish Cup – Shunsuke Nakamura with it in 2007

Scott Brown and Fraser Forster collect the Scottish Cup in 2013. Celtic had changed into the hoops to collect the trophy after the game had been played in a very un-Celtic black strip

Celtic collect the Scottish Cup in their 'Invincible' season of 2017

*Tom Rogic, scorer
of the dramatic late
winner in the Scottish
Cup Final of 2017*

Brendan Rodgers. No one will ever understand why he walked away!

And these are the people that it is all about – the fans!

*Callum McGregor and Scott
Sinclair with the Scottish Cup in
the rain at Hampden in 2019*

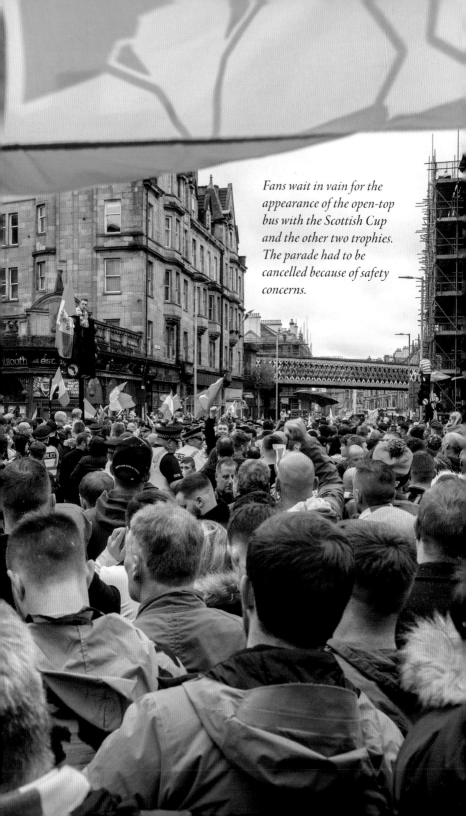

Fans wait in vain for the appearance of the open-top bus with the Scottish Cup and the other two trophies. The parade had to be cancelled because of safety concerns.

but windy, the ground was hard and the ball seemed a bit light.

McPhail scored in the first half, beating two defenders and then lobbing the goalkeeper. It turned out to be the only goal of the game, as Celtic defended grimly (famously, Fallon and Rollo, their hair brushed back and playing with grim determination, 'kicked a'thing that cam ower the half-wey line' and the half-back line of Evans, Boden and Baillie held out similarly) for the next 75 minutes until the glorious sound of Jack Mowat's final whistle indicated that Hunter, Fallon and Rollo; Evans, Boden and Baillie; Weir, Collins, McPhail, Peacock and Tully had won the 16th Scottish Cup for the club. It was a glorious day for Celtic and their supporters, so many of whom now lived abroad and relied on the BBC World Service to keep them abreast of what was going on. So mid-morning in Canada and the USA, evening in India and early morning in Australia saw scenes of Celtic celebration – and that is before we begin to talk about Ireland, England or Scotland. That night saw dancing in the streets of the Gorbals. Was this the return of paradise?

The real tragedy of all this, however, was that the success was not maintained or developed. The club continued to be badly run. 1952 saw a miserable 1-2 defeat in the Scottish Cup to Third Lanark after an equally dreadful 0-0 draw, while the chairman Mr Kelly saw fit to pick a fight with Mr Graham of the SFA over the flying of the Irish flag at Parkhead. It was a successful piece of politics – it is always fun to see officialdom make a fool of itself by, in this case, making an order which it couldn't enforce – but most supporters would rather have seen a good team on the park.

1953 was coronation year, and glory would come to Celtic in the all-British Cup, but the Scottish Cup brought more misery for the side. Eyemouth were swept aside, there was a stumble at Stirling before Celtic eventually won through in the replay at Parkhead, and then came a famous game at Falkirk on 21 February. A fine 3-2 win after being behind was good enough, but it was also the game where Charlie Tully scored direct from a corner kick, was made to take it again because the ball had apparently been outside the arc, and he scored again! It was also the game in which the great Jimmy Delaney, now playing in his twilight years for Falkirk, was badly fouled by Celtic's Frank Meechan. Celtic fans turned on Meechan and gave him 'pelters' for treating a great Celt like that!

That game was great Celtic stuff, but in many ways typical of Celtic in this era. A moment of spectacular greatness, but followed by a lapse into mediocrity. Celtic went to Ibrox in the next round, seemed to believe all the press propaganda about Rangers and collapsed dismally to a 0-2 defeat.

But then came 1954. By this time, Jock Stein as captain had begun to make his leadership qualities have an effect on the team, gradually winning over men like Charlie Tully who was initially reluctant to accept him. It was the year of the first league and cup double since 1914, and the Scottish Cup campaign was an epic one. Three times Celtic were drawn away from home at small, tight, difficult grounds at Falkirk, Stirling Albion and

Hamilton Academical – all potential banana skins – but the team won through by the odd goal in each case, thrilling and animating the fans by doing so.

Then came Motherwell again in the semi-final. Motherwell were (incredibly) now in Division 'B'. 102,424 were at Hampden to see Celtic 2-1 up but failing to get a crucial third goal, and the inevitable happened when Motherwell scored with a header virtually on time. The replay was held on the holiday Monday, 5 April, before 92,662 fans, and they saw a 3-1 win for Celtic with goals from Willie Fernie, Neil Mochan and an own goal from Motherwell's defender Willie Kilmarnock – an event which led to decades of quiz questions about how Kilmarnock could score against Motherwell, yet Celtic won the game?

The scoreline in the other semi-final the following Saturday was an incredible Rangers 0 Aberdeen 6. It was a result which, when announced over the radio, the announcer emphasised and then left a pause to allow for gasps. Not unnaturally this result was greeted with a certain amount of incredulity, then joy and euphoria in Celtic households, but it had to be tempered with the thought that Aberdeen would be formidable opponents. Their star centre-forward, however, Joe O'Neill (Celtic daft, not surprisingly with a name like that!), who had scored a hat-trick against Rangers, was injured for the final, and this may have given Celtic a decisive advantage.

It was another great Scottish Cup Final played in front of a capacity Hampden crowd with a huge number of Aberdonians, now in red as distinct from the black and gold of 1937, mingling happily with Celtic fans, all singing their comparatively new song 'The Northern Lights of Old Aberdeen'. It was a final in which Celtic and Aberdeen fans famously got on, with Celtic fans still congratulating the Dons on their 6-0 tanking of Rangers.

Half-time saw the game goalless. Then Celtic went ahead through a scrappy own goal, Aberdeen equalised almost immediately when Paddy Buckley for once managed to get the better of Jock Stein, before a fine piece of Willie Fernie magic on the right led to a tap-in from Celtic's makeshift centre-forward Sean Fallon. Then the famous half-back line of Evans, Stein and Peacock took a grip of the game and Celtic held out to win 2-1. It was the 17th Scottish Cup win, and the names of Bonnar, Haughney and Meechan; Evans, Stein and Peacock; Higgins, Fernie, Fallon, Tully and Mochan entered the Celtic folklore of great Scottish Cup Final teams.

We now, however, enter a dark era of our club's Scottish Cup history. Ten years of horror. One would like to have said 'we didn't even come close'. That in fact is not true. On four occasions we reached the final, and on another four the semi-final. So we did come close! That is what makes it all the harder to bear. Better surely to depart the tournament in January blaming it all on a hard pitch or a penalty decision that the referee gave or did not give rather than the gut-crunching disaster of a defeat in the spring when the snows have gone, the birds are twittering in the trees and the world looks a nice place – except for the bulldozer-type flattening of a cup-final defeat when you could have won it, often with a few unanswered questions.

The four cup-final defeats (three of which went to replays) all have one thing in common – the wrong team selection. Teams were picked more or less on the whim of the chairman and defied analysis even by the press, let alone the fee-paying public with the green and white scarves. The chairman, Mr Kelly, was a great chairman for Celtic in the political sense of the word. He has already been praised for his stance against the silly SFA diktat of the flying of the Irish flag, and students of bigotry remain amazed as to how he managed to win the support of Rangers, but be violently opposed by Hibs. (Yes, Hibs! Jealousy is a terrible thing!) In other respects he also managed to live up to the ideals of Willie Maley and indeed his own father, James Kelly, in his insistence that the world must see the best side of Celtic FC. Where he differed from these two great men was that he knew little about man-management and absolutely nothing about football tactics – but sadly, he thought he did!

Dear reader, the squeamish among you may not like what is to come in the Celtic horror stories. They are painful and some of them are still difficult to understand and to accept, but the remarkable thing was that so many of the loyal support stayed with the club and came out successfully at the other end. Those of us who were too young to really remember any pre-war great days began to imagine that it always had to be like this. So, having been warned, let us begin. In the *Aeneid* of Virgil, the good Aeneas, leader of the refugees from Troy, is asked by Queen Dido to say what happened. Aeneas describes his grief as 'infandum' (unspeakable) but 'although my mind shudders at the recollection, I will begin'.

Season 1955 saw Celtic second in both major competitions to Aberdeen and Clyde. The season was thus by no means a failure (one of the very rare seasons when Celtic came second in the league in this era), particularly as we came a lot closer than Rangers did, but the Scottish Cup Final of that year remained an unhealed wound for many years. The passage to the final has been described as 'undistinguished'. Recreation Park, Alloa was the first port of call, a place where Celtic had not been for many years. It was a 4-2 victory. Then followed a trip to Kilmarnock for a game on a frosty pitch which ended 1-1 at an overcrowded Rugby Park before Celtic won the replay on the Wednesday afternoon with a goal from Jimmy Walsh. Hamilton Accies, now in Division 'B', had made life difficult for Celtic in last season's quarter-final and did so again this year, but Fernie and Collins got the goals to get Celtic through.

Eerie parallels prevailed from last year as well in the semi-final. 'B' Division Lanarkshire opposition (Airdrie, this time rather than Motherwell), a pretty dreadful draw in the first game, the replay played on the holiday Monday at the beginning of April but this time John McPhail scored twice to put Celtic into the final to play neighbours Clyde on 23 April.

Soap opera drama abounded in the run-up to the game about whether the game was to be televised live or not. Television had only arrived in Scotland in 1952, and only a very few owned a 'box' or a 'set', but it was growing, and the country had already seen the World Cup of 1954. The televising of the game depended on the sale of tickets, but eventually the decision was reached that the game could be shown live. It was Scottish football's first-ever domestic match to be televised live, and Scottish patriots were appalled that the BBC sent an English commentator – the erudite and Celtic-sympathising Kenneth Wolstenholme – to do the game on the grounds that they didn't want regional accents!

Clyde's manager was Paddy Travers, who had been a player with Celtic the last time that the teams had met at this stage – in 1912! He did not get a place in that final (the inside-forwards were Jimmy McMenemy and Patsy Gallacher!) but he had won the cup as a manager for Clyde in 1939 and he might have expected to be given the Celtic job after the retirement of Willie Maley. Clyde, as often the case, full of Celtic supporters, had a fine team – full-back Harry Haddock and left-winger Tommy Ring were Scotland internationals – but it was generally expected that Celtic would win.

The first game was played on a sunny but windy day. The standard of play was not high, but Celtic, with a fine goal by Jimmy Walsh in the first half with the wind behind them, were looking good. In the second half, Clyde did not seem able to capitalise on the wind – until that fatal corner well within the last five minutes. It was not a good one from Archie Robertson and was heading straight for goalkeeper Johnnie Bonnar! Whether it was the wind playing tricks, the sun in Bonnar's eyes or simply a lapse of concentration, we don't know, but the 106,831 crowd and the many more crowded round a flickering black and white TV and looking forward to the presentation of the cup saw Bonnar, the hero of 1953 and 1954, allow the ball to slip through his fingers into the net, and Clyde were thus granted a reprieve. It was the same kind of goal as Alan Craig of Motherwell in 1931, but this time the grief was Celtic's.

Even then, Celtic were not too despondent. There was still a replay, but this was when the Bob Kelly death wish took over. There had been a somewhat undignified (and even slightly comic) moment when Bobby Collins, the 'wee barra', the smallest man on the park, had indulged in a shoulder-charging interlude with the Clyde goalkeeper. Everyone had a laugh, and duly forgot all about it, but it was bad enough for Mr Kelly to drop Bobby for the replay! The forward line was also rejigged and Sean Fallon brought in again as centre-forward. It had worked in 1954 but would not do so in 1955.

The weather conditions could not have been worse, and were a total contrast from Saturday. No TV this time and only 68,631 were there, all assuming that the absence of Bobby Collins was due to an injury. The news was greeted with joy in the Clyde dressing room. Clyde played confidently and scored through a rebound from the Celtic-daft Tommy Ring (whose brothers shunned him the following night when he went to show his mother his Scottish Cup medal), and Celtic's rejigged forward line never got going. It was a wet and totally painful experience.

But if 1955 was bad, 1956 was a great deal worse. This time the team selection was simply bizarre, and although there were injuries to Stein and Collins (a genuine injury this time), the whole performance of the team in the final was a mystery, and led to all sorts of dark insinuations. The passage to the cup final was more straightforward this year. Good wins at Morton and Ayr, then tighter wins over Airdrie at Parkhead and Clyde at Hampden in the semi-final (some sort of revenge for last year) saw Celtic meet Hearts in the final on 21 April 1956. No TV this year, and a huge crowd of 132,842 with Edinburgh well represented, and many Hearts supporters paying their first visit to Hampden. It was Hearts' first Scottish Cup Final since 1907!

Tribute must be paid to Hearts. A fine team patiently assembled by Tommy Walker (they would win the league in 1958 and 1960, had already won the League Cup in October 1954 and would do so on another three occasions) with many good players like the famous inside trio of Conn, Bauld and Wardhaugh, Dave Mackay, Johnny Cumming and Freddie Glidden, they were a good side and might well have defeated Celtic in any case. They also, in 1956, had a civilised support, something that was not always true of Celtic in those awful days of the 1950s. Nor was it true of Hearts in more recent years!

The team selection, however, was crucial. The absence of Stein for most of the season had been generally solved by fielding Eric Smith at right-half to allow Bobby Evans to play centre-half. This had been a partial success at least but the forward line was more of a problem. Yet, to cover for the absence of Collins, there were adequate replacements like John McAlindon, Jimmy Walsh and Jim Sharkey, all of whom were good enough, particularly Sharkey who had scored in the semi-final against Clyde. Yet Mr Kelly, in a move which still defies any kind of reasoning, brought right-back Mike Haughney to the inside-right position, played left-back Frank Meechan at right-back, and in the outside-right position gave a chance to a youngster called Billy Craig who had played only three games for the club.

It was the Haughney move which was the biggest disaster, for although he scored Celtic's only goal (which might have been disallowed for a foul on the goalkeeper), he was otherwise anonymous as Celtic were, frankly, outplayed by a superior team, something that cannot really be said very often of Celtic in a cup final.

The supporters were shattered and in their distress looked for other causes of this defeat. Some of them landed on the goalkeeping. Such stories would grow arms and legs in view of subsequent events, and should be examined in the context of the events of the following year of 1957. The pain was intense in 1956, but it does not excuse the awful behaviour at the end of the game, Hearts supporters (often with wives and small children) compelled to run the gauntlet of two separate gangs of Celtic supporters lining up in ominous and threatening silence as they made their way to the Mount Florida railway station.

By the time the 1957 Scottish Cup campaign began, Celtic had for the first time won the Scottish League Cup, beating Partick Thistle in a replayed cup final and restoring a little credibility after the puzzling events of April 1956. In the Scottish Cup, Mosset Park, Forres was the first port of call, and the locals saw a great Celtic performance with a 5-0 victory. It was totally different on 16 February when Rangers came to Celtic Park and played out a thrilling 4-4 draw. Rangers were ahead 2-0 at one point, but then Celtic made it 4-2 before

Rangers equalised twice in the last ten minutes – one a soft penalty and the other a blunder by John Jack – all of which did no harm at all to the Glasgow conspiracy theorists, especially when 80,000 turned up at Ibrox the following Wednesday.

This time on a hard and heavily sanded pitch, Celtic made no mistake with Johnny Higgins scoring first, then Neil Mochan before half-time. Celtic simply played the game out in the second half with Rangers fans departing in droves long before the final whistle. Higgins and Peacock were the men who scored the goals in the quarter-final match in early March at Celtic Park against St Mirren, which Celtic won with more comfort than the 2-1 scoreline would suggest.

And thus we come to the semi-final against Kilmarnock at Hampden on 23 March. 109,145 saw the first game, and it might have been better for the green and white hordes if John Higgins had missed his header for that Mochan cross which gave Celtic their late and not really entirely deserved equaliser. However, 76,963 came back again for the replay, a teatime kick-off at Hampden on Wednesday. It was an odd, disappointing and mysterious Celtic experience.

The wind was described as 'capricious', but newspapers, not least the respected *Glasgow Herald*, unite in talking about the sheer amount of mistakes made by the Celtic defence, centre-half John Jack and goalkeeper Dick Beattie in particular, who was described as a 'nervous wreck' by the end. The highlights can be viewed on YouTube and one leaves the reader to make up his own mind, but it was all a huge disappointment. Years later in 1965 when Beattie was 'done' for match-fixing when with Portsmouth, Celtic supporters thought back to this match and said 'Ah!' Some of them even wondered about the 1956 final against Hearts – but it must be stressed that no evidence of anything untoward has ever emerged, at least as far as Celtic are concerned. It is also true that it is a gut reaction to blame a bad defeat on corruption – the same was said about the 1926 Scottish Cup Final and the Glasgow Cup Final of 1908/09, again with no evidence. And it is also possible that Kilmarnock, a fast-emerging team with some fine players, quite simply were the better team!

In 1958, Celtic, only a few months after the famous 7-1 win over Rangers in the Scottish League Cup Final, started off with a tight win against Airdrie at Broomfield. Celtic were 4-0 up but began to lose goals through their own carelessness and the inspired play of Ian McMillan who would soon be transferred to Rangers. It ended up 4-3 and Celtic were very much indebted to the saving of the same Dick Beattie who did so badly against Kilmarnock the previous year, and indeed who had been one of the stars of the 7-1 game, famously having his photo taken while holding up seven fingers!

Stirling Albion came to Parkhead next and were dispatched 7-3. The next round tie on 1 March was also played at Parkhead – but by agreement with Clyde. This had followed a league game earlier in the season when a wall had collapsed at Shawfield, killing a young boy and injuring many. When the teams were drawn to play at Shawfield (where the damage was still being repaired), both teams agreed to play the game at Celtic Park. A

65,000 crowd appeared on a nice day after a snowy week, and saw a poor Celtic team badly beaten 0-2 by the Clyde side who went on to win the cup that year. The decline from the 7-1 win in October had been swift.

1959 saw the 'Kelly's Kids' youth policy in full swing. It was a good idea, based consciously on the 'Busby Babes' idea of Manchester United, but the policy was ill-thought out and badly organised with the one man who could have made it work, Jock Stein, given too little say in it. In any case, youth policies, by definition almost, do take time. However, Celtic started off by beating Albion Rovers 4-0 at Parkhead, then drew 1-1 with Clyde at Celtic Park on a Wednesday afternoon after the pitch was waterlogged on the Saturday. A really exciting replay then followed at the now repaired Shawfield on Monday, 23 February with a 5.30pm kick-off under Clyde's floodlights. Bertie Peacock scored the decisive goal in extra time, and the reward was a home tie on Saturday, 28 February against Rangers!

Before a restricted crowd of 42,000 – a successful effort to beat hooliganism – the Celtic youngsters turned it on, scored on either side of half-time through John Divers III and Matt McVittie and stayed in control of the game until Rangers scored with virtually the last kick of the ball. It was too late to make any difference, even though it reduced Celtic fans listening to the game on the radio to an apoplexy of desperation as they urged the referee Jack Mowat to blow for full time!

Hopes that the Scottish Cup might be returning to Celtic Park increased when Celtic beat Stirling Albion 3-1 on a glue pot of a pitch at Annfield. Celtic took advantage of a mysterious decision of Stirling Albion to play against the wind and the rain and were 3-0 up at half-time with goals from John Divers, Sammy Wilson and Ian Lochhead. The Binos pulled one back in the second half but to no further effect.

And so to Hampden for the semi-final on 4 April against St Mirren. 73,885 stood and gawped in amazement at the way that Celtic folded before a rampant Buddies team which simply swept them aside. It was totally incomprehensible, and the 4-0 score might have been a great deal more, as Celtic's young forwards failed to get moving, and experienced defenders like Evans and Peacock simply buckled under it all. It was a shambles of a team which was Celtic in name only. Most supporters were angry, although a realistic assessment was that the occasion was simply too much too soon for so many of the young Celts.

The shambles continued in 1960. There was, however, one significant event in March, little talked about at the time, but one which would have massive reverberations for the club. Jock Stein was allowed to leave his vague and ill-defined job as youth-team coach to become manager of Dunfermline Athletic, currently struggling at the foot of the table. Insofar as anyone noticed, we were glad to see that our ex-captain had got himself a job – but he would not do well, no one thought, at perpetually struggling East End Park on a low budget with a club who were no strangers to the Second Division.

Even when, in his first game, Stein's new team beat a poor Celtic side in what was (for Celtic) a meaningless league fixture, we just shrugged our shoulders. It was only next year that we realised just what had happened. Years later in a famous BBC interview, Jock said that one of the reasons that he left was because he may have been given to understand that, as a non-Catholic, he might have reached his limit at Celtic FC. If this is so, it reveals just what a fool the chairman was – and how Celtic would suffer for the next five years because of his folly!

The 1960 Scottish Cup featured a prolonged struggle to get the better of St Mirren. It is often felt that one draw can happen, but that another one after that is 'kinda pushin' yer luck'. Loads of goals, appalling defending, poor weather, a few postponements, surprisingly large crowds and eventually on Leap Year Day of 29 February, Neil Mochan scored all five goals in a 5-2 win at Parkhead in a game where season ticket holders of both clubs were allowed in free! There followed, the following Saturday, a trip to Borough Briggs in Elgin (the ground where Jimmy Delaney had finished his career a few years earlier) and a narrow 2-1 win with two goals in the last ten minutes which avoided a major embarrassment. 'Getting out of the Highland jail' was the phrase used. There was then a more respectable (but still not yet a comfortable) 2-0 win over Partick Thistle to set up a semi-final against Rangers.

Oh dear! A harbinger of things to come! A good, possibly even unlucky, draw in the first game on 2 April where young Steve Chalmers scored against a Rangers side who were no great shakes, and people were beginning to ask, cautiously, if the Celtic youth policy was beginning to work. 79,786 were there at Hampden, and 71,977 came back for the replay on the Wednesday night with a teatime kick-off for the game that might well go down as the start of the Rangers complex of the early 1960s. The Celtic team which had apparently won their spurs on Saturday folded piteously on Wednesday and Rangers, who would soon lose the league to Hearts and be hammered mercilessly by Eintracht Frankfurt, ran out 4-1 winners. 1-1 at half-time had been followed by awful defending in the second half, and the torrential rain which came on more or less at the full-time whistle was looked upon as either the wrath of the gods or a token of what was waiting for us in the next few years. Dunfermline Athletic, incidentally, escaped relegation that year.

Dunfermline Athletic! Ah, yes! 1961. Sixty years has not erased the memory of that dull April night, and the effect that that night has had on the rest of our lives has been egregious and significant. Even though the correct decision was made nearly four years later, and we went on to unbelievable heights, Wednesday, 26 April 1961 will remain a scar. At about the same time, the USA were making a fool of themselves (not for the first or last time) by trying to invade Cuba in what became known as the Bay of Pigs fiasco. It was hardly a bigger fiasco than ours.

But to begin at the beginning. 1961 was actually a year in which we (poor deluded fools!) could believe that a good team was emerging. There were still inconsistencies, and league form was predictably dreadful, but the Scottish Cup saw good wins against Falkirk, Montrose and Raith Rovers (neither of these three being the most demanding of opposition, it has to be said, but we won convincingly) and then on 11 March a quarter-final against Hibs, who had a fine team and a good goalkeeper called Ronnie Simpson, now back in Scotland after a great career with Newcastle United. The Edinburgh men were winning 1-0 before 56,000 at Parkhead until late in the game when Steve Chalmers scored the equaliser – the scenes of relief and joy being so remarkable that even BBC TV had to turn one of its antiquated cameras to behind the goal to record the scene for the highlights programme.

Easter Road was, frankly, dangerous that Wednesday night of the replay. The crowd was given as 39,243. You had to be gullible if you believed that. There were at least 10,000 more inside than that, and the gates had to be closed with thousands still outside. The game was, like the first game, very even, but in extra time it was the unlikely figure of John Clark, a young defender who had played only a handful of games for the club over three seasons, who got the winner.

Airdrie were competently dispatched 4-0 at Hampden on 1 April. Everyone expected that the opponents would be St Mirren in the final, but in fact, it was Dunfermline who edged through after a replay. We were glad that it would not be St Mirren, so often our nemesis in the past, and looked forward to seeing provincial Dunfermline who had never been within a million miles of the Scottish Cup on any previous occasion and did not look like doing so now against our young lions who were fast developing and firing on all cylinders, not least that great right-half called Pat Crerand.

Optimism, that most dangerous of emotions, grew. Seven years had passed since 1954. Ignoring war years, that had been the longest absence of the Scottish Cup from Celtic Park this century, and one had to go back to 1892–1899 for another such gap. Time to bring back the Scottish Cup! Sadly, optimism developed into something approaching complacency and so many people who really should have known a lot better underestimated Jock Stein.

One of those who did just that was chairman Bob Kelly, who allowed Bertie Peacock to go to play in a silly friendly international in Italy for Northern Ireland. Granted, Peacock was past his best, but, having played with Jock Stein, Bertie certainly knew the way that Jock's mind worked, and the fact that his country was still interested in him says something, does it not? Peacock was not chosen for the first game of the Scottish Cup Final and was allowed to go to Italy for the replay. This was a bad mistake.

The game should have been won on Saturday, 22 April. 113,618 saw what could only be described as a poor game, a 0-0 draw, in which Dunfermline were far from overawed and did themselves proud. Celtic fans were less happy, but surely the replay would be a different matter? The more perceptive also thought that Peacock should get a game. The excellent John Clark should not be replaced at left-half, but Peacock had once played in the forward line as well. He could do a job there beside Willie Fernie.

The folly of allowing Peacock to disappear abroad became apparent when Jim Kennedy, the left-back, went down with appendicitis on the Tuesday and would have to be replaced by debutant Willie O'Neill. Surely there was still time for Peacock to be recalled? This was 1961, in many ways a far less sophisticated time as far as communication was concerned, but there were still telephones and aeroplanes. The defensive-minded Clark could play at left-back, and Bertie could play at left-half? It did not seem too difficult to work that out ... but it never happened. The money spent in paying the airfare would surely have been worth it.

87,866 saw this shattering game which kicked off at 6.15pm, floodlights not yet having arrived at Hampden Park. Pat Crerand was inspirational in the constant drizzle and bad light, but the forwards simply could not score. Eddie Connachan, the Celtic-daft Dunfermline goalkeeper, played out of his skin but he was helped by some woefully inept Celtic shooting. Half-time saw still no score and the danger signal was up. Dave Thomson scored for Dunfermline in the 67th (yes, the 67th!) minute and Celtic still could not score. Desperation grew, and then Frank Haffey in the Celtic goal lost concentration and Dunfermline's veteran Charlie Dickson scored again into the King's Park goal behind which stood thousands of sullen and angry Celtic supporters.

Full time came to a hail of stones and bottles from the misguided of the Celtic support, in stark contrast to the demeanour of the player who accepted defeat graciously, and indeed to the majority of the Celtic support who departed in morose but dignified silence. The pain of this game, however, would simply not go away – and still hasn't. A lifetime later, those of us who recall that game remember how we hated Jock Stein and his white coat that night!

Nothing can ever excuse hooliganism, but those at the top of the club had a responsibility to recognise that the anti-social behaviour was born of frustration, and that something really should be done at club level. 1962's hooliganism was far worse. It came, ironically, at the end of a season where the standard of play from the team had been a great deal better, and where there were clear and definite signs that a good team was slowly emerging, or as the phrase was in 1962, 'the young Kelly Kids have arrived'.

But had they? Season 1961/62 was characterised by some inspiring football, but also some dreadful naivety, exemplified by an appalling inability to beat smaller teams like Falkirk, Stirling Albion, Airdrie and Raith Rovers. That was the Scottish League, but the Scottish Cup saw some epic games – and a little naivety here as well.

The Scottish Cup started before Christmas this year with an easy win over Cowdenbeath, and then at the end of January with a more difficult but still impressive win at Second Division Morton. This set up a game at Tynecastle against Hearts on 17 February. In some ways it was Celtic's best-ever cup tie, for they were 2-1 down for a long time in the second half, fought back to make it 3-2, then Hearts pulled it back level before Pat Crerand with a twice-taken penalty edged Celtic home to win 4-3. Hearts protested long and hard about refereeing decisions, and the weaker element of the Celtic support would have agreed that a draw and a replay might have been a fairer result, but the game nevertheless was a great advert for Scottish football and for Celtic. A spring was now in our step.

Next came Third Lanark to Celtic Park in early March. Again this was another amazing game. 3-1 down at half-time and looking down and out to a good Thirds side, once again the Celtic youngsters fought back with loads of energy and self-belief to make it 4-3 but then themselves conceded a late equaliser to make it 4-4. One wondered what the fuss was all about the following Wednesday night at Hampden (Cathkin was rightly considered too small for the huge Celtic crowd) when Celtic won 4-0 at a canter with Steve Chalmers and John Hughes among the goals in both games.

The semi-final draw paired Rangers with Motherwell at Hampden and Celtic with St Mirren at Ibrox. It looked a good draw, particularly when Celtic travelled to Paisley on the Monday evening before the semi-final for a meaningless Scottish League game and won 5-0 in a fine display of attacking football.

But sometime between the Monday night and the Saturday afternoon, two unwelcome and dangerous guests arrived at Parkhead. One was called Naivety and the other was called Complacency. Naivety failed to tell Celtic that St Mirren's performance on Monday might have been what is known in the trade as an 'ambush', and Complacency said seductively that all you have to do is turn up at Ibrox on Saturday and everything will be all right.

Hardly anyone in the press, or in either support, gave St Mirren much of a chance this bright and breezy day at Ibrox on 31 March 1962. It became another day of infamy. The first hint, however, that something might be wrong came when captain Dunky MacKay won the toss and chose to play against the wind. This was not in itself a cause for concern, although conventional football wisdom at the time tended to say that it was best to go with the elements in the first half on the grounds that conditions might change in an hour's time. What was concerning, however, was the outbreak of bickering from other members of the team with several men clearly seen shouting at their captain for being a fool. This may or may not have played a part in what followed, but it certainly hinted at unsettlement in the Celtic ranks.

The wily old Willie Fernie now played for the Saints and scored first. Taking full advantage of the wind, St Mirren scored a further two, and the half-time score was a barely credible St Mirren 3 Celtic 0 with several operators of half-time scoreboards at other grounds refusing to put this score up, convinced that someone was having them on. At Hampden where Rangers were playing Motherwell in the other semi-final, it was widely believed to be a hoax.

The second half saw a slight improvement in the play but no dent in the scoreline and after several periods of obvious unhappiness on the terracings, after about 80 minutes, some Celtic supporters (and they could not in all honesty be described as a 'small minority') invaded the park in an attempt to get the game stopped. Referee Mr McKenzie took the players off. Lack of intelligence can never be used as an excuse for such attempted bullying and mob rule, and chairman Bob Kelly consulted his fellow directors and, to his credit, conceded the game, there and then, to the St Mirren directors. Thus by the time that the pitch was cleared and the players came back (Celtic did score once) the game was in fact over and Celtic were, once again, out of the Scottish Cup.

The club lost a great deal of credibility in all this, but the real punishment for players and fans came in the crushing disappointment. Yet again no trophy for Celtic. Was there ever to be an end to this nightmare?

Celtic might well have been banned from the Scottish Cup of 1963 in the wake of that Ibrox disgrace, but for fairly obvious financial reasons, they weren't. It might have been as well if they had been banned, for 1963's Scottish Cup Final was as sorry a night as one could have imagined, and frankly, one of those nights on which one despaired about the club, because no one at the top of the hierarchy seemed to *want* to do anything about it. It was the 75th year of the club. Celebrations for that anniversary were not so much muted as non-existent. There was nothing to be happy about.

The 1963 Scottish Cup was badly distorted by the big freeze-up, possibly worse than 1947 or any other year. There was perhaps less snow than in 1947, but the freeze-up lasted longer, from mid-January until well into March. Celtic managed to play one Scottish Cup tie on Wednesday, 28 January at Brockville. Newspaper reports are virtually unanimous that the game should not have gone ahead, but it did and Celtic beat Falkirk 2-0 with goals from John Hughes and Charlie Gallagher. It was Wednesday, 6 March before the next game could be played and it was another good result – a 3-1 win over Hearts at Parkhead, in spite of Hearts scoring first through a man called Willie Wallace. The following Wednesday, we had Gala Fairydean getting a great welcome from the Parkhead crowd before a 6-0 home win, and then at the end of the month, Celtic were at a crowded Love Street, Paisley to play St Mirren (more or less a year exactly since the infamous game at Ibrox between the two teams) but this time Celtic won 1-0 with a fine goal from the grossly undervalued Frank Brogan.

So far, so good. In a dreadful game at Ibrox in the semi-final on 13 April, Celtic beat a Raith Rovers side heading for relegation, 5-2, while on the same day Rangers beat Dundee United by the same score in a game which similarly failed to get anyone excited in spite of the plethora of goals. It was thus the first Old Firm Scottish Cup Final since 1928, and this year it was scheduled for 4 May because of the freeze-up when it would normally have been at least a fortnight earlier. Celtic fans were apprehensive (and with good cause) but a commonly held phrase was 'You never know' in the build-up to this game.

But there was, for Celtic, another factor. Their one undeniable star player, Pat Crerand, had now been transferred to Manchester United. This had happened in February in the middle of the freeze-up, but it was a long story. Crerand had clearly been unhappy about so much that was going on at Parkhead, but he was now away. The transfer fee was about £60,000 but predictably, it had not been used. This was sad because there were so many good talented players of a Celtic persuasion going around other clubs, and they would have loved to join us.

In fact, there was a lot to be happy about in the first game in the Hampden rain when both teams scored just before half-time and the game finished 1-1. Rangers were undeniably the better side on a territorial basis, and Frank Haffey in the Celtic goal had an outstanding game, but there was always the chance that Celtic could just nick a winner near the end. But 1-1 it was, and the Celtic fans applauded their team with vigour at the end. Wee Jimmy Johnstone had been a revelation, Frank Brogan had been a constant threat on the left wing and Jim Baxter had never dominated the game as the press had told us he would. Rangers did not look unbeatable, but the intervening 11 days made sure that they became so, as 'headless chickens' became the order of the day at Celtic Park.

The final could not be replayed until a week come Wednesday because there was a Scotland v Austria game on the first Wednesday (a game, incidentally, which is a story in itself and had to be abandoned because of the brutal tactics of the Austrians), and Celtic played off three league games. They beat Clyde and Motherwell but also paid an awful visit to Dundee United where they lost 0-3 in a terrible display. It was this performance against a Dundee United team which even their most ardent supporters could not rate any higher than 'ordinary' which effectively killed Celtic, and led to one of the most vile and sustained outpourings of sheer filth from so-called supporters that one could imagine with the honest Steve Chalmers the victim of most of it.

Leadership was clearly lacking and the team that took the field for the cup final replay was defeated more or less from the start. Out were the two successful wingers from the first game, Johnstone and Brogan. The forward line which was cobbled together read Craig, Murdoch, Divers, Chalmers and Hughes, arguably no one in his best position – and the word 'shambles' would not quite cover their display. 'They had all the teamwork and cohesion of a starving mob at a bread riot' as it was graphically but tastelessly described. On a night like this, you needed Pat Crerand, the one Celtic player of undeniable class – but he was away. The directors and the chairman just seemed to think that magically Celtic would learn to cope without him.

Nemesis arrived in full force that night of the cup final replay on 15 May, visiting agony and torture on the Celtic fans for the folly and indeed wickedness of their leaders. Rangers were 2-0 up before half-time and then when they scored again in the 70th minute, 50,000 spectacularly and almost in unison turned their backs on Celtic and went home. One recalls the eerie silence of the departure punctuated by the odd oath or curse of Bob Kelly or Pat Crerand – the obvious targets – and yet, one veteran supporter, who clearly knew the story of Pandora's box in which all the evils of the world were released, but also hope was liberated, said quietly and sagely 'They'll come again!'

Celtic fans had seen many false dawns in their time, but 1964 did seem to bring some sort of improvement, apart from one key area, namely their chronic inability to stand up to a Rangers team who were not, in all truth, all that good, as their repeated failures in Europe proved. By the time that the Scottish Cup began after the new year, the Celtic death wish had seen four defeats to Rangers. But Celtic accounted for Eyemouth, and then two weeks later on Burns Night, a very interesting encounter with Morton, the runaway Second Division leaders, saw a great 3-1 win which included a magnificent individual John Hughes goal and a goal scored direct from a corner by Charlie Gallagher. The Celtic Supporters Association handbook for the following year talks about 'the laughable spectacle of the good people of Greenock, from the provost downwards, brainwashed by the press into believing that they would beat Celtic'.

Still on the crest of a wave from that one, Celtic beat Airdrie 4-1 at Parkhead in the next round to put them into the quarter-finals against – Rangers! But there was another more positive dynamic here. Celtic, in contrast to Rangers, were still in Europe and actually doing well! On the Wednesday before the cup tie at Ibrox, they beat Slovan Bratislava away to qualify for the semi-final. They came home to a deserved heroes' reception and they were actually clapped on to the field by Rangers for their performance! Whether this was a stunt to unnerve Celtic, or designed as an anti-hooligan measure, we cannot be sure. It may even have been a genuine gesture of respect from Rangers. For whatever reason, Rangers deserve a certain amount of credit.

In any case, things looked good for Celtic. The weather was virtually perfect, the Celtic end was in good voice and the players *looked* confident. But the conquerors of Slovan Bratislava were prisoners of 1964 when the unwritten, unseen but omnipotent law was in force that Celtic were not allowed to beat Rangers. This law, supported by the *Scottish Daily Express* and the BBC, was sadly invoked today again. A good first half finished with a goal for Rangers. Soon after half-time, Rangers scored again ... and Celtic collapsed pitifully with no real resistance or fightback. Six weeks later they blew up in Europe as well when the omens looked good.

1964 was awful. Rational people would have given it all up, but we were Celtic supporters.

Season 1946/47: First Round

25/01/1947	Dundee	away	1-2	McAloon

Season 1947/48: Semi-Finalists

07/02/1948	Cowdenbeath	home	3-0	McPhail 2, W. Gallacher
21/02/1948	Motherwell	home	1-0	Paton
06/03/1948	Montrose	home	4-0	McPhail 2, Weir, Paton
27/03/1948	Morton	Ibrox	0-1	

Season 1948/49: First Round

22/01/1949	Dundee Utd	away	3-4	J. Gallacher 2, Tully

Season 1949/50: Third Round

28/01/1950	Brechin City	away	3-0	Weir 2, McPhail
15/02/1950	Third Lanark	away	1-1	Weir
20/02/1950	Third Lanark	home	4-1	McPhail 3, Tully
25/02/1950	Aberdeen	home	0-1	

Season 1950/51: Winners

27/01/1951	East Fife	away	2-2	J. Weir, Collins
31/01/1951	East Fife	home	4-2	McPhail 2, Peacock, Collins
10/02/1951	Duns	home	4-0	J. Weir 2, Peacock, D Weir
24/02/1951	Hearts	away	2-1	J. Weir, McPhail
10/03/1951	Aberdeen	home	3-0	McPhail 2, Tully
31/03/1951	Raith Rovers	Hampden	3-2	J. Weir, McPhail, Tully
21/04/1951	Motherwell	Hampden	1-0	McPhail

Season 1951/52: First Round

30/01/1952	Third Lanark	home	0-0	
04/02/1952	Third Lanark	away	1-2	Rollo

Season 1952/53: Quarter-Finals

24/01/1953	Eyemouth Utd	away	4-0	McGrory 4
07/02/1953	Stirling Albion	away	1-1	McGrory
11/02/1953	Stirling Albion	home	3-0	McGrory 2, Peacock
21/02/1953	Falkirk	away	3-2	McGrory, Tully, Fernie
14/03/1953	Rangers	away	0-2	

Season 1953/54: Winners

17/02/1954	Falkirk	away	2-1	Fernie, Higgins

27/02/1954	Stirling Albion	away	4-3	Mochan 2, Higgins, Haughney (pen)
13/03/1954	Hamilton Accies	away	2-1	Fernie, Haughney (pen)
27/03/1954	Motherwell	Hampden	2-2	Mochan, Fallon
05/04/1954	Motherwell	Hampden	3-1	Mochan, Fernie, og
24/04/1954	Aberdeen	Hampden	2-1	Fallon, og

Season 1954/55: Finalists

05/02/1955	Alloa	away	4-2	Walsh 2, Peacock, Haughney (pen)
19/02/1955	Kilmarnock	away	1-1	Smith
23/02/1955	Kilmarnock	home	1-0	Walsh
05/03/1955	Hamilton Accies	home	2-1	Collins, Fernie
26/03/1955	Airdrie	Hampden	2-2	Fernie, Walsh
04/03/1955	Airdrie	Hampden	2-0	McPhail 2
23/04/1955	Clyde	Hampden	1-1	Walsh
27/04/1955	Clyde	Hampden	0-1	

Season 1955/56: Finalists

04/02/1956	Morton	away	2-0	Tully, Collins
18/02/1956	Ayr United	away	3-0	Collins 2, Mochan
03/03/1956	Airdrie	home	2-1	Collins, Tully
24/03/1956	Clyde	Hampden	2-1	Sharkey, Haughney (pen)
21/03/1956	Hearts	Hampden	1-3	Haughney

Season 1956/57: Semi-Finalists

02/02/1957	Forres Mechs	away	5-0	McPhail 3, Higgins, Mochan
16/02/1957	Rangers	home	4-4	McPhail, Higgins, Collins, Fernie
20/02/1957	Rangers	away	2-0	Higgins, Mochan
02/03/1957	St Mirren	home	2-1	Higgins, Peacock
23/03/1957	Kilmarnock	Hampden	1-1	Higgins
27/03/1957	Kilmarnock	Hampden	1-3	Collins

Season 1957/58: Third Round

01/02/1958	Airdrie	away	4-3	Byrne 2, Collins, Fernie
15/02/1958	Stirling Albion	home	7-2	Byrne 2, Smith 2, Wilson 2, Mochan
01/03/1958	Clyde	away	0-2	

Game played at Celtic Park for safety reasons

Season 1958/59: Semi-Finalists

31/01/1959	Albion Rovers	home	4-0	Wilson 2, Jackson, og
18/02/1959	Clyde	home	1-1	McVittie
23/02/1959	Clyde	away	4-3	Wilson 2, McVittie, Peacock
28/02/1959	Rangers	home	2-1	Divers, McVittie
16/03/1959	Stirling Albion	away	3-1	Divers, Wilson, Lochhead
04/04/1959	St Mirren	Hampden	0-4	

Season 1959/60: Semi-Finalists

13/02/1960	St Mirren	away	1-1	Byrne
24/02/1960	St Mirren	home	4-4	Mochan 2, Divers 2
29/02/1960	St Mirren	home	5-2	Mochan 5 (1 pen)
05/03/1960	Elgin City	away	2-1	Divers, Smith
12/03/1960	Partick Thistle	home	2-0	Smith, Colrain
02/04/1960	Rangers	Hampden	1-1	Chalmers
06/04/1960	Rangers	Hampden	1-4	Mochan

Season 1960/61: Finalists

28/01/1961	Falkirk	away	3-1	Peacock 2 (pens), Auld
11/02/1961	Montrose	home	6-0	Hughes 2, Chalmers 2, Byrne, og
25/02/1961	Raith Rovers	away	4-1	Hughes, Chalmers, Fernie, og
11/03/1961	Hibs	home	1-1	Chalmers
15/03/1961	Hibs	away	1-0	Clark
01/04/1961	Airdrie	Hampden	4-0	Hughes 2, Chalmers, Fernie
22/04/1961	Dunfermline	Hampden	0-0	
26/04/1961	Dunfermline	Hampden	0-2	

Season 1961/62: Semi-Finalists

13/12/1961	Cowdenbeath	home	5-1	Chalmers 2, Jackson, Hughes, Divers
27/01/1961	Morton	away	3-1	Carroll, Divers, Jackson
17/02/1962	Hearts	away	4-3	Divers 2, Chalmers, Crerand (pen)
10/03/1962	Third Lanark	home	4-4	Chalmers 2, Hughes, F. Brogan
14/03/1962	Third Lanark	away	4-0	Hughes 2, Chalmers, Byrne

Game played at Hampden for safety reasons

31/03/1962	St Mirren	Ibrox	1-3	Byrne

Season 1962/63: Finalists

28/01/1963	Falkirk	away	2-0	Hughes, Gallagher
06/03/1963	Hearts	home	3-1	Murdoch, McNamee, Hughes
13/03/1963	Gala Fairydean	home	6-0	Murdoch 3, Hughes 2, Divers
30/03/1963	St Mirren	away	1-0	F. Brogan
13/04/1963	Raith Rovers	Ibrox	5-2	McKay 2 (pens), Chalmers, Divers, F. Brogan
04/05/1963	Rangers	Hampden	1-1	Murdoch
15/05/1963	Rangers	Hampden	0-3	

Season 1963/64: Quarter-Finals

11/01/1964	Eyemouth	home	3-0	Chalmers 2, Gallagher
25/01/1964	Morton	away	3-1	Hughes, Gallagher, Johnstone
15/02/1964	Airdrie	home	4-1	Chalmers, Hughes, Johnstone, Murdoch (pen)
07/03/1964	Rangers	away	0-2	

CHAPTER FIVE

THE GREAT DAYS
1965–1977

IT WAS probably sometime in November or December 1964 that Celtic's chairman Bob Kelly realised that he had been wrong. This took a lot of admitting because although all Celtic supporters could work out without a great deal of bother what was going on, Kelly lacked anyone in his own close circle to have a 'quiet word' in his ear. He was so surrounded by sycophants and parasites that he lived in his own fool's paradise where he was unaware of anything else other than himself, and he was so sure that he was right. But things at the other 'paradise' had reached a critical point.

Things had been looking up – for a spell. The team had at long last stood up to Rangers in the rain of September 1964 and had then reached the League Cup Final, but had then predictably, albeit narrowly and even unluckily, blown it. Celtic had then gone into freefall and the crowds were showing every sign of deserting them – for good, this time. Words like 'finished' were freely used. It was then, in this darkest of dark hours, that Kelly realised that he had made the wrong decision in March 1960 when he let Jock Stein go.

If this 1960 decision had been made on the basis of Stein's nominal Protestantism (Stein, though by no means a godless man, was far from a regular church attender), then it showed Kelly's own bigotry and lack of awareness of the situation, and how Celtic had suffered for it! But now in late 1964, reputedly over a lunch table in a restaurant when Stein, now manager of Hibs, had approached Kelly to discuss an approach that Wolverhampton Wanderers had made for him (a somewhat dubious story, one feels), Kelly bit the bullet (and, oh, how it must have hurt!) and Stein was offered the job. Stein accepted with alacrity but imposed one or two conditions, particularly full undisputed control of team selection and team matters, and the return of Bertie Auld from Birmingham City.

In later years, Kelly would have everyone believe that this was all part of a grand plan, as if Stein had been 'farmed out', as it were, to Dunfermline and then Hibs so that he could one day return to become manager of Celtic. This, frankly, was transparent moonshine.

Celtic, having spent an awful Christmas, New Year and January, did not make the announcement until Sunday, 31 January 1965. Even then, Stein would not take over as manager until 8 March, by which time Celtic would have played three Scottish Cup games that year. But the psychological effect was galvanising. On 6 February Celtic went to their old cup tie rivals St Mirren. Before a packed Love Street crowd (Love Street was always packed when Celtic arrived in the Scottish Cup!),

Celtic turned it on with one goal from Chalmers and two from Lennox. They then had a surprisingly difficult trip to Hampden to play Queen's Park. They appeared in an all-green strip for the first time for a while and edged home only through a solitary Bobby Lennox goal.

And then we came to the significant day of Saturday, 6 March when Kilmarnock came to Celtic Park. Stein was due to take over on the Monday, and therefore this was McGrory's last day as manager before he moved to his new role as public relations officer. It was also the last day that Celtic ever played in the 'Hibs reverse' strip of white with green sleeves. There was a bit of history with Kilmarnock who, in a meaningless League Cup sectional game at Rugby Park earlier in the season, had turned nasty and injured McNeill and Murdoch. It was therefore all the more rewarding to beat them 3-2 that day with goals from Lennox, Auld and Hughes.

But there was even more to be happy about on that sunny, spring day. Across the country in Edinburgh in what was virtually Hibs's last kick of the ball under Jock Stein's managership, full-back John Fraser scored the goal which put Rangers out of the Scottish Cup! Possibly, some said, Stein won the Scottish Cup for Celtic before he even arrived at Celtic Park!

Three weeks later Stein took charge of the team for his first-ever Scottish Cup tie with them, and it was the semi-final v Motherwell at Hampden. It was a difficult game at Hampden on a sunny but windy day and Motherwell twice went ahead through Joe McBride, who gave Billy McNeill a difficult time of it. But Lennox put Celtic on level terms the first time, then it was Bertie

Auld with a penalty kick who levelled the score, and then Celtic scored in the very last minute what seemed like the winner before it was controversially knocked off for offside. 2-2 it was, but Celtic made no mistake in the Wednesday night replay with goals from Chalmers, Hughes and Lennox.

In the other semi-final, between Dunfermline Athletic and Hibs (Jock Stein's two former teams) Dunfermline won through and thus the 1965 Scottish Cup Final was a reprise of 1961, the key difference being that Stein was now the manager of Celtic, as distinct from Dunfermline! Nevertheless, Dunfermline were well managed by Willie Cunningham. They were also going for the Scottish League, and while some folk saw this as a disadvantage, other more perceptive journalists and supporters felt that it was good for the Pars to have to play every game. As it happened, they blew up the week before the Scottish Cup Final when they needed to beat St Johnstone to stay top of the league and could only draw.

Celtic, meanwhile, played their meaningless league fixtures with no apparent concern whether they won or not – and there were some absolutely dreadful performances – but all the time, Jock Stein and the players themselves were always learning, notably that Bobby Murdoch, an indifferent inside-forward, would make a superb right-half.

League form was indeed shocking but it was almost as if this cup final had been all 'meant' and that God, as we always suspected, really was a Celtic supporter after all! 108,000 were there on a typical spring day of 24

April and they saw a tremendously entertaining game with chivalrous opponents both on the field and off. Dunfermline scored first through Harry Melrose, then a Charlie Gallagher shot hit the bar and the ball soared straight up into the air. Bertie Auld ran forward, jumped and edged it over the line with his head. Dunfermline then scored just on half-time when some idiot on the PS system started to speak and distracted goalkeeper John Fallon.

Depression at half-time. Was this to be another heartbreak? Would the ten barren Scottish Cup years now become 11? 'We'll forgive everything, Cellic, as long as ye's win the day!' The huge swaying crowd at the Celtic end remained still hopeful, and were rewarded with a fine well-worked goal between Auld and Lennox, and Auld put it away. A long second half, a good save by John Fallon from Alex Edwards, another replay looming, and then it happened. The Charlie Gallagher corner kick, Captain Courageous rising like a bird (I think I see him yet!) and then delirium at the distant Celtic end and indeed all over the ground. Indeed, all over the world!

Nine long minutes to go. Nine long minutes of holding on to the pole that said 25 to mark the gangway 25, gripping it ferociously, willing the minutes to pass, trying to make pacts with God about going to church every Sunday for the rest of your life as long as we won the day. And then Hugh Phillips, one of the best referees of the time, pointed to the tunnel and paradise was regained. 'Parkhead is paradise once more!' wrote a journalist of the *Scottish Daily Express*, a newspaper which from now on showed every sign of jumping ship from the sinking Rangers to the resurgent Celtic.

The rest of the day remains a blur. The cup being presented. The fear that this was all a dream and that we were about to wake up. The juxtaposition of silverware with green and white was not a common sight for many of us! And the veteran who had seen Patsy Gallacher and Tommy McInally and Jimmy McGrory, not to mention his RAF days when he played his own glorious part in the liberation of Africa and Italy, averring that he had never seen anything like that, and the other man, well-dressed, tie and soft hat, middle class, middle-aged, a teacher perhaps, a banker, a doctor or a dentist, not in any way inebriated by anything other than the sweet joy of ecstasy, collapsed over a garden hedge in Aitkenhead Road, saying that he didn't think he could have taken it if they had lost today again. And then that summer of 1965 – glorious even when it rained – it was 'the dawn of the free'!

Such was the experience of supporting this very special club in 1965 and glory be to Fallon, Young and Gemmell; Murdoch, McNeill and Clark; Chalmers, Gallagher, Hughes, Lennox and Auld!

In 1966 the Scottish Cup campaign began with the visit of Stranraer, the first time that the clubs had ever met in any competition, and Stranraer had been around since 1870! Celtic, not surprisingly, won 4-0, and the next game was at Dens Park, Dundee. Heavy snow put the game off on the Saturday but Celtic, without necessarily being totally in command, won on the Wednesday night with goals from Steve Chalmers and Joe McBride.

The quarter-final in the first week of March saw Celtic at Tynecastle. In spite of the game being all-ticket, Tynecastle, not for the first time in its history, showed its inability to cope with a huge Celtic crowd and the game had to be stopped for a long period in the first half while the police managed to usher the encroachers back on to the terracing. It transpired that someone had managed to open an exit gate at the Gorgie Road end and to allow in hundreds of ticketless fans.

When the game restarted, it was a thriller with Celtic twice equalising before going ahead and looking likely winners until Johnny Hamilton scored a late leveller. The replay attracted 72,000 to Parkhead on the Wednesday night, when they saw a totally different game with Celtic in command throughout and Jimmy Johnstone absolutely superb. Jimmy scored the first goal and the others were thanks to Bobby Murdoch and Steve Chalmers, while Willie Wallace, still in 1966 a Hearts player, scored a late consolation goal.

The semi-final brought together Celtic and Dunfermline at Ibrox on a windy and unpleasant day at the end of March. But this was a poorer Dunfermline team than a year ago, and Celtic won comfortably 2-0 with goals from Chalmers and Auld in what was generally agreed to have been a very poor game of football. This set up another Old Firm Scottish Cup Final, but everything was intertwined with other competitions, notably the European Cup Winners' Cup semi-final which Celtic lost unluckily to Liverpool.

Bad luck was also a major factor in the Scottish Cup Final itself. The first game was really rather a tame 0-0 draw, and the replay saw an even game with little to separate the teams. But it was Rangers who got the goal, admittedly a good one from Kai Johansen, and they were able to hold out against Celtic's late pressure. It was unfortunate ... but it would also be rather difficult to become jealous of Rangers over the next few years!

Celtic's 4-0 win over Arbroath (good though it was) was not the main topic of conversation in Scotland, even among Celtic supporters, on the never to be forgotten day of 28 January 1967. This was, of course, the day that Berwick Rangers beat the other Rangers at Shielfield Park a mile or two across the English border. It was a remarkable result. It strained credulity and was much celebrated in all Scotland and perhaps revealed that Rangers were no longer 'Scotia's Darling Club', as all their erstwhile allies in the press, radio and TV turned on them with astonishing ferocity. We were almost sorry for them! And yet, only a few years ago, with breathtaking arrogance, Rangers had produced a plan to streamline the Scottish League which involved the exclusion of five clubs. And yes, you've guessed it, Berwick Rangers were one of them!

Major giant-killings were by no means common in Scottish Cup history. There were more examples in England but until 1967, one would have to think hard to come up with many examples. Celtic had lost to Arthurlie in 1897, Dundee to Fraserburgh in 1959, but a giant-killing of this magnitude was hard to find.

This did not mean that Celtic would necessarily win the Scottish Cup, but it certainly helped. Highland

League Elgin City enjoyed their day out at Celtic Park but failed to 'do a Berwick' as they crashed 0-7, but then as in 1965, Queen's Park put up some resistance. This game was at Celtic Park, three days after Celtic's great defeat of Vojvodina in the European Cup. The mood was upbeat and cheerful – but the defending was astonishingly slapdash and careless and Queen's Park scored three goals, including one in the first minute. Fortunately, Celtic scored five, but it was far from a comfortable afternoon in the Parkhead rain.

Sean Connery (James Bond) tried to muscle in, but his antics impressed no one, and when some 30 years later he became a parasite at David Murray's Ibrox, we recalled this vainglorious episode in 1967 and shook our heads.

This was also the game in which Jimmy Johnstone was suspended by the club for a violent headbutt on a Queen's Park player who had fouled him. Cynics wondered whether the club suspension was anything to do with getting Jimmy out of the Scottish League v English League game the following midweek, but in any case, Jimmy was back in action for the big games to come – something that did little to dispel the suspicions of the doubters!

The semi-final was against Clyde at Hampden on Saturday, 1 April. It was a damp, unpleasant day and a 0-0 draw. It was one of the worst games that Celtic had played all season, although they should have had a penalty kick late in the game. The replay was a different matter altogether as Bertie Auld simply turned it on, scoring a great goal from the edge of the box, and Celtic ran out 2-0 winners with a degree of comfort.

This set up a final against Aberdeen, who had defeated Dundee United by an own goal in the other semi-final at Dens Park. Aberdeen in 1967 were enjoying a comparatively new resurgence on the Scottish scene after well over a decade of dreadful underachievement. Now under Eddie Turnbull, at one time a crusty inside-left with Hibs, they were not to be ignored and both league games between Celtic and Aberdeen had been draws. This final had all the makings of a close game in the tradition of 1937 and 1954 but two things happened in the previous midweek. One was that in Prague, Celtic had qualified for the European Cup Final and were thus on a high, and the other was that Aberdeen's manager Eddie Turnbull was taken ill at the Gleneagles Hotel and was unable to travel with them. To what extent this had any real effect on the game we cannot say, but Celtic scored twice through Willie Wallace on either side of half-time and Simpson, Craig and Gemmell; Murdoch, McNeill and Clark; Johnstone, Wallace, Chalmers, Auld and Lennox won Celtic's 19th Scottish Cup.

We all know what happened after that in Lisbon – but there was a reaction in the autumn, a dismal one, with defeats in Europe, South America and then at Celtic Park in late January 1968 when the team went down in the Scottish Cup to a good Dunfermline Athletic side. This time, although there were one or two absentees from the Celtic ranks, there were no real excuses. Dunfermline simply played better and won, then went on to win the Scottish Cup itself.

1969 saw a very spectacular Scottish Cup Final – possibly the best Celtic cup final of them all in the eyes of some supporters, but the passage to the final hardly filled the fans with enthusiasm. Two attempts were needed to get the better of both Glasgow teams, Partick Thistle and Clyde. Both games saw scrappy, possibly even lucky, games at the grounds of the opposition, but far better performances at Parkhead, the 8-1 game against Partick Thistle in particular, showing just how good Celtic could be. Then in the quarter-final on 1 March Celtic won 3-2 at Parkhead against St Johnstone who came very close to earning a replay at Muirton, which would not have been undeserved.

The semi-final saw Celtic take on Morton at Hampden. The kick-off was delayed because Hampden had not opened enough turnstiles (incredible, but true!) but eventually Morton came running out in all white. But wait a second! Morton had a guy who looked like Jimmy Johnstone and another who looked like Billy McNeill, and if you looked hard enough from the high terracings of Hampden, you could see that there was a green trim to the strips! Then the real Morton came out wearing blue! The real Morton also scored first, but normal service was soon resumed and Celtic won 4-1 with goals from Wallace, McNeill, Chalmers and Johnstone. In the other semi-final, Rangers beat Aberdeen by the surprisingly high score of 6-1 and now the third Old Firm cup final of the 1960s beckoned.

It wouldn't have been an Old Firm cup final if there weren't any shenanigans beforehand, and they came mainly from Ibrox. There was, for example, an attempt in a newspaper to get Colin Stein's (Rangers centre-forward and nothing to do with Jock) suspension for violent conduct broken or delayed so that he could play in the 'showpiece' final, something that Rangers themselves disowned long before the attempt collapsed in ridicule. There was an attempt from Ibrox to get the prices for their own supporters reduced even though they now had a roof over their head, whereas Celtic supporters would stand in the open, and then most crassly of all, Rangers told the world that Ibrox would be open on the night of the cup final for the victory parade. Against all this, Celtic, who would be without Ronnie Simpson, Jimmy Johnstone and John Hughes, used Jock Stein's most formidable weapon – the eloquent and dignified silence.

Knowing Rangers' inability to be pragmatic and to change to varying circumstances, Stein gave orders that at least one man should stay on each wing at all times, thus pulling a Rangers defender out and giving more room for Celtic to come through the middle. Yet the first Celtic goal came from a corner kick taken by Lennox and headed on by the unchallenged McNeill. This had followed, we were told, repeated instructions to 'watch McNeill at corner kicks' and constant practice at Ibrox over the past week in how to deal with Billy – including the use of the elbow, if necessary! Basically, Alex Ferguson failed to go up with McNeill, and Kai Johansen, the hero of 1966, failed to cover his post.

Before half-time, Lennox and then Connelly had added another each, and Steve Chalmers ran on and scored yet another in the second half. In fact, Rangers were lucky to get off with 4-0 as Fallon, Craig, Gemmell, Murdoch, McNeill, Connelly, Auld, Brogan, Lennox, Wallace and Chalmers won Celtic's 20th Scottish Cup. It was an occasion that no one who was there would forget for the rest of his/her life. The game was a nasty one, and some spectators of the blue variety felt that the game should be stopped and entered the playing arena with a view to exercising their debating skills to that effect. All this, however, merely added to the fun, as the other boys in blue, the Glasgow police, relentlessly and sadistically pushed them back to watch more of the game!

Celtic's first Scottish Cup game in the 1970s was at Celtic Park against the team that they seemed to meet sooner or later in every Scottish Cup, namely Dunfermline (they had done so in 1961, 1965, 1966 and 1968). Today was a tight game, but Celtic's two late goals when all seemed lost, from John Hughes and Harry Hood were enough to win a game which, one feels, did an awful lot to begin the sad decline of the Pars.

Dundee United were duly walloped 4-0 in the next round at Celtic Park, and then we had a bruising Old Firm battle at Celtic Park on 21 February. The pitch was a gluepot, as happens when thick frost is followed quickly by a rapid thaw, the crowd were well pumped up and the behaviour of both sets of players was appalling. Rangers, now under Willie Waddell and with nothing left in their season other than the Scottish Cup, approached this game with a grim outlook – they had to win, but also knew within themselves that Celtic were a great deal better. After all, Willie Waddell, their new manager and until recently a journalist in the *Scottish Daily Express* had told them that often enough!

The mood was set when Jim Craig scored an own goal and was congratulated by a couple of Rangers players for so doing. Not surprisingly, he reacted to this, and on several occasions after this, mayhem appeared in 'clashes' in which fists flew. Referee Mr Wharton, a huge man, to his credit involved himself as a peacemaker, but was never totally successful, with several players on either side lucky to avoid the long walk. The only one sent off was Alex MacDonald of Rangers, a worthy candidate to be sure but unlucky not to have some company, but in between all this, Celtic played some good football and Lennox, Hay and Johnstone scored the goals. A few days later, both teams were summoned to SFA headquarters and even Glasgow City Chambers to be told what bad boys they were. Even politicians got involved (it was general election year, after all!) and 'the carpet' was distinctly crowded! We braced ourselves for the usual clichés about 'what was wrong with Scottish society' and indeed, they duly arrived.

Things were tight for Celtic in the semi-final at Hampden against Dundee, which looked for all the world as if it were heading for a replay (something that Celtic could ill afford with their fixture schedule) when an error by Ally Donaldson in the Dundee goal allowed Lennox to score the vital winner and to set up a repeat of the 1967 final against Aberdeen.

The Scottish Cup Final hurt. Celtic were on the wrong end of three refereeing decisions from Bobby Davidson. One was when a ball hit Bobby Murdoch in the chest and a penalty was allowed; another was when a good goal by Bobby Lennox was disallowed for an alleged foul, and the third was when the same player was clearly brought down by Martin Buchan and no penalty given – and all this before half-time!

This was bad enough and Jock Stein certainly had his say about Mr Davidson. But there were other factors at work as well. Hard as anyone might try to deny it, Celtic's eye was off the ball. The following Wednesday night at the same stadium was when Celtic took on Leeds United. Anyone believing that the manager and the players did not have this at the back of their minds was deluding himself.

The other thing is that, even allowing for all the unfortunate and undeniably wrong refereeing decisions, the score at half-time was still only Aberdeen 1 Celtic 0. One might have expected a Celtic team to fight back from that, something that they had become famous for in cup ties. But they didn't. In a crazy last ten minutes Aberdeen scored twice and Celtic once, and Aberdeen lifted their second-ever Scottish Cup. For Celtic, this was a poor game, and for their supporters a devastating experience, slightly disguised, and indeed made up for, by the great victory over Leeds United in the European Cup. But the danger signals were up for the European Cup Final. They were sadly ignored.

1971 started with the dreadful Ibrox disaster in the new year with the death of 66 Rangers supporters. For understandable reasons, football suffered because of this, but Celtic's Scottish Cup campaign began with a rare visit from Queen of the South, a club who had fallen on bad times. They provided few problems for Celtic in a 5-1 home victory. Then yet again, Celtic had to face Dunfermline Athletic! (What's a Scottish Cup campaign without a visit from the Pars?) This time Celtic struggled to find form in the first game at Parkhead, a 1-1 tough, uncompromising draw with the two best players on the park being ex-Celts John Cushley and Joe McBride, now playing for Dunfermline. Stein was unhappy, talked about 'lack of appetite', promised changes for the replay but put out basically the same team with a few positional alterations, and a far more committed performance saw a 1-0 win at East End Park, the only goal of the game coming from Harry Hood.

The quarter-final against Raith Rovers was a 7-1 canter, the only remarkable thing about it being the *casus belli* between Jock Stein and John Hughes who went home in a huff before the game started, when he discovered that he was not playing. Relationships had been bad for some time, but they now deteriorated beyond repair. The semi-final paired Celtic against Airdrie on 3 April. Semi-finals are seldom great games but this was an exception. The weather was pleasant, and a 3-3 draw entertained the crowd, even though questions were asked about Celtic's defence who were 3-1 up soon after half-time, squandered two goals and might even have lost at the end.

The replay was a less entertaining game but a more professional Celtic performance. 2-0 was the score but Celtic had two great performers. One was Jimmy Johnstone and the other was young Kenny Dalglish whose first real game this was, as distinct from a few appearances as substitute. He impressed, and so did Celtic as Johnstone and Hood got the goals that set up yet another Old Firm final.

The avowed concern for the 'welfare of the spectators' on the part of the authorities in the wake of the New Year disaster tarnished a little when they twice allowed six-figure crowds into Hampden for the Scottish Cup Final and its replay, especially when the TV authorities offered to televise the replay. But the BBC and STV did not, apparently, offer enough money, and of course, as we are all sadly aware, money takes precedence over public safety and even common sense and common decency as far as the SFA are concerned. Twas ever thus, and twill ever be thus, one fears.

The crowds that assembled for both these games were well entertained. The Scottish Cup Final of 1971 was in a real sense the showdown. Celtic had now won the Scottish League six times in a row, putting them in the same bracket as Willie Maley's great side of 1905–1910 and Jock Stein made sure that Rangers all knew about this, but Rangers had won the Scottish League Cup last October, so each side had won an honour this season already. What was distasteful was the urging on of Rangers in some sections of the press in order, as it were, to honour those who had perished on 2 January. '66 reasons why Rangers should …' became a common motif. It was an embarrassment to most decent Rangers supporters, and a source of anger to all Celtic followers who had shared in the grief of the supporters who had been lost.

The first game on 8 May 1971 looked as if it was going to be won by Celtic who were ahead through Bobby Lennox for a long time in the game, but Rangers equalised in the last five minutes through a Derek Johnstone header. It was disappointing, but possibly a fair result. For the replay on Wednesday, 12 May, Stein made one change, bringing in young Lou Macari for

Willie Wallace and sending out Williams, Craig, Brogan, Connelly, McNeill, Hay, Johnstone, Hood (Wallace), Macari, Callaghan and Lennox to bring home Celtic's 21st Scottish Cup.

It was a warm and very pleasant spring evening and Celtic, attacking the goal in front of their own supporters, scored twice before half-time, Lou Macari sweeping home an easy one in the aftermath of a corner, and Harry Hood sinking a penalty kick after Jimmy Johnstone had been manhandled by Ron McKinnon. The 2-0 half-time score was fair and although Rangers got one back through a fortuitous Jim Craig own goal, Celtic finished well on top with the central defensive pairing of Billy McNeill and George Connelly outstanding throughout, and Jimmy Johnstone simply superb. It was Celtic's seventh league and cup double.

The success was repeated in 1972. The campaign began with three games at Celtic Park – an unremarkable 5-0 win over Albion Rovers in early February was followed by a more creditable 4-0 defeat of Dundee, a win that was better than it seemed, for Dundee were no bad side in 1972. Then Hearts came to Glasgow on 18 March. This was a game that Celtic felt they had won but then a moment of slackness in defence allowed Hearts a late equaliser. Dixie Deans had scored for Celtic in the first half, and then in the second half, with perhaps an eye on the European Cup quarter-final next Wednesday, Celtic seemed to settle for that. Most supporters were looking for another goal to kill the game, but the game settled into a dour midfield contest. Celtic are not really very good at that type of game, and they paid the penalty in the 88th minute when Renton equalised for Hearts to the shock of so many Celtic fans who had already gone home, sure that they had won!

This led to a contentious replay at Tynecastle on Monday, 27 March. It was not all that contentious on the field of play, for the game was settled by a Lou Macari header, and this time Celtic played a containing game with a little more professionalism and ran out 1-0 winners. The problems were with the crowd. In the first place an all-ticket crowd of 40,000 was allowed in – far too many for that cramped stadium with its problems of access. Then the 16,000 Celtic fans were forced to disembark from their buses about two miles away from the ground. Haymarket station also brought fans by train, and although that particular distance is considerably less than two miles, it nevertheless meant that there were an awful lot of angry Celtic fans walking about the streets of Edinburgh.

Then with the game reaching its climax, serious fighting broke out in the covered enclosure opposite the main stand. It seemed to have owed its genesis in Hearts supporters singing songs normally associated with Rangers, but Celtic fans were not exactly angels either, and the fighting was bad enough for fans to invade the field to avoid it, and for the game to be stopped. There was the humbling spectacle of Celtic and Hearts players ushering young supporters away from it all. Fortunately, Mr Paterson did not make a bad situation worse by abandoning the game, as he might have done, and eventually the game proceeded as the Edinburgh police took away the worst of the many offenders. Football hooliganism was one of the many unpleasant fashions in British society in 1972.

For more reasons than one, full time was a relief, and Celtic now had Kilmarnock in the semi-final, played eccentrically and inexplicably on a Wednesday night after the same two teams had played in the Scottish League on the Saturday! Celtic won both games 3-1, the semi-final being played at Hampden and Celtic wearing all yellow for a change strip – something that was equally inexplicable and unnecessary. More predictably, Deans scored twice and Macari once before a crowd of 48,398.

Hibs then surprised themselves by beating Rangers in the replay of the other semi-final at a time when the country was bracing itself for yet another Old Firm Scottish Cup Final. So it was an 'all green' final instead, of the type last seen in 1923. The 106,102 crowd who assembled at Hampden on the mild, pleasant, but not all that sunny day of 6 May 1972 saw one of the best Celtic Scottish Cup Finals of them all as they beat Hibs 6-1 and Dixie Deans joined the great Jimmy Quinn (and maybe Sandy McMahon as well) in scoring a Scottish Cup Final hat-trick.

It is important to realise too that this performance was even better than it sounded. It was not achieved against a poor team. Hibs were a good footballing side at the peak of their powers under newly appointed Eddie Turnbull who was carrying on the good work of Bill Shankly. To an extent, one could say that Hibs 'froze' on the big occasion, but in fact they were swept aside by the splendid Celtic team of Williams, Craig, McNeill, Connelly,

Brogan, Murdoch, Johnstone, Dalglish, Callaghan, Macari and Deans.

Bobby Murdoch and Jimmy Johnstone were outstanding as McNeill scored first, then came the Deans hat-trick (a header, the famous dribble round the defender and the goalkeeper followed by a somersault, and then a crisp striker's goal) and finally two from Lou Macari as Celtic won the Scottish Cup for the 22nd time.

Much was made of the fact that by 1973, the Scottish Cup had been around for 100 years. The reckoning was technically correct although pedants could raise an objection or two. The first Scottish Cup Final had not been played until 1874, and the 100 years made no allowance for war years. So when Princess Alexandra was prevailed upon to come to the Scottish Cup Final of 1973, it was on decidedly shaky historical grounds! The first Scottish Cup tie (as distinct from the final) was indeed played in 1873, so there was, one supposes, a tenuous connection.

With one exception, Celtic's path to the Scottish Cup Final had been uneventful. Deans and Dalglish scored two each as Celtic beat East Fife 4-1 at Parkhead. More might have been expected from Motherwell at Fir Park, but they were easily swept aside 4-0, Deans scoring another two against his old team.

And then came the visit of Aberdeen. Celtic had scored early, but it was disallowed for offside and an hour had been played when Jimmy Johnstone and Jim Hermiston clashed on the far side of the field in front of the Jungle. At first glance, it did not look anything other than a bit of pushing and shoving, and referee Bobby

Davidson (the referee of the 1970 Scottish Cup Final and who had had a few other run-ins with Jock Stein since then) was following the ball and did not see it.

But linesman Jim Renton did, and after prolonged consultation, Hermiston and Johnstone were summoned, having themselves apparently decided to drop the matter and play football instead. Hermiston was booked (this was before the days of yellow and red cards) and then Jimmy Johnstone was ordered off. He had, apparently, aimed a kick at Hermiston. All hell now broke out as Jimmy trooped from the field and it was a long time before the police were able to restore order.

The game continued. Even with ten men, Celtic still should have won. Dalglish should have finished the job near the end, but didn't, and it was Pittodrie for the replay. A crowd of over 33,000 turned up and they were scantily rewarded with a rather dour cup tie with defences on top. It was decided only when Billy McNeill headed home a Harry Hood lob into the box with four minutes to go and extra time looming. It was the only goal of the game.

There followed two games of excruciating boredom in the semi-final against Dundee. 0-0 on 7 April and 0-0 after 90 minutes on 11 April, but class will out (eventually) and the extra time period of the replay saw Celtic win through. Jock Stein appeared at the end of 90 minutes and encouraged George Connelly to go forward, but it was Jimmy Johnstone who scored. Once he scored, the fun was over, and Dalglish scored a second one before Johnstone scored again. Dundee had put up a brave fight, but had been worn down.

The Scottish Cup Final on 5 May 1973 was looked upon as a climax to the season. Rangers, who had last really challenged for the flag in 1969, fought well this season, and it was only the week before the Scottish Cup Final that Celtic clinched their eighth league championship at Easter Road. They were less lucky this week. Rangers won 3-2 in a tight game, and underneath all the hype, as the press showed their true colours, the simple fact was Celtic and Rangers were two evenly balanced sides, and the key factor was the injury to Celtic's left-back Jim Brogan. It would not have been an outrage if Celtic had won instead, but Rangers were due one of their very few days in the sun. As for the press, they lauded Rangers 'not without cause, but without end'.

1974 saw Celtic win their ninth Scottish League title in a row. They also won the Scottish Cup back. But 1974 was a strange year, played under the shadow of Scotland having qualified for the World Cup for the first time since 1958 and everyone, for a change, talking with animated enthusiasm about the national side! Not only that, but football was allowed to be played on a Sunday for the first time ever. This was because of the three-day week caused by the miners' strike and the fact that some people would be working on a Saturday. Half-hearted protests from mainstream churches and more full-blooded ones from the lunatic fringe had no effect on the decision. After all, money was involved! Celtic's first-ever Sunday game was a Scottish Cup match on 27 January, Dixie Deans scoring a hat-trick as Celtic won 6-1 against Clydebank at Parkhead.

Three weeks later, the scoreline was repeated, this time against Stirling Albion, and three weeks after that and still on a Sunday in spite of a change of government following a general election, Celtic and Motherwell served up a real cracker in front of 46,000 at Celtic Park. Harry Hood twice equalised for Celtic after Motherwell had gone ahead, but no one was able to force a winner and the action shifted to Fir Park in midweek. It was another cracking cup tie in front of a large crowd, but it was Dixie Deans who, once again, was the difference with a diving header. Goalkeeper Dennis Connaghan, however, saved the day for Celtic with a couple of good saves. Jock Stein rarely praised his goalkeepers, but he made an exception tonight.

It was Tayside now that stood between Celtic and their 23rd Scottish Cup. On Wednesday (Why? Were there no Saturdays?), 3 April, Celtic took on Dundee in one of a long series of semi-finals between the teams. Unlike last year's game and in spite of the scoreline being only 1-0, this was a rather easy win for Celtic with Jimmy Johnstone scoring the only goal of the game. There was a little 'previous' here, however. Dundee had beaten Celtic in the Scottish League Cup Final the previous December, and Tommy Gemmell, now of Dundee, had rather enjoyed that. Now when told that he was to mark Jimmy Johnstone, Tommy said 'Jimmy who?' At full time he realised he should never have said that.

Dundee United had now reached their first-ever Scottish Cup Final by beating Hearts in the other semi-final. Under young manager Jim McLean, they had many fine developing players and were notoriously hard to beat on their own Tannadice pitch. But sadly for the Dundee United men, today was to set the tone for their 'final hurdle' complex and their predictable ability to 'freeze' on the day at Hampden. 75,959 saw Celtic go two goals up through Hood and Murray before half-time, and then after a fairly dull second half, Deans scored a third at the end. The game was punctuated by some pointless and irrational hooliganism for the sake of it (this was the mid-70s after all!) and a couple of stray dogs also found their way on to the park but Connaghan, McGrain, McNeill, Brogan, Murray, McCluskey, Johnstone, Hood, Deans, Dalglish and Hay were the men who won Celtic's 23rd Scottish Cup.

The success was repeated in 1975, and it was all the more important to do so this year because the Scottish League had gone after a few dreadful performances at the turn of the year. It would be the first year since 1965 that Celtic would not be Scottish champions. It had been clear that an era was coming to an end, but it was also clear that one or two players were not up to scratch on a consistent basis. However, the Scottish Cup campaign began at Easter Road on Burns Night. Hibs, with their customary clumsy public relations and their incessant desire to pick a pointless fight with Celtic, put up the prices for Celtic's visit, and were rewarded with a 2-0 defeat, the goals scored by Deans and Murray in one of Celtic's better performances of 1975. And poor Hibs had no other Scottish Cup tie in which to increase their prices!

An injury-hit Celtic then beat Clydebank 4-1 even though the Bankies scored first, but then we had a real humdinger of a cup tie at Boghead, Dumbarton.

It was a 15,000 all-ticket game, almost a throwback to Dumbarton's great days of the 1890s, and Dumbarton had two ex-Celts in John Cushley and Willie Wallace and a future one in Tom McAdam. Frankly, the Sons of the Rock deserved a replay and Celtic were far from their best but Ronnie Glavin and Paul Wilson scored the goals in what was really a thrilling cup tie – full-blooded, loads of bookings, the crowd in constant excitement. It was a 2-1 victory and Celtic were glad to get away without any damage.

Then came the annual Scottish Cup semi-final against Dundee on 3 April. It was a fine spring night (once more we have to ask why a midweek for a semi-final?), but the football was dreadful until Tommy Gemmell was caught in possession by Ronnie Glavin and Celtic were in their seventh successive Scottish Cup Final, of which they had won four and they duly made it five a month later on 3 May.

The opponents were Airdrie, playing their first Scottish Cup Final since 1924 when they had actually won the trophy. They were not always an easy team to like, yet one had to give them credit for surviving in a grim environment with a small support and with their funny little cricket-style pavilion behind one of the goals. The word 'romantic' often found its way into Scottish newspapers to describe a potential Airdrie Scottish Cup win, but Celtic, still smarting from the loss of the Scottish League, were far too long in the tooth for that.

Yet from the Celtic point of view, there was indeed some romance and certainly some poignancy. The poignancy concerned Paul Wilson. Sometimes underperforming, and often subjected to ignorant racial abuse (even, incredibly, from those who called themselves Celtic supporters!), Paul suffered a tragedy in the week of the game when his mother died. Stein, perhaps believing in the therapeutic nature of football and possibly even recalling the precedent of 1915 when McMenemy and Dodds won a Glasgow Cup Final for Celtic a few days after each had lost a brother in the Great War, decided that Paul should play, if he wished to. Paul did and two headed goals in a 3-1 victory (the other goal was a penalty by Pat McCluskey) won Celtic's 24th Scottish Cup in a final where Airdrie, to their credit, battled hard throughout. Celtic's team was Latchford, McGrain, Lynch, Murray, McNeill, McCluskey, Hood, Glavin, Dalglish, Lennox and Wilson.

And it was at the end of this game that Billy McNeill announced his retirement. He had won seven Scottish Cup winners' medals, and it was a fitting occasion to signal his departure. He may, however, have had cause to wonder if he was doing the right thing a couple of months later when Jock Stein was involved in a horrendous road accident which almost killed him. In fact his injuries knocked him out of football for all the 1975/76 season. The Scottish Cup campaign of 1976 collapsed ignominiously at the first time of asking at Fir Park, Motherwell when the team blew a 2-0 half-time lead to lose 3-2. 1976 was not a happy time for Celtic.

But the wheel turned again in 1977. Stein was back. Occasionally lacking his old sparkle, and with a team who contained few superstars – there were McGrain and Dalglish, but the rest were honest journeymen, youngsters like Burns and Aitken, and veterans like Pat Stanton who suddenly began to win medals when he appeared for Celtic after a decade of consistently brilliant personal performances, but for an underachieving side at Hibs! Joe Craig was bought from Partick Thistle to score goals.

Credit must also be given to Stein for bringing back ex-Ranger Alfie Conn from Tottenham. Stein knew that Rangers were struggling with a nasty support and the now universal condemnation of their religious policy. Stein delivered the knockout blow when he signed Conn, adding for the benefit of the press that he had consulted some of his senior players, mentioning casually Danny McGrain and Kenny Dalglish. The astute members of the press and public noticed immediately that Stein, McGrain, Dalglish and indeed the new signing Conn all had something in common! It was connected with how they normally spent their Sunday mornings! And all this time, Rangers were hamstrung with bigotry – a policy which denied them many players and which guaranteed them the hatred of a large section of Scottish society and the growing contempt of journalists like Ian Archer of *The Glasgow Herald*, who simply did not understand it all.

Stein's sagacity deserved success, and a league and cup double followed, but it was not one of Celtic's better campaigns. Replays were needed to beat Airdrie and Ayr United after awful first games in both cases, but then there was a better performance to beat Queen of the South on a spring Sunday at Celtic Park, and this time when Celtic met Dundee in the semi-final (for the fourth season out of five), the score was 2-0 with two good goals by Joe Craig.

And so to Rangers in the final on a rainy and deserted Hampden Park, most fans of both persuasions having decided to watch the game on TV (the first time that a Scottish Cup Final had been televised since 1957). Celtic continued to win all the psychological battles as well, making sure that they appeared with 'league champions' on their tracksuits and giving better and more frequent interviews to the TV and press than Rangers did. Alfie Conn was, of course, spotlighted as much as possible.

The game was dire and hinged on the penalty kick awarded by Mr Valentine of Dundee. If you support Celtic, of course, it was a penalty for handball, but if you support Rangers, it hit the defender's knee and was awarded illegally by the referee whom they now called Bob Vatican as a result of his perceived Romanising tendencies.

What is beyond any doubt is that Andy Lynch sank it, and that Celtic held out in a poor second half that was more or less completely devoid of good football to keep the score at 1-0. Chances for a cushion goal which might have relieved the pressure were squandered once or twice, but full time came and Celtic had now won the Scottish Cup 25 times. The team was Latchford, McGrain, Lynch, Stanton, MacDonald, Aitken, Dalglish, Edvaldsson, Craig, Wilson and Conn with Doyle and Burns as substitutes. It was by no means the greatest Celtic team there had ever been, but it was good enough. Since 1965, Celtic had now won the Scottish Cup eight times out of 13.

Season 1964/65: Winners

06/02/1965	St Mirren	away	3-0	Lennox 2, Chalmers
20/02/1965	Queen's Park	away	1-0	Lennox
06/03/1965	Kilmarnock	home	3-2	Lennox, Auld, Hughes
27/03/1965	Motherwell	Hampden	2-2	Lennox, Auld (pen)
31/03/1965	Motherwell	Hampden	3-0	Lennox, Chalmers, Hughes
24/04/1965	Dunfermline Athletic	Hampden	3-2	Auld 2, McNeill

Season 1965/66: Finalists

05/02/1966	Stranraer	home	4-0	Gallagher, Murdoch, Lennox, McBride
23/02/1966	Dundee	away	2-0	Chalmers, McBride
05/03/1966	Hearts	away	3-3	Chalmers, McBride, Auld
09/03/1966	Hearts	home	3-1	Chalmers, Johnstone, Murdoch
26/03/1966	Dunfermline	Ibrox	2-0	Chalmers, Auld
23/04/1966	Rangers	Hampden	0-0	
27/04/1966	Rangers	Hampden	0-1	

Season 1966/67: Winners

28/01/1967	Arbroath	home	4-0	Murdoch, Gemmell, Auld, Chalmers
18/02/1967	Elgin City	home	7-0	Lennox 3, Wallace 2, Hughes, Chalmers
11/03/1967	Queen's Park	home	5-3	Gemmell (pen), Wallace, Murdoch, Chalmers, Lennox
01/04/1967	Clyde	Hampden	0-0	
05/04/1967	Clyde	Hampden	2-0	Lennox, Auld
29/04/1967	Aberdeen	Hampden	2-0	Wallace 2

Season 1967/68: First Round

| 27/01/1968 | Dunfermline Athletic | home | 0-2 | |

Season 1968/69: Winners

25/01/1969	Partick Thistle	away	3-3	Hughes, Wallace, Murdoch
29/01/1969	Partick Thistle	home	8-1	Callaghan 2, Lennox, Hughes, Gemmell, Johnstone, McNeill, Wallace
12/02/1969	Clyde	away	0-0	

189

24/02/1969	Clyde	home	3-0	Chalmers, Hughes, Murdoch
01/03/1969	St Johnstone	home	3-2	Chalmers, Hughes, Lennox
22/03/1969	Morton	Hampden	4-1	Chalmers, McNeill, Wallace, Johnstone
26/04/1969	Rangers	Hampden	4-0	McNeill, Lennox, Connelly, Chalmers

Season 1969/70: Finalists

24/01/1970	Dunfermline	home	2-1	Hughes, Hood
07/02/1970	Dundee United	home	4-0	Hughes 2, Macari, Wallace
21/02/1970	Rangers	home	3-1	Lennox, Hay, Johnstone
14/03/1970	Dundee	Hampden	2-1	Lennox, Macari
11/04/1970	Aberdeen	Hampden	1-3	Lennox

Season 1970/71: Winners

23/01/1971	Queen of the South	home	5-1	Hood 2, Callaghan, Wallace, McNeill
13/02/1971	Dunfermline Athletic	home	1-1	Wallace
17/02/1971	Dunfermline Athletic	away	1-0	Hood
06/03/1971	Raith Rovers	home	7-1	Lennox 3, Gemmell (pen), Callaghan, Wallace, Davidson
03/04/1971	Airdrie	Hampden	3-3	Hood 2, Johnstone
07/04/1971	Airdrie	Hampden	2-0	Johnstone, Hood
08/05/1971	Rangers	Hampden	1-1	Lennox
12/05/1971	Rangers	Hampden	2-1	Macari, Hood (pen)

Season 1971/72: Winners

05/02/1972	Albion Rovers	home	5-0	Callaghan 2, Macari, Deans, Murdoch
26/02/1972	Dundee	home	4-0	Lennox 2, Dalglish, Deans
18/03/1972	Hearts	home	1-1	Deans
27/03/1972	Hearts	away	1-0	Macari
12/04/1972	Kilmarnock	Hampden	3-1	Deans 2, Macari
06/05/1972	Hibs	Hampden	6-1	Deans 3, Macari 2, McNeill

Season 1972/73: Finalists

03/02/1973	East Fife	home	4-1	Deans 2, Dalglish 2
24/02/1973	Motherwell	home	4-0	Deans 2, Dalglish, Lennox
17/03/1973	Aberdeen	home	0-0	

21/03/1973	Aberdeen	away	1-0	McNeill
07/04/1973	Dundee	Hampden	0-0	
11/04/1973	Dundee	Hampden	3-0	Johnstone 2, Dalglish
05/05/1973	Rangers	Hampden	2-3	Dalglish, Connelly (pen)

Season 1973/74: Winners

27/01/1974	Clydebank	home	6-1	Deans 3, Lennox 2, Davidson
17/02/1974	Stirling Albion	home	6-1	Hood 2, Murray 2, Dalglish, Wilson
10/03/1974	Motherwell	home	2-2	Hood 2
13/03/1974	Motherwell	away	1-0	Deans
03/04/1974	Dundee	Hampden	1-0	Johnstone
04/05/1974	Dundee United	Hampden	3-0	Hood, Murray, Deans

Season 1974/75: Winners

25/01/1975	Hibs	away	2-0	Deans, Murray
15/02/1975	Clydebank	home	4-1	Dalglish 2, McNamara, MacDonald
08/03/1975	Dumbarton	away	2-1	Glavin, Wilson
02/04/1975	Dundee	Hampden	1-0	Glavin
03/05/1975	Airdrie	Hampden	3-1	Wilson 2, P. McCluskey (pen)

Season 1975/76: First Round

| 24/01/1976 | Motherwell | away | 2-3 | Dalglish, Lynch |

Season 1976/77: Winners

29/01/1977	Airdrie	away	1-1	Doyle
02/02/1977	Airdrie	home	5-0	Craig 4, Glavin
27/02/1977	Ayr United	home	1-1	Glavin
02/03/1977	Ayr United	away	3-1	Glavin (pen), Doyle, Aitken
13/03/1977	Queen of the South	home	5-1	Glavin 3 (2 pens), Craig, Dalglish
06/04/1977	Dundee	Hampden	2-0	Craig 2
07/05/1977	Rangers	Hampden	1-0	Lynch (pen)

CHAPTER SIX

FITFUL, SPORADIC BUT OCCASIONALLY SPECTACULAR

1978–2000

WHAT A dreadful year 1978 was. Neither the club, the supporters nor Jock Stein himself ever recovered from the awful mistake of selling Kenny Dalglish on the eve of the 1977/78 season. The actual agreeing to the sale was bad enough, but what really hurt was that no great attempt was made to spend enough of the money on an adequate replacement. The perception was that the directors had done very well out of this, thank you. Their day would come – it was a long time in the distance, 16 years in fact – but it all started in 1978 with this rather eloquent statement that Celtic did not want to win another European Cup, and that making money was more important!

The fans' views did not seem to be of any great importance.

Celtic, with Stein giving every sign of suffering from depression, muddled on. As happens when you are down, you suffer more misfortunes, notably in this case a serious injury to Danny McGrain, and that was after other injuries to Alfie Conn and Pat Stanton. No recovery came before the New Year and the Scottish Cup saw a spectacular 7-1 demolition of Dundee, but then a feckless draw against Kilmarnock at Parkhead was followed by a 0-1 defeat at Rugby Park in a game that saw the young and still not yet very mature Roy Aitken sent off. A writer described Celtic's return across Fenwick Moor that night as being akin to Napoleon's retreat from Moscow. He was not far off the mark. The feelings of devastation were similar.

1978 was a low point of our existence – and that was before Scotland went to Argentina! – but 1979 saw Billy McNeill back in charge. But there was no immediate Scottish Cup success for Billy. In a very hard winter, Celtic managed to get through Montrose and Berwick, but then they came up against Alex Ferguson's Aberdeen, the club that Billy had recently left to return home to Celtic. A respectable 1-1 draw at Pittodrie was followed by a defeat at Parkhead brought about by some shameful defending in the first half and a brave linesman in the second half. After Celtic had pulled one back, time and time again, they were denied by offside. Sometimes it was because of the excellence of the Aberdeen offside trap, other times it was because the linesman could not believe that the Celtic forwards, even the ageing Bobby Lennox, were so fast. All in all, it was not a pleasant game with neither Celtic's players nor their fans reacting well to this defeat.

It is a shame that the 1980 Scottish Cup is remembered for all the wrong reasons around hooliganism. 1909 was a riot because fans were wanting extra time; one cannot really find any other reasons for 1980's disgrace. It was a violent riot and the clear and obvious failure of the Scottish educational system. It even disgraced the fair name of sectarianism! It certainly had nothing to do with religion. It was, in fact, thuggery. Nor can any great purpose be served by saying that it was all 'their' fault, and that Celtic fans were the injured innocents. No, they weren't. Lack of intelligence was shared equally.

1980 was not really a great Celtic season. The league was squandered in a particularly heartbreaking way and Celtic's fans really needed a Scottish Cup triumph to cheer them up. They had beaten Raith Rovers 2-1 in a rather underwhelming Parkhead victory, but there then followed a real cracker of a Scottish Cup tie against old foes St Mirren. Celtic were going out of the cup in the first game at Parkhead when Murdo MacLeod headed in a Davie Provan cross with more than half of the 32,000 crowd already on their way home in disgust.

The replay at a packed Love Street on Wednesday, 20 February is a story in itself. Celtic won with ten men, Tom McAdam having been sent off by the overzealous Mr Foote (thus triggering a few missiles being thrown on to the park by some of our more challenged supporters), who then awarded a penalty to each side and incurred the wrath of the St Mirren supporters in the first minute of extra time by (correctly) waving down a linesman's flag and allowing Johnny Doyle to run through and score what proved to be the winner from a fairly tight angle, to give Celtic victory in a tingling 3-2 contest.

Then there was a competent 2-0 win over a strong Morton side at Parkhead in the quarter-final, before Hibs were swept aside 5-0 at Hampden in the semi-final. Hibs were a dreadful team that year, but they had engaged George Best who, when he turned up, showed that he still had his footballing ability. That same semi-final day, Rangers, rather surprisingly, beat Aberdeen at Parkhead, and thus we had yet another Old Firm Scottish Cup Final, the sixth since 1963.

Celtic were clear favourites, but still suffering from the psychological problems resulting in allowing their 1980 Scottish League challenge to self-destruct. More pertinently, they also had both their central defenders, Tom McAdam and Roddie McDonald, out suspended. The weather was good, if a little windy, and unlike 1977, it was actually a good game to watch. Both teams had chances, but neither could put one away and 90 minutes came and went without anyone scoring. The extra-time goal was an odd one – a Danny McGrain drive which George McCluskey stuck out his foot at, and the ball deceived everyone in blue. One would have to admit that there was an element of luck here, but, over the piece, Celtic were possibly the better team in what was an intriguing contest. Full time came with the ball in Peter Latchford's hands, and Celtic's Latchford, Sneddon, McGrain, Aitken, Conroy, MacLeod, Provan, Doyle, McCluskey, Burns, McGarvie and Lennox as a substitute had won our 26th Scottish Cup.

It would be nice to leave it like that, but the historian must now record the brainless things that happened. The police were nowhere in sight. Celtic fans invaded the park to congratulate their heroes, Rangers fans invaded the park to give vent to their personality disorders, the TV commentators and journalists, whilst masquerading as 'shocked' and 'saddened', nevertheless enjoyed every minute of it as thickos from each side showed off Scotland to the world. 'Here comes another charge!' said the excited Archie McPherson and Alec Cameron, as if they were at Culloden or Bannockburn. The Scottish Tourist Board was never likely to use this footage to attract people to Bonnie Scotland, but the long-term effect of all this was that alcohol was banned from future football matches – and maybe that was a good thing.

There now followed four dark years of Celtic's Scottish Cup history. 1981 and 1982 saw Celtic win the Scottish League, but the cup proved elusive for Billy McNeill and his men. 1981 saw a trip to Berwick Rangers, then home ties against Stirling Albion and East Stirlingshire. None of these provided any bother but the semi-final threw up Dundee United, now reaching their peak with two Scottish League Cups under their belt and already doing well in Europe. The first game was a dull 0-0 draw, but in the replay, there were four goals, two for each side, before half-time and then Mike Conroy had the misfortune to score an own goal to put his own team out of the cup. A week later Celtic won the league – at Tannadice! – and as everyone predicted, Dundee United blew up in the replay of the Scottish Cup Final, and allowed Rangers to win the cup.

It was Aberdeen who defeated Celtic in 1982. It was a tight game at Pittodrie but it was Aberdeen who got the goal and Celtic who didn't. Don Morrison of the *Sunday Mail* makes the damning comment that 'too many Celts didn't want to know until the last 15 minutes'. This game had followed a win over Queen of the South. 1983 and 1984 also saw Aberdeen deliver the *coup de grâce*, but the circumstances were totally different.

Clydebank and Dunfermline were beaten 3-0 at Celtic Park in 1983, but it was 4-1 for Celtic against Hearts in the quarter-final. Hearts, by now in the First Division and replete with ex-Rangers men who had seen better days – Sandy Jardine, Alex McDonald and Willie Johnston – were a bitter team and with even more bitter supporters in the early 1980s thanks to a long run of non-success. Today they were even more upset when Willie Johnston, just back after serving a suspension, was sent off again (the 19th time in his career) for appearing to headbutt Davie Provan. Celtic's goals were scored by Murdo MacLeod, Frank McGarvey and two from Charlie Nicholas.

Ah! Charlie Nicholas! Subject of much transfer speculation and in many ways the man of the moment. But could he cope with it all? Why did he not appear for Celtic in the semi-final against Aberdeen? Well, all Glasgow and all Scotland knew very soon, for Glasgow is a difficult place to keep a secret. No one ever tried all that hard to deny the gossip – but the tragedy was that Celtic lost 0-1 and departed the Scottish Cup at the semi-final stage. With Nicholas, it might have been different.

Charlie Nicholas departed that summer – he had been working hard for that for some time! – and so too did Billy McNeill because the directors would not give him a contract! 1983 was far from a high point in Celtic history. And it was Davie Hay in charge of a rather unfortunate team whose performances did not quite live up to expectations given the quality of players at Davie's disposal – Paul McStay, Murdo MacLeod, Tommy Burns, Roy Aitken and others.

League form in 1984 was sporadic and inconsistent, and the League Cup was lost in an unlucky cup final where penalty kicks played a disproportionate part, but the final of the Scottish Cup was even less lucky. It was reached by three rather spectacular away performances, then a less impressive but still competent semi-final 2-1 win over St Mirren at Hampden. The away performances saw another trip to Berwick for a 4-0 win, then a 6-0 defeat of East Fife (better than it sounds, for East Fife had defeated Hibs in a previous round), followed by a truly spectacular demolition of Motherwell, also 6-0.

All this paired Celtic against Aberdeen in the final of 19 May. All Scottish Cup Final defeats are painful, but there are degrees of pain and this one rates highly, not least because Celtic needed to win it to prevent a barren season. Aberdeen were a thoroughly professional outfit (as befitted a team managed by Alex Ferguson) with a streak of nastiness running through them, including a certain amount of gamesmanship which occasionally bordered on cheating, and it gives no happiness to note that so many of the culprits that day were destined in later years to play a part, successful and otherwise, in Celtic's history. Aberdeen were undeniably deserved winners of the Scottish League, but one would have to question their Scottish Cup triumph.

They were leading by an Eric Black goal with at least two things wrong with it, when the moment that defined this final happened. Roy Aitken's tackle on Mark McGhee would have earned a red card nowadays, but in 1984, referees usually cut a player a little slack. But McGhee knew how to stay down, and Gordon Strachan knew how to influence the referee, and the result was that Celtic played a proportion of the first half, all the second half and extra time with ten men.

They played heroically, and when Paul McStay scored the equaliser late in the second half of normal time, hopes rose that we might be in for the greatest Celtic cup-final comeback of them all. It would have been totally deserved, but tragically, in extra time it was Aberdeen's Mark McGhee who scored, his charge up the field, arm extended, fist clenched, difficult to reconcile with the 'ferocious' tackle and 'serious damage' inflicted on him by Aitken an hour earlier. When McGhee later joined Celtic, it was felt that he was never totally accepted by some supporters. There were good reasons for that.

Thus, 1984 was bad, and for a long time 1985 looked as if it was going to be even worse, but this time the late comeback did get its reward, and some supporters said that they thought it was 'all meant' by the omnipotent! Once again, supporters had been kicked in the teeth by dismal failures in the other two domestic competitions, not to mention some sheer blatant nobbling of UEFA in Europe by a team called Rapid Vienna. The Scottish

Cup was once again looked to with desperation rather than hope.

It was not a great pathway to the final. A narrow win over Hamilton Accies after having been laid off by bad weather for about a month was followed by an easier 6-0 win over Inverness Thistle. The last ten minutes of this game showed that Celtic supporters had a sense of humour. Buoyed up by the news from their transistor radios that Rangers were losing at Ibrox to Dundee, and having enjoyed their own team's imminent victory over the Highlanders, the Jungle decided to support Inverness and willed them to score a goal. But the players would not cooperate!

Then came a very close call at Dundee in a 1-1 draw at Dens Park followed by a tight 2-1 win at Parkhead. Both games might well have gone the other way, especially the first game. The replay owed a little of its success to Dundee having a man sent off, but Maurice Johnston scored a magnificent winner. The first game against Motherwell in the semi-final was similarly tight. Celtic were poor, and possibly even lucky, that day, and not a great deal better in the replay until the last quarter of the game when they eventually broke through and scored three times.

All this did not inspire a great deal of confidence in the team for the 1985 Scottish Cup Final against Dundee United, that most boringly and flairlessly competent of defensive sides who did, however, have an Achilles heel when they came to Glasgow. After a first half of sheer boredom, Dundee United went ahead early in the second half and looked like keeping it that way. Spirits dropped and manager Davie Hay put his head on the block by taking off the ineffective Tommy Burns and Paul McStay. His gamble lay in pushing Roy Aitken forward with instructions to simply 'take a grip of the game'. At this point, we could hardly guess that we were about to see one of the best Celtic Scottish Cup Final comebacks of them all.

Aitken, the victim of 1984, became the hero of 1985. Within minutes, as Celtic surged forward, Provan had scored with a free kick, and then Aitken himself charged down the right wing to cross for Frank McGarvey to apply the finishing touch. It was one of Celtic's greatest cup finals and 'up there' alongside 1892, 1904, 1925, 1931 and 1965. It saved Davie Hay's job and it gave the long-suffering Celtic supporters something to cheer about. The team was Bonner, W. McStay, McGrain, Aitken, McAdam, MacLeod, Provan, Johnston, Burns (McClair), P. McStay (O'Leary) and McGarvey, with a particular poignancy in the fact that Willie McStay and Paul McStay had now, as brothers, emulated the great feats of the great uncles in the 1920s. It is surely unique in world football to have two sets of brothers from the same family winning cup medals – 60 years apart!

1986's Scottish Cup campaign was a disappointing failure. A 2-0 win over St Johnstone was weak, but then they were very lucky to get the better of lowly Queen's Park in front of a poor 11,000 crowd at Parkhead one dull February day after Queen's Park had gone ahead with a penalty. And inadequate defending brought its due rewards when Celtic went down by the odd goal in seven at Easter Road at the beginning of March. It was one of those games described in the media as 'great entertainment'. Celtic fans were not nearly so charitable. The flurry of goals at the end were entertaining and there were a couple of penalties as well, but the late winner for Hibs was hard to take, especially as Celtic had also exited the Scottish League Cup in a penalty shoot-out at the same ground earlier in the season. As in 1979, the cup had proved a disappointment, but the league made up for it.

1987 saw Celtic fall after seeming to have done the hard bit. Three games were necessary to separate Celtic and Aberdeen. 2-2 at Pittodrie on a frosty pitch after Celtic had been 2-0 up at half-time said a great deal about Celtic's ongoing 'defensive frailties', but then a tense 0-0 draw at Celtic Park was followed by a trip to a neutral ground at Dens Park when Brian McClair scored the goal which won it. As Rangers were already out, having blown up spectacularly when Hamilton Accies came to Ibrox, Celtic must have now fancied their chances, but they fell at Tynecastle in an undistinguished affair with Hearts scoring a late goal. This was a rather large nail in the coffin of manager Davie Hay.

But 1988 was very different. It was Celtic's centenary season, and Billy McNeill (who, many thought, should never have been away in the first place) was back as manager. After an uncertain start, Billy and Celtic swept to a double, winning the Scottish Cup in a final with eerie resemblances to that of 1985.

It would be a mistake, however, to say that the Scottish Cup was a canter. There were some horrible performances, not least the first game against Stranraer at Parkhead where Stranraer missed a penalty and an open goal and Celtic held on to their 1-0 lead. Then in a televised TV game at Parkhead between Celtic and Hibs, the score was 0-0, and 'both teams were lucky to get nil' as the saying went. The Celtic fans were reduced to singing the praises of Dunfermline Athletic, who had defeated Rangers the day before! The replay at Easter Road before a 24,000 all-ticket crowd saw Billy Stark score the only goal of the game after a fierce Peter Grant drive hit the underside of the bar and bounced out.

Partick Thistle were less bother in the quarter-final, but then came the epic semi-final against Hearts, a game that did little to dispel the anti-Celtic hysteria which had been prevalent at Tynecastle for some time, particularly since 'Albert Kidd' day at Dens Park in May 1986. Hearts had been leading through a dubious goal which looked like a foul on the goalkeeper, and as full time approached, their supporters began some premature celebrations. They should have known better, for Mark McGhee managed to score a goal, threading a ball through the whole Hearts defence after goalkeeper Henry Smith had dropped a ball, then Henry dropped another one for Andy Walker to score. It was an excellent example of a death wish. It was as if Hearts' players knew and expected that this was going to happen all along.

And so to Dundee United in the final. It was almost a carbon copy of 1985. But there was a guest this year: one Margaret Thatcher, Prime Minister of Great Britain. This was a crass and unbelievably stupid idea, for no one in either Glasgow or Dundee has ever been known to vote Tory (well, not many!), and whoever dreamed this one up got his own reward in terms of crowd reaction when the crowd held up a red card and shouted 'Thatcher! Thatcher! Get tae f***.' 'What are they saying?' asked Mrs T of SFA secretary Ernie Walker. A pause, then 'I think they are wishing you luck' answered Ernie, who had never been known to be stuck for an answer.

It was a bright sunny day, and Celtic, already league champions, were looking for icing to put on the cake. Kevin Gallacher (grandson of Patsy) scored for United soon after half-time, but Frank McAvennie scored twice, the second one virtually on the final whistle to win Celtic's 28th Scottish Cup in incredible style. The team was McKnight, Morris, Rogan, Aitken, McCarthy, Whyte (Stark), Miller, McStay, McAvennie, Walker (McGhee) and Burns, and once again, there was the definite feeling that it was all 'meant'.

One had to spare a thought this day for the Fife schoolteacher who had, through connections in schools football, earned himself a seat in the centre stand, not all that far away from where Mrs Thatcher was sitting. This man was a rabid supporter of both the Labour Party and Rangers (an unusual combination, perhaps, contradictory even, but by no means unheard of), and at full time when the Scottish Cup was being presented by Mrs Thatcher to Roy Aitken, the pressure of the crowd prevented him from leaving and he had to stay and watch.

Season 1988/89 was a difficult one. The 5-1 defeat at Ibrox in late August was bad enough, but what was 100 times worse was the imploding in its aftermath. We never really recovered from that, and by New Year, the league was gone. But there was still the Scottish Cup in which we definitely had the last laugh. In the Scottish Cup, Dumbarton and Clydebank didn't cause an awful lot of trouble, but then Edinburgh blocked our path.

Hearts came to Parkhead in mid-March. Frank McAvennie, last year's hero, had announced that he was wanting to leave Celtic – and wondered why he got booed – but that was not the main topic of discussion. This was the 'real rammy' soon after Celtic went 2-0 up, when Alan McLaren and Tosh McKinlay of Hearts and Mick McCarthy of Celtic were all dispatched to the pavilion well before half-time. It all followed the award of a penalty to Celtic which Aitken converted. McLaren was going to be yellow carded for dissent but kept arguing and the colour changed to red. Then McKinlay was guilty of an over-the-ball tackle on Billy Stark, and McCarthy retaliated. Referee Davie Syme had his moments in his career, a few of them involving Celtic, but this was one of his better days, and he was spot on here. In the wide open spaces of the second half, Hearts pulled one back, but Celtic still won 2-1.

Then came Hibs in the semi-final on the day after the Hillsborough disaster. Laudably, the SFA did not give in to any psychological or emotional blackmail from those who wanted the game postponed and the game went ahead after due respect was paid to the victims. In a strange atmosphere, Celtic beat a poor Hibs side rather easily 3-1.

It was thus again Celtic v Rangers in the Scottish Cup Final of 1989. Rangers had, of course, won the Scottish League and were expected to win here as well. 20 May was a very warm day, but it was Celtic who had the edge.

Joe Miller scored the only goal of the game after a poor passback, improbably blamed on long grass by a Rangers defender. Rangers tried hard, even bringing on Graeme Souness himself, their player-manager, at one point when they got really desperate, but Celtic held out to the end to win the 29th Scottish Cup, the winners being Bonner, Morris, Rogan, Aitken, McCarthy, Whyte, Grant, McStay, Miller, McGhee and Burns, with Stark and Fulton being the unused substitutes.

This cup final was one of the very few occasions at this time when Celtic won the propaganda battle, and it all concerned Maurice Johnston. Few men have ever been more demonised in Celtic history than this man – and in his case it is entirely justified – but at this point in time, Johnston was a Celtic player, apparently. He had been photographed beside Billy McNeill at Celtic Park with a green and white scarf along with his attractive girlfriend, and had made his infamous statement that Celtic 'were the only team that he wanted to play for'. He had not yet signed, but that did not yet matter and all this took place in the run-up to the Scottish Cup Final. We all know what happened later that summer, but for the moment, Mojo was a Celt. Or so it seemed.

It is to be hoped that Celtic supporters enjoyed their Scottish Cup triumph of 1989, for another six years of agony were to pass before another triumph came along. 1990 was a particularly painful final, but there was at least one great day to savour on the way there. The context was that this was a truly awful Celtic team. Having failed to land Maurice Johnston, they relied far too much on an underperforming Polish forward called

Dariusz Dziekanowski and were enfeebled even more by the departure of Roy Aitken thanks to a combination of a vicious journalistic campaign and the ungrateful Parkhead boo-boys who had incredibly short memories. It was a strange and bewildering business, and it also betokened the undeniable fact that something was wrong at Celtic Park.

The league had gone long before the start of the Scottish Cup campaign. A trip to Forfar for the first time since 1914 in the Scottish Cup saw a narrow squeak but Celtic squeezed through, and then came the one bright spot of 1990 – the 1-0 defeat of Rangers at Celtic Park on a heavy pitch. It was the day that a Rangers player did some damage to the dressing room woodwork in his frustration. Tommy Coyne it was who scored the only goal of the game, and TV coverage showed quite clearly him being pushed by his ex-Dundee teammate John Brown in what can only be described as a tantrum. And then we had the vandalism to the dressing room door by the Rangers captain, and it was a fair comment that Rangers did not handle their reverse in any kind of a gentlemanly manner. Someone even said that the door was 'butchered'!

It was great to see Maurice Johnston that day. Now without a friend in the world for his colossal treachery and not really welcomed by those he had joined, he was relentlessly abused by the Celtic crowd that day, some of whom at least showed a sense of humour when they called him a 'Catholic b******' in what was, without a shadow of a doubt, the first time that Celtic supporters had used that particular form of abuse!

For a while after that, things took a turn for the better, particularly with a good 3-0 win over Dunfermline at Parkhead in a replay after a 0-0 draw at East End Park. Clydebank then played the one and only Scottish Cup semi-final in their history to lose 0-2 to Celtic, and Celtic approached the Scottish Cup Final against Aberdeen with at least a ray of hope, although most supporters would have admitted in their heart of hearts that Aberdeen were the better side, an impression strengthened some ten days before the final when Aberdeen beat Celtic with embarrassing ease in a league match at Celtic Park.

And yet for the final on 12 May 1990, Celtic raised their game. Ninety minutes came and went with no goal scored, and it was a similar story in the extra-time period. Neither side dominated, but one always felt that a goal could come. But it didn't. Celtic's hopes of three Scottish Cups in a row thus depended on a penalty shoot-out, now insisted upon by the TV companies, although one felt that a team should be entitled to one replay.

Celtic tend not to do well in such lotteries, and today was a collector's item of heartbreak. Eight Celtic players scored their penalties, but two didn't, and Celtic's misery was complete, the agony compounded when Charlie Nicholas (the deserter of 1983 and now playing as a despised soldier of fortune for Aberdeen) scored one of their penalties. The final nail in the coffin came when the last penalty was scored by an Aberdeen player who claimed that God was on his side as he ran up to take his penalty. In a country which already confuses football with religion rather too much, this was tactless, to put it mildly.

But for Celtic it was a case of *Vae victis* ('woe to the conquered')! The intensity of the pain was to an extent assuaged by the performances of Packy Bonner in the goal for Ireland in the 1990 World Cup in Italy, but the summer was a time without hope or any kind of confidence that the corner was ever going to be turned. Those at the top seemed even to lack the desire to compete.

1991 contained an element of déjà vu. There was another trip to Forfar (this time a slightly more comfortable victory), another victory over Rangers at Parkhead (with even worse behaviour from the defeated) and another heartbreak at the end (but this year in the semi-final). Between Forfar and Rangers, this year there was an easy 3-0 defeat of St Mirren. It was the Rangers game, however, on 17 March (Hail Glorious Saint Patrick!) which had all the country talking. Two first-half goals from Gerry Creaney and Dariusz Wdowczyk put Celtic on top, but then Peter Grant was sent off (incredibly, but technically correctly) for breaking too early from the wall at a free kick!

Rangers might now have had a chance, but they chose instead to demonstrate their skills of pugnacity rather than football, and three of them were deservedly red-carded by Edinburgh referee Andrew Waddell, never the darling of Celtic Park nor a close personal friend of Billy McNeill but on this occasion absolutely correct, for varying kinds of lashing out. Manager Graeme Souness, sitting in the stand for previous misbehaviour, did at least apologise, but it had been a Frankenstein monster of his own creation.

But all this did not hide the fact that this was still a poor Celtic team, and they got their comeuppance in the semi-final at the hands of Motherwell who really should have won the first game which ended in a 0-0 draw, but made no mistake in the replay which they won 4-2, effectively bringing to a sad end the second reign of Billy McNeill as manager. But Nemesis was waiting for the Celtic board as well, and she was now edging closer. The board followed the sacking of Billy McNeill with the appointment of Liam Brady, who had been a great player for Arsenal, Juventus and Ireland ... but who knew nothing about Scotland, and who had never managed even a minor football team! It was an astonishingly bad appointment!

But sheer bad luck and a spot of bribery of ballboys (yes, ballboys!) sealed Celtic's fate in the Scottish Cup of 1992. This was in the pouring rain of Hampden on the last day of March in the semi-final against Rangers. New manager Liam Brady had shown more than a little naivety in the early part of the season, but the team had now, apparently, turned a corner and were beginning to play well, reaching the semi-final by beating Montrose, Dundee United and Morton. But the semi-final in some ways cost Brady his job in the long term, and yet it was not entirely his fault. A long string of missed chances, one definite penalty turned down by referee Andrew Waddell (who had already sent a Rangers player off), several other reasonable appeals turned down, and then, as has now come to light, a confession by Rangers' assistant manager, Archie Knox, that he bribed ballboys to slow the game down by not returning the ball to Celtic players when it was their throw-in! Bizarre but true and now openly admitted!

One could hardly believe that, nor could one believe that Rangers in fact survived that second-half battering. But Celtic did not score, and the screw turned even tighter on the board, whose team had not been within a hundred miles of winning the Scottish League either. The Scottish Cup campaigns of 1993 and 1994 are too painful to recall in detail. Celtic went down to Falkirk at Brockville in 1993 after eventually getting the better of Clyde, and then (with Lou Macari now the manager) to Motherwell in 1994. By this time quite a few Celtic fans were now doing things that were unbelievable and unforgiveable, not least to themselves. They were actually hoping that their team would lose so that the board would become further discredited and collapse all the sooner. A cup run might have allowed the board to regroup and earn some money, but it didn't happen. The fans did, in March 1994, get their wish as far as the board was concerned, and no forgiveness is really possible for those who allowed this club to sink to such a state.

Season 1994/95 was a strange one. Celtic had a new chairman, a new manager and a new (albeit temporary) home at Hampden while Parkhead was flattened and redeveloped. It was not an easy season either, for the damage done by the old board had been extensive and long-lasting. In the most painful of circumstances imaginable, Celtic lost the Scottish League Cup Final to Raith Rovers, and the league campaign didn't really even get started, so it was once again the Scottish Cup that was the trophy sought to bring an end to so many years of misery.

The road to the final was uninspiring and depressing. St Mirren, Meadowbank and Kilmarnock all came to Hampden Park and failed to score any goals – something that said more about their own incompetence than any brilliance on Celtic's part. Hibs faced Celtic in the semi-final at Ibrox one Friday night. Both teams were wearing hideous strips, parodies of their proper strips, there was very little good football on view and Andy Walker missed a dreadful penalty kick. It was nothing like a Scottish Cup semi-final, and it was only with the greatest reluctance that 30,000 fans turned up the following Tuesday night to see the replay. This time at least Celtic looked like Celtic and therefore played like Celtic. Collins, O'Donnell and Falconer scored the goals as Celtic won 3-1.

That was on 11 April. The final was played on the ridiculously late date of 27 May, a good six weeks later! During this long wait, Celtic were constantly reminded that their opponents Airdrie were only a First Division club, just as Raith Rovers had been in the Scottish League Cup Final. The pressure was intense. Celtic had a side that could only be described as mediocre (if that), but this game meant absolutely everything to the fans. Because of the perpetual renovations at Hampden which seemed to have been going on for ever, only 37,000 tickets were available, so most of us were compelled to watch TV to see this nerve-wracking and frankly dreadful football match, in which an early Pierre van Hooijdonk header was all that separated the teams. Long before the end, we were all devoting our attention to the little digital clock in the corner of the television screen and willing it to go round!

The men who received the Scottish Cup and their medals from the Duchess of Kent were Bonner, Vata, Boyd, McNally, McKinlay, McLaughlin, Grant, McStay, Collins, Donnelly (O'Donnell) and van Hooijdonk (Falconer). This team will never be in any sort of competition for the greatest Celtic side of all time, but nevertheless, they deserve their place in Celtic history. It was possibly the worst Scottish Cup Final of them all in terms of quality (although one has to admit that there is some strong competition for this award, and in any case, there is seldom a good quality Scottish Cup Final, as they are all so tense) but nevertheless that day of 27 May 1995 was the day that Celtic were rescued in playing terms. They had been rescued more than a year before from the wicked men, but if they had not won today, Celtic would still have been mired in the mud and would have remained the laughing stock of the world. These guys at least shut them up! And for that we must be totally grateful. And how nice it was to see genuine Celtic men like Peter Grant, Paul McStay and Tommy Burns at long last getting something to be happy about!

The cup was presented that day by the Duchess of Kent, a minor royal, but a pretty lady who seemed to enjoy herself, although she would have been more at home at Wimbledon watching tennis. A year before she had become the first royal in modern times to convert to Roman Catholicism, something that may explain the comparative lack of vitriol from the Celtic support!

But as Paul McStay collected the Scottish Cup from the gracious lady, it was as well that he did not know that this was emphatically NOT the start of a new era. The next five years were more collectors' items of heartbreaks. Some sort of limited success was achieved in other competitions (although not very much, to be honest). But the Scottish Cup brought three semi-final defeats in a row, a final defeat and then the Inverness fiasco of 2000.

And yet in 1996, the main problem was, once again, sheer hard luck. In the Scottish Cup, the first team that Celtic met was a team called Whitehill Welfare from outside Edinburgh. The game was played on a frozen pitch at Easter Road, and Celtic won comfortably 3-0. They then beat Raith Rovers 2-0 at the fast-developing Parkhead, thus going a long way to banishing the spectre of that League Cup Final of last season, and then came a televised game against Dundee United, at that time in the First Division. Things were looking bad for Celtic as United were 1-0 up and heading for victory until Pierre van Hooijdonk equalised in the 89th minute and Andy Thom virtually on time made it 2-1. It made for great television, but it set up a semi-final against Rangers, and Celtic in season 1995/96 suffered very badly from an inferiority complex as far as Rangers were concerned.

In fact, Celtic only began to play well once the damage was done and the team was 0-2 down. Van Hooijdonk scored late on, and then Simon Donnelly had at least two reasonable chances, but it was not to be, and victory went, once again, to those who did not deserve it.

Yet Celtic had their revenge in a way the following year in 1997. In the quarter-final, played, for television reasons, on a Thursday night, a good header from Malky Mackay and a penalty from Paolo di Canio saw Celtic through against Rangers at an exultant Parkhead. They had already beaten Clydebank (at Firhill because of Clydebank's problems with their ground) and Hibs, the latter after a replay at Celtic Park and a very difficult first game in Edinburgh.

But then, predictably, when the job seemed more or less done, Celtic infuriatingly threw it all away against Falkirk in the semi-final at Ibrox.

They were ahead in the first game on a hot, sunny day until careless defending allowed the Bairns to equalise with a late header, and then on an awful Wednesday night in the rain, we suffered one of the worst nights we had experienced for many years (and in the 1990s, that is saying something!) as we went down 0-1 to a first-half Paul McGrillen goal. No one's agony, however, was greater than that of Tommy Burns, whose last game in charge this game had to be. There seemed to be no end in sight to our pain.

But a good, if comparatively unknown, manager in Wim Jansen was appointed, along with a new general manager called Jock Brown, one-time TV commentator and, less respectably, a players' agent. For a while this arrangement worked well, but it soon became apparent that Jansen and Brown did not really get on. Nevertheless, 1997/98 saw the welcome capture of the Scottish League Cup and the breaking of the ten in a row for the league championship.

But the Scottish Cup was once again a heartbreak. Morton were competently dispatched 2-0 and then at East End Park one Monday night there was a 2-1 win over Dunfermline which was a lot easier than it sounds. In the quarter-final for the second year in a row a late winner broke the spirits of a hard-working but technically inferior Dundee United. This game was at Tannadice, and it was a particularly sad moment for a nice young Dundee United defender called Erik Pedersen who scored a late own goal which he could not really get out of the way of. Poor Erik! His wife had given birth to a baby a few hours earlier. But for Celtic the dream of a treble was still alive.

Sadly it was Rangers who again put us out in the semi-final, actually played at 'neutral' Parkhead because Hampden was once again being refurbished. It was another of these gnawingly frustrating games when Celtic played as well as Rangers but conceded two goals before Celtic pulled one back virtually at the death when the damage was done. However, the pill was sweetened by the winning of the league, and in the Scottish Cup Final at Celtic Park, the lesser of the two evils, Hearts, won their first Scottish Cup since 1956.

1999 was an awful year. Win Jansen, the hero of the previous campaign, suddenly resigned, a couple of days after winning the league in May 1998, not even bothering to hide the fact that he could not hit it off with Jock Brown. He was eventually replaced by a likeable central European called Jo Venglos for whom the task was simply too much. He had a good past record with other clubs, but was not the first or the last to discover

FITFUL, SPORADIC BUT OCCASIONALLY SPECTACULAR

that managing Celtic is an extraordinary job, particularly as he had to deal with quite a few players who, for one reason or another, played up and turned ill-willy – all to the detriment of the club. Such disputes are unnecessary and awkward.

The Scottish Cup of 1999 saw good competent home wins over Airdrie and Dunfermline, then an impressive win at Cappielow, a place where Celtic now seldom visited. For the third year in a row we defeated Dundee United, this time at Ibrox in the semi-final by 2-0, and this time it should have been a lot more. And so it was Rangers in the final on 29 May at the now repaired Hampden.

The game cannot be seen without the context of the terrible events of Sunday, 2 May where Rangers won the league at Celtic Park, and Celtic players and fans simply lost the plot, especially when a coin was thrown at referee Hugh Dallas, something that nothing could possibly excuse or justify. Celtic would suffer for this, but nowhere more so than in this depressing cup final a month later. It was only 0-1, but the players had no one who could lift them, and Dr Venglos disappeared soon after. Late in the game a net-bound shot hit a Rangers player on the shoulder. No penalty was the correct decision, but it was an example of how when your luck is out, it stays out!

The year 2000 is synonymous with disaster as far as the Scottish Cup was concerned with the 3-1 defeat at home to First Division Inverness Caledonian Thistle remaining the low point of many people's lives. One would like to think that it might have been different if the game had been played on its original date of 29 January but high winds presented a danger to the fragile roofing of Celtic Park. The game was redated for Tuesday, 8 February. Crucially, on Saturday, 5 February Celtic had lost to Hearts at home after being 2-0 up, and the fans (and players) were turning on manager John Barnes.

Several Celtic players that night – Eyal Berkovic and Mark Viduka in particular – gave every impression of not trying. Arguments and fisticuffs were reported in the dressing room at half-time. Viduka did not appear in the second half, having apparently refused to play, and a shambles of a team re-emerged after the interval. Yet the team were only at half-time 1-2 down and a meaningful fightback was by no means out of the question.

Ian Wright was given the job of rescuing Celtic. He had been a brilliant player for Arsenal, but he was now 36, and quite a few Celtic supporters wondered why he had been signed in the first place. Wright tried – he certainly cut out the clowning – but lacked fitness and with no one else able to turn things round for Celtic, Inverness deservedly won 3-1. Seldom has Celtic Park seen such anger on the part of the fans who had remained. The players were kept in the stadium for their own protection until about 1am, but even then, there was a crowd waiting to vent their anger and John Barnes, Terry McDermott and Eric Black, the management team, were out on their neck by the end of the week. They had clearly not understood what Celtic was all about. Only Arthurlie in 1897 could compare with this game for tragedy and heartbreak. Fortunately, however, what Arthurlie and Inverness had in common was that they brought significant and necessary regime change. Possibly it all had to happen. Maybe, but it was painful.

Season 1977/78: Second Round

06/02/1978	Dundee	home	7-1	McCluskey 3, McAdam 2, Burns, MacDonald
27/02/1978	Kilmarnock	home	1-1	MacDonald
06/03/1978	Kilmarnock	away	0-1	

Season 1978/79: Quarter-Finals

31/01/1979	Montrose	away	4-2	McCluskey 3, Lynch (pen)
26/02/1979	Berwick Rangers	home	3-0	Lynch (pen), Burns, og
10/03/1979	Aberdeen	away	1-1	Doyle
14/03/1979	Aberdeen	home	1-2	Lennox

Season 1979/80: Winners

26/01/1980	Raith Rovers	home	2-1	Lennox, Doyle
16/02/1980	St Mirren	home	1-1	MacLeod
20/02/1980	St Mirren	away	3-2	Doyle 2, Lennox (pen)
08/03/1980	Morton	home	2-0	Casey, McCluskey
12/04/1980	Hibs	Hampden	5-0	Lennox, Provan, Doyle, McAdam, MacLeod
10/05/1980	Rangers	Hampden	1-0	McCluskey

Season 1980/81: Semi-Finals

24/01/1981	Berwick Rangers	away	2-0	Nicholas, Burns
14/02/1981	Stirling Albion	home	3-0	McGarvey, McCluskey, Burns
08/03/1981	East Stirlingshire	home	2-0	Conroy, MacLeod
11/04/1981	Dundee United	Hampden	0-0	
15/04/1981	Dundee United	Hampden	2-3	Nicholas 2 (1 pen)

Season 1981/82: Second Round

| 23/01/1982 | Queen of the South | home | 4-0 | McGarvey, McGrain, Halpin, McCluskey (pen) |
| 13/02/1982 | Aberdeen | away | 0-1 | |

Season 1982/83: Semi-Finals

29/01/1983	Clydebank	away	3-0	Nicholas 2, McCluskey
19/02/1983	Dunfermline	home	3-0	McGarvey 2, McCluskey
12/03/1983	Hearts	home	4-1	Nicholas 2, MacLeod, McGarvey
16/04/1983	Aberdeen	Hampden	0-1	

219

Season 1983/84: Finalists

28/01/1984	Berwick Rangers	away	4-0	McClair 2, McGarvey, Melrose
18/02/1984	East Fife	away	6-0	Burns 2, McGarvey, McClair, Colquhoun, MacLeod
17/03/1984	Motherwell	away	6-0	McClair 2, Reid, Burns, McGarvey, MacLeod
14/04/1984	St Mirren	Hampden	2-1	McClair, McStay
19/05/1984	Aberdeen	Hampden	1-2	McStay

Season 1984/85: Winners

30/01/1985	Hamilton Accies	away	2-1	McGarvey 2
16/02/1985	Inverness Thistle	home	6-0	McStay 3, Johnston, McGarvey, MacLeod
09/03/1985	Dundee	away	1-1	Johnston
13/03/1985	Dundee	home	2-1	McGarvey, Johnston
13/04/1985	Motherwell	Hampden	1-1	Burns
17/04/1985	Motherwell	Hampden	3-0	Johnston 2, Aitken
18/05/1985	Dundee United	Hampden	2-1	Provan, McGarvey

Season 1985/86: Quarter-Finals

25/01/1986	St Johnstone	home	2-0	Grant, Johnston
15/02/1986	Queen's Park	home	2-1	McClair, Aitken
08/03/1986	Hibs	away	3-4	McClair 2 (1 pen), McGhee

Season 1986/87: Second Round

01/02/1987	Aberdeen	away	2-2	McClair, McInally
04/02/1987	Aberdeen	home	0-0	
09/02/1987	Aberdeen	Dens Park	1-0	McClair
21/02/1987	Hearts	away	0-1	

Season 1987/88: Winners

30/01/1988	Stranraer	home	1-0	McAvennie
21/02/1988	Hibs	home	0-0	
24/02/1988	Hibs	away	1-0	Stark
12/03/1988	Partick Thistle	away	3-0	Walker, Burns, Stark
09/04/1988	Hearts	Hampden	2-1	McGhee, Walker
14/05/1988	Dundee United	Hampden	2-1	McAvennie 2

Season 1988/89: Winners

28/01/1989	Dumbarton	home	2-0	Walker, Burns
18/02/1989	Clydebank	home	4-1	Burns 2, McAvennie, Stark
18/03/1989	Hearts	home	2-1	McGhee, Aitken (pen)
16/04/1989	Hibs	Hampden	3-1	McCarthy, McGhee, Walker
20/05/1989	Rangers	Hampden	1-0	Miller

Season 1989/90: Finalists

20/01/1990	Forfar Athletic	away	2-1	Morris (pen), Dziekanowski
25/02/1990	Rangers	home	1-0	Coyne
17/03/1990	Dunfermline Athletic	away	0-0	
21/03/1990	Dunfermline Athletic	home	3-0	McStay, Coyne, Miller
14/04/1990	Clydebank	Hampden	2-0	Walker 2
12/05/1990	Aberdeen	Hampden	0-0	

Aberdeen won 9-8 on penalties

Season 1990/91: Semi-Finals

26/01/1991	Forfar Athletic	away	2-0	Wdowczyk, Coyne
26/02/1991	St Mirren	home	3-0	Miller, Creaney, og
17/03/1991	Rangers	home	2-0	Creaney, Wdowczyk
03/04/1991	Motherwell	Hampden	0-0	
09/04/1991	Motherwell	Hampden	2-4	Rogan, og

Season 1991/92: Semi-Finals

22/01/1992	Montrose	home	6-0	Creaney 3, Coyne 3
11/02/1992	Dundee United	home	2-1	Creaney, Coyne
07/03/1992	Morton	home	3-0	Creaney 2, Collins
31/03/1992	Rangers	Hampden	0-1	

Season 1992/93: Second Round

09/01/1993	Clyde	away	0-0	
20/01/1993	Clyde	home	1-0	Coyne
06/02/1993	Falkirk	away	0-2	

Season 1993/94: First Round

29/01/1994	Motherwell	away	0-1

Season 1994/95: Winners

28/01/1995	St Mirren	home (Hampden)	2-0	van Hooijdonk, Falconer

18/02/1995	Meadowbank	home (Hampden)	3-0	van Hooijdonk 2, Falconer
10/03/1995	Kilmarnock	home (Hampden)	1-0	Collins
07/04/1995	Hibs	Ibrox	0-0	
11/04/1995	Hibs	Ibrox	3-1	Falconer, Collins, O'Donnell
27/05/1995	Airdrie	Hampden	1-0	van Hooijdonk

Season 1995/96: Semi-Finals

27/01/1996	Whitehill Welfare	Easter Road	3-0	van Hooijdonk 2, Donnelly
17/02/1996	Raith Rovers	home	2-0	Donnelly, Thom
10/03/1996	Dundee United	home	2-1	van Hooijdonk, Thom
07/04/1996	Rangers	Hampden	1-2	van Hooijdonk

Season 1996/97: Semi-Finals

26/01/1997	Clydebank	Firhill	5-0	Cadete 2, Mackay, van Hooijdonk, di Canio
17/02/1997	Hibs	away	1-1	O'Donnell
26/02/1997	Hibs	home	2-0	O'Donnell, di Canio
06/03/1997	Rangers	home	2-0	Mackay, di Canio (pen)
12/04/1997	Falkirk	Ibrox	1-1	Johnson
23/04/1997	Falkirk	Ibrox	0-1	

Season 1997/98: Semi-Finals

24/01/1998	Morton	home	2-0	Brattbakk, Jackson
16/02/1998	Dunfermline	away	2-1	Mahe, Brattbakk
08/03/1998	Dundee United	away	3-2	Brattbakk, Wieghorst, og
05/04/1998	Rangers	Celtic Park (neutral)	1-2	Burley

Season 1998/99: Finalists

23/01/1999	Airdrie	home	3-1	Larsson, O'Donnell, og
13/02/1999	Dunfermline Athletic	home	4-0	Larsson 3, Brattbakk
08/03/1999	Morton	away	3-0	Viduka 2, Larsson
10/04/1989	Hibs	Ibrox	2-0	Blinker, Viduka
29/05/1999	Rangers	Hampden	0-1	

Season 1999/2000: First Round

08/02/2000	Inverness Caley Thistle	home	1-3	Burchill

CHAPTER SEVEN

THE GLORIOUS 21ST CENTURY? WELL ... SOMETIMES!

2001–2020

THERE WAS something symbolic about the year 2000 as far as Celtic were concerned. At long last, in the summer of that year, they appointed a good manager in Martin O'Neill, and not only that, they backed him with cash to buy the right sort of players. It was as if everyone took a deep breath, recognised that the horrendous 1990s were now over, and that it was time to move on, and to show the world what Celtic were capable of. One often feels that those who moan about the first 20 years of the 21st century should really think about what things used to be like. Only twice in the history of the club have things been so good – Maley's team when he was in his prime in the Edwardian era, and Stein's team in similar circumstances from the mid-1960s until the mid-1970s. As far as the Scottish Cup is concerned, Celtic have won it nine times in the 21st century and proportionately that beats any other 20 years one cares to mention. That is not to deny, however, that there have also been some horrendous disappointments.

The 2001 Scottish Cup campaign began one cold January night in Stranraer when Celtic won 4-1, and this brought them up against a team that they have tended to meet quite often in the Scottish Cup – Dunfermline Athletic. The first game at East End Park on 17 February was characterised by a flurry of late goals and the Pars were rather lucky to earn a Parkhead replay. The replay was not played until 7 March but it was a comfortable 4-1 win. Four days later Hearts came to Parkhead for the quarter-final, a televised Sunday game, and the 1-0 victory, with the goal scored by the man of the season Henrik Larsson, was far more emphatic than the scoreline would suggest.

By the time that Celtic faced Dundee United in the semi-final on 15 April, we had already won the Scottish League Cup and the Scottish League and the question was being asked whether the seemingly unstoppable Henrik Larsson could beat the goalscoring records of Jimmy McGrory. Significantly, none of our older supporters objected to the words 'Larsson' and 'McGrory' being used in the same breath, and that was surely significant!

Today Celtic won 3-1, Larsson scoring two of them. One of them was a superb diving bullet header (of the type that we used to get told that Jimmy McGrory often scored) and Celtic were comfortably into the Scottish Cup Final to meet Hibs. The McGrory/Larsson diving header is, of course, one of the perennial aspects of following

Celtic, and another recurring theme of Scottish football appeared at the final. Since Hibs had won the cup in 1902, beating Celtic at Celtic Park (and had foolishly sneered at Celtic when they did so), their supporters had emerged from the grim Leith tenements to travel to Glasgow for Scottish Cup Finals and to be beaten by Patsy Gallacher in 1914, Joe Cassidy in 1923, Dixie Deans in 1972 and now by Henrik Larsson in 2001 (Gary Hooper would continue the tradition in 2013).

Not for the first nor last time, the Hampden pitch had come in for criticism in the semi-final. There had also been American football played there, and pop concerts, not to mention a whole season of Queen's Park home games. For a while, the SFA resisted any criticisms of the surface, but eventually relented and returfed the whole pitch for the Scottish Cup Final.

It had been hoped that Larsson could score a hat-trick and thus also be mentioned in the same breath as Jimmy Quinn and Dixie Deans (who had both scored hat-tricks in Scottish Cup Finals), but Henrik scored only twice. Jackie McNamara scored first in the first half, then Henrik scored a great goal early in the second half before killing Hibs's fast-vanishing hopes with a penalty near the end. It was a very satisfactory Scottish Cup Final, marred only by it being the start of the lamentable habit of both Hibs and Celtic being compelled to change because of a 'colour clash'. There is no colour clash between the green and white hoops of Celtic and the green with white sleeves of Hibs! There wasn't in 1972, but by 2001, the Scottish Cup Final was being run by more feeble men! So Celtic played in yellow and Hibs played in white, but both had loads of green elsewhere. And the supporters of both sides proudly wore the green!

Celtic's team was Douglas, Mjallby, Vega, Valgaeren, Agathe, Lambert (Boyd), Lennon, Moravcik (McNamara), Thompson (Johnson), Sutton and Larsson. They changed into their hoops for the trophy presentation, to show that they really were Celtic! They had now won their first treble since 1969, and on 26 May 2001, there was not really very much wrong with the world. Martin O'Neill had clearly been the right choice, and the talismanic Swede had now come good. His talent had been simmering up to this point, but it now really sparkled and shone.

The football played in 2002 was possibly even better than that played in 2001, although it did not bring the same reward in terms of trophies won, the team unfortunately losing to Rangers in both domestic cup competitions, tragically so in the Scottish Cup Final. The competition began with a 5-0 win over Alloa, played eccentrically at Brockville, the home of Falkirk, a stadium that had even less going for it than Recreation Park, Alloa did. We had the rare experience of hearing the stadium announcer at Celtic Park in a game before the Alloa match basically telling supporters not to go! He warned supporters about how bad the facilities at Brockville were, particularly for female supporters! Then Celtic won 2-0 at Kilmarnock in a game that only just went ahead, surviving the twin Saturday evening threats of a power cut and a few thunderstorms. An own goal and Henrik Larsson saw us through to the next round.

Aberdeen had been making improvements of late, and the Monday night quarter-final at Pittodrie in late February looked a tough one, especially when it was announced that Henrik Larsson had not made it because of injury. The game was idiosyncratically refereed by Hugh Dallas but Celtic's two goals by Hartson and Petrov were enough to see Celtic through, even though Hartson was red carded near the end and Rab Douglas saved an Aberdeen penalty at the death. Celtic won 2-0.

It is not often that Ayr United reach the semi-finals of the Scottish Cup, but they duly did so in 2002, having also reached the League Cup Final as well. In an early Saturday evening start on 23 March, Ayr put up a brave fight to go in 0-0 at half-time. Henrik Larsson, however, scored soon after the break, but it was not until Alan Thompson scored two late goals that Celtic could breathe easily.

And so to the final between Rangers and league champions Celtic on 4 May 2002. Possibly O'Neill made a mistake in not playing Lubo Moravcik in what would have been his last game for the club, and one feels that had the game reached extra time, Lubo might have been deployed. One or two others were struggling with their fitness, but even so Celtic were twice ahead through Hartson and Balde – but couldn't hold on to their lead for very long, and then tragically, Rangers scored the winner in the last minute. It had been a very even game, and it was tough luck on Celtic.

2003 was a curious year about which one does not know whether to laugh or cry. There was a great (albeit ultimately unsuccessful) European experience which involved collecting the scalps of Blackburn Rovers, Liverpool and others, but the club won nothing, losing the Scottish League and the Scottish League Cup to Rangers in the most heartbreaking of circumstances, and exiting the Scottish Cup to our old foes Inverness whom we seriously underestimated, having our eye on other things.

There had been two easy wins over the Saints of Mirren and Johnstone, both 3-0 at Celtic Park, but then we were put up to Inverness for the quarter-final. It was played on a Sunday evening at the end of an eventful week. A week earlier, we had lost the League Cup Final to Rangers after John Hartson had had a perfectly good goal chalked off and had also missed a penalty, but then we had climbed a mini-Everest by beating Liverpool in the UEFA Cup on the day, more or less, that the Second Gulf War was starting. For those of us with long memories who recalled 1966 when Celtic were robbed of victory against Liverpool by a dreadful refereeing decision, it was a sweet moment.

All this meant, however, that preparations to deal with Inverness were rather too far from our thoughts, and Martin O'Neill made the mistake of sending out a strange-looking team for the laudable purpose of giving some men a rest. But history tells that you cannot, as it were, negotiate with the Almighty on such matters, especially if you have not spent enough time working on your research about your opponents. Your best available men are always required for cup ties, and Celtic went down 0-1. Dennis Wyness of Inverness scored on the stroke of half-time, and Celtic's forwards were unable to earn even a draw, let alone the win that the supporters craved. Martin O'Neill got few things wrong – but this was one of them.

2004 was far better. On a miserably cold, wet day at Celtic Park in January, the campaign began with a 2-0 win over Ross County, even though one of the goals looked like a push on the goalkeeper. There followed a fine 3-0 win over Hearts at Tynecastle, and then Rangers came to Celtic Park in the Scottish Cup. It was a scrappy game, with neither side looking particularly impressive but it finished well when Henrik Larsson scored the only goal of the game. Celtic had been marginally the better team.

The semi-final was played on 11 April at Hampden against Livingston. It was a comparatively easy 3-1 victory with Sutton scoring twice and Larsson once to set up a final against Dunfermline, the team that Celtic almost seemed destined to play sooner or later in the Scottish Cup. There were one or two side issues here. There was a certain 'previous' with Dunfermline who, some Celtic players and Chris Sutton in particular felt, did not try as hard as they could have on the last Sunday of last season when Rangers won the league; Dunfermline had, three weeks earlier, beaten Celtic on the day that the SPL trophy for 2004 was being presented, thereby spoiling a party, and there was also the factor that the Scottish Cup Final would be Henrik Larsson's last game for the club. It would be nice for him to finish his time at the club with a cup-final hat-trick, especially as it was now exactly 100 years since Jimmy Quinn had scored the first.

He scored twice, but Petrov scored the other in a final that was not always easy for Celtic fans to watch, for the Pars were 1-0 up at half-time. Larsson's two goals, however, came at the right time, the first one a particularly memorable piece of Larsson football when he picked up a through ball and ran on to score to the sound of all the seats tipping up as the crowd stood up to see. Once again Celtic were changing into their hoops (they had been wearing a green jersey with silk pants this time) at full time to collect the Scottish Cup for the 32nd time. The team was Marshall, Varga, Balde, McNamara, Agathe, Lennon, Petrov, Pearson (Wallace), Thompson, Larsson and Sutton. It was a fitting way for Henrik Larsson to take his departure. It is odd that he won only two Scottish Cup medals in 2001 and 2004. He deserved more. In both finals he came close to scoring a hat-trick, but not quite.

2005 was a strange Scottish Cup year with the 1-0 victory in the final against Dundee United looked upon as very much the consolation prize for the loss of the Scottish League. It was also the swansong of Martin O'Neill as Celtic manager. But the campaign had kicked off gloriously with a narrow but decisive 2-1 victory over Rangers at Celtic Park on 9 January. A goal from Sutton and another from Hartson proved better than the one from Ricksen of Rangers, even though at the very end, Rangers had a glorious chance to equalise which they ballooned over the bar.

Then yet again, we met Dunfermline at East End Park, winning 3-0 with all goals coming before half-time and the second half, frankly, a bit of a bore with

Dunfermline unable to break down the Celtic defence and Celtic, for their part, having no great desire to humiliate the Pars. The quarter-final put Celtic to Clyde's ground at Broadwood for the first time, and although the Bully Wee did well to hold Celtic until nearly half-time, they had no answer to a rampant side in the second half and Celtic won comfortably 5-0.

Tougher opposition was forthcoming in the semi-final against Hearts at Hampden. Hearts had beaten Celtic the week before at Parkhead in the league and they were very optimistic about this game, so much so that their supporters felt emboldened enough to embarrass themselves by booing and jeering during a minute's silence for Pope John Paul II, who had died the week before. They had their own silences, however, when Chris Sutton and loanee Craig Bellamy scored at the start of each half, and even though they pulled a goal back in the second half, Celtic were comfortable winners.

This put Celtic into the final to play Dundee United. But it was a quiet and chastened Celtic support that made its way to Hampden that dull and misty day of 28 May. In every way, this looked like the absolute opposite of a 'normal' Scottish Cup Final when everything is usually sunny, cheerful and optimistic. The previous Sunday had been Black Sunday when Celtic blew the Scottish Premier League after being ahead in their game against Motherwell, and then Martin O'Neill announced that he was giving up his job as Celtic's manager in order to look after his sick wife. In truth O'Neill's judgement had been questioned for some time, for the run-in had included defeats to both Hearts and Hibs at Parkhead. There had been an almost catatonic inability to see that changes were required, and that the forwards in particular needed to be shaken up.

But all was forgiven in the Hampden drizzle as Celtic won 1-0 against a spirited but fairly talentless Dundee United. Highlights were few and far between after Alan Thompson had scored for Celtic with a soft goal in the tenth minute, but we did see Chris Sutton run up to take the penalty which would have killed the game and then kick the ground, and then just at the death, United's Alan Archibald hit the bar with a fierce drive from distance. But soon after that, referee John Rowbotham signalled time on Celtic's 33rd Scottish Cup triumph, the winning team being Douglas, Agathe, Balde, Varga, McNamara, Petrov, Lennon, Sutton, Thompson (McGeady), Hartson (Valgaeren) and Bellamy. Martin O'Neill collected the trophy that night, as his Celtic managerial career came to an end.

It was as well for Gordon Strachan in his first year of management that he won the Scottish Premier League and the Scottish League Cup, for his Scottish Cup campaign of 2006 lasted one game – against Clyde at Broadwood. He made the catastrophic mistake of giving a Celtic debut to two players in the one game, something that was almost an insult to Clyde and certainly a gross underestimation of the lower-league club's abilities. The Chinaman Du Wei was clearly lost at centre-half and Roy Keane, at long last getting his life's desire to play for Celtic, was clearly surprised by the pace of the Clyde forwards and did not look 100 per cent fit. Clyde scored twice before half-time (and missed a penalty as well!) and it was not until the 82nd minute that Maciej Zurawski pulled one back – but too late and thus Sunday, 8 January 2006 must now join 9 January 1897, 22 January 1949 and 10 February 2000 as days of Scottish Cup infamy for Celtic. Astonishingly, Gretna (a club which rose and fell with spectacular speed in the early 2000s) appeared in the Scottish Cup Final that year, and took Hearts to penalty kicks!

2007 saw Celtic win the Scottish Cup for the 34th time, but it was a poor campaign. At least two games and possibly three can be pointed to as being good examples of how Celtic actually won over inferior opposition, but only through sheer professionalism and knowing how to win rather than proving themselves the better team or playing in a manner indicative of Celtic. The first Saturday of the new year saw a 4-0 win at Celtic Park over Dumbarton (no problem there) and then came Celtic's best game of the Scottish Cup when Celtic travelled to Livingston and won 4-1 after having conceded the first goal. Derek Riordan scored two goals for Celtic that day.

And then came a trip to Inverness at the end of February. Inverness, Celtic and the Scottish Cup had been bad news in the past, and this time it looked as if something similar was going to happen, because well within the last five minutes it looked like Inverness were going to win by the only goal of the game. Celtic had been involved in Europe and we all feared Gordon Strachan had taken his eye off the Scottish Cup ball in the same way as Martin O'Neill had done in 2003 at the same ground. But centre-half Steven Pressley headed in from two yards to earn a replay, and then with virtually the last kick of the ball, a curling cross from Kenny Miller won the game. How ironic it was that two players, possibly better identified with Rangers than Celtic, won the day!

More fecklessness was in evidence at the Hampden semi-final against St Johnstone with the Perth men clearly worthy of a draw. In fact, they scored first but Vennegoor of Hesselink scored once with a penalty and another from open play in a poorly attended game, watched by 28,339. This victory paired Celtic up against relegated Dunfermline in the final on 26 May 2007. It was the fourth time they had met at this stage. It did not seem as if it was going to be a great game – and it wasn't.

In fact, this game really must join the ranks of Celtic's poorer Scottish Cup Finals (along with the likes of 1995 and 2005) with a lot of us really asking ourselves whether we could take another 30 minutes of extra time, until the unlikely figure of Cameroon right-back Jean-Joël Perrier-Doumbé scored a scrappy goal which was befitting for a scrappy cup final played by two poor and tired teams. But the Scottish Cup joined the Scottish Premier League thanks to the efforts of Boruc, Perrier-Doumbé, McManus, Pressley, Naylor, Nakamura, Lennon (Caldwell), Hartley, McGeady, Miller (Beattie) and Vennegoor of Hesselink. This was Neil Lennon's last game as a player of Celtic and he was far from happy with manager Gordon Strachan when he was taken off, ostentatiously walking past his manager and the team bench and heading straight towards the dressing room. He did, however, come back for the celebrations of the 34th Scottish Cup victory.

2008 was a disappointment. The SPL was eventually won spectacularly at the end of the season, but we exited the Scottish Cup very tamely, going down to Aberdeen at Celtic Park in the quarter-final after having seemed to have done the difficult bit at Pittodrie. The defeat of gallant Stirling Albion was routine and competent, and then Celtic really turned it on one lunchtime with a spectacular 5-1 win over Kilmarnock at Rugby Park at the start of February with one goal scored by an impressive new signing called Georgios Samaras, earning for himself the instant nickname 'gorgeous Georgios'. Sadly the earnest and likeable Greek did not always live up to this billing.

Five weeks later Celtic looked as if they were going out of the Scottish Cup to Jimmy Calderwood's Aberdeen at Pittodrie. It was not that they weren't playing well, merely that the chances were being spurned. Then, as often happens, it was Aberdeen who went ahead and they looked more than capable of holding on to the lead, until Vennegoor of Hesselink managed to scramble a rather lucky equaliser. It was celebrated more than it deserved, but it did seem to indicate that we could turn it on at Parkhead in nine days' time. The danger signal had been up a week earlier when Celtic dominated Dundee United in a league match but could not score. The same happened here with Celtic doing everything but score to the frustration of the 33,000 crowd, and Aberdeen then, predictably, got a goal. This time there was no reprieve and Celtic exited the Scottish Cup.

2009 saw Celtic win a tough match against Dundee at Parkhead with the First Division side well worthy of a replay in the eyes of the press and the more honest Celtic supporters, but Celtic had the sheer professionalism to win through. The next round game against Queen's Park at home was, arguably, one of Celtic's worst ever Scottish Cup performances even though they won 2-1. Manager Gordon Strachan himself used words like 'very poor', and after Queen's Park pulled a goal back within the last ten minutes, there was more than a little anxiety lest the amateurs score what would have been a not undeserved equaliser. That way, we could have got to Hampden a little earlier than normal!

And then we come to the events of the last week in February and the first week in March. On 28 February we had a spectacular 7-0 win over St Mirren in the league at Celtic Park, and we all thought that we had turned the corner after a run of uninspiring performances. There followed a tough but worthy 2-1 win at Rugby Park, Kilmarnock and we all headed to New St Mirren Park for our first-ever game at that new venue, rather too full of confidence following last week's 7-0 win, and we lost. There had been a historical precedent in 1962 (5-0 in the league, but 0-3 in the cup semi-final) and it is what is known as an 'ambush'. But Celtic failed to heed the lesson of history.

A silly penalty was given away this Saturday lunchtime, and once again we could not convert chances. St Mirren were well worth their win, and manager Gordon Strachan did himself few favours by snarling at the press. He earned himself a reprieve by winning the League Cup the next week, but his failure to win the league and the fact that he had made too many enemies, particularly in the media who can, of course, exercise a malign and disproportionate influence on things, meant that he was out by the summer. But this game at St Mirren was a nail in his coffin.

If 2008 and 2009 were disappointments, then 2010 was a positive disaster. Tony Mowbray was the manager for the first three Scottish Cup games – all wins away from home, competent rather than creditable against Morton and Dunfermline and then a better performance against Kilmarnock in a good 3-0 win with a Robbie Keane hat-trick, but league form was absolutely atrocious and culminated in a 4-0 defeat by St Mirren in Paisley in which the players looked as if they were playing to get their manager sacked – and if that is what they were trying, they succeeded. The honest and decent Tony Mowbray, who had found the job too much for him, was on his way the following day. His big mistake had lain in how he handled the January transfer window. The function of this 'window' is to supplement and to cover for injuries. Mowbray tried to rebuild his team at this time!

But Celtic were still in the Scottish Cup under caretaker manager Neil Lennon. League form had actually improved, but today, Saturday, 10 April 2010, saw a performance to rival those against Inverness Caledonian Thistle in infamy, but this one was from the other Highlanders, Ross County, who deservedly won 2-0 against a Celtic team which was a Celtic team in name only. 2009/10 is the only season in the 21st century (apart from 2002/03 with the extenuating circumstances of a run to the UEFA Cup Final) in which nothing was won. There were some awful players at Celtic Park that season, most of whom it would be prudent not to name.

Neil Lennon was now in charge for season 2010/11. It was only the Scottish Cup which prevented a barren season in 2011, but it was quite a campaign! Things began with a 2-0 win at Berwick – a fairly unexciting game well populated by TV crews hoping in vain for a shock. Then at the start of February we had a visit to Ibrox. It was 2-2 but in some ways a travesty of a game. It was the day that the 'Broony' gesture was born after Scott had scored Celtic's second equaliser. Fraser Forster was red carded for bringing down the detestable Naysmith, who was subsequently himself red carded for simulation (and had the cheek to complain about it!), but even when Celtic were ten men against 11, they were clearly the better team, a point emphasised in the replay at Parkhead.

It had to be played almost a month later, and although the score was a narrow 1-0 with the only goal of the game scored by Mark Wilson soon after half-time, the 'other score' was 3-0 for Rangers in terms of red cards with Bougherra, Whittaker and Diouf all showing the world what Rangers were all about, then managers Neil Lennon and Ally McCoist sharing pleasantries and inviting each other out for a pint at full time and having to be separated by the police and officials. It was a game much dissected and analysed, with a few of the hoary old clichés about 'what was wrong with Scottish society' being trotted out. But the bottom line was that Celtic were through to the next round.

The next game at Inverness was postponed at the first time of asking because of a waterlogged pitch, and it was played in midweek, but couldn't be televised because of the Champions League! Not that it mattered. Celtic came from behind to win 2-1, but the narrowness of the scoreline needn't fool anyone. It was comfortable, and so too was the semi-final against Aberdeen, a team with a major inferiority complex about Celtic about this time. The game at Hampden saw the Dons bravely hold out until half-time, but then subside 0-4 to a rampant Celtic side who were thus into the final to play Motherwell.

In more or less perpetual rain on 21 May 2011, Forster, Izaguirre, Majstorovich, Wilson, Mulgrew, Loovens, Brown, Ki, Samaras (Stokes), Commons (Forrest) and Hooper (McCourt) beat Motherwell 3-0 to win the club's 35th Scottish Cup. It was an easy victory. Motherwell might have complained that Daniel Majstorovich should have been sent off for a second yellow card, but they could not complain about anything else as goals by Ki, an own goal and a fine free kick from Charlie Mulgrew saw Celtic home. It was Neil Lennon's first trophy as manager, and made up for the unprofessional throwing away of the SPL at Inverness a few weeks earlier. For Lennon personally, the Scottish Cup brought some good news that he could have done with, for he had been attacked by a Hearts fan at Tynecastle four days previously. Astonishingly, Hearts fans cheered their hero! Clearly the wounds that Albert Kidd inflicted in 1986 had still not healed.

2012 was the year made famous for its Valentine's Day when Rangers, paying the price for decades of bad management and simple dishonesty, including the refusal to cough up their income tax (!), went into administration. They had gone bust, and their players who used to kiss jerseys and talk about undying love for the club disappeared like snow off a dyke when there was no money left! By that time, in the Scottish Cup, Celtic had defeated Peterhead at Balmoor and Inverness at Inverness, and Rangers themselves had succumbed to Dundee United, one of many clubs who turned viciously on them and lifted not one finger to help them. Dundee United then hosted Celtic in the quarter-final and lost 0-4, a result which was a little hard on the Tannadice men, but showed a certain ruthlessness in this Celtic side.

There was then a painful semi-final against Hearts. Already SPL champions, but surprisingly defeated in the Scottish League Cup Final by Kilmarnock, Celtic did not play as well as they might have done against Hearts, and were thus sitting ducks for a couple of penalty decisions from referee Euan Norris (well, one 'decision' and one 'non-decision'!). Hearts were given a penalty kick when the ball hit Joe Ledley, then Celtic were refused one when a similar thing happened at the other end! All this late in the game, and it did little to lessen the perception that referees were institutionally anti-Celtic. But then again, Jock Stein used to say that Celtic needed to be four or five goals better than everyone else so that 'refereeing friction' did not matter! Celtic, by not taking a grip of the game, had rendered themselves vulnerable to the referee's opinion.

The 2013 Scottish Cup actually began in December 2012 as far as Celtic were concerned. This might not have been the best idea in the world, as we did find several Premier League teams out of the Scottish Cup and therefore their season over before Christmas. Celtic escaped this fate, but only just in two dreadful games against Arbroath, a team two divisions beneath Celtic. The first game was a 1-1 draw at Celtic Park, a dreadful performance with some of the fringe players getting a rare chance and failing to take advantage, as Arbroath's late (and not undeserved) equaliser took the game to a replay at Gayfield.

Gayfield, a matter of yards away from the North Sea, was a place that Celtic had not visited for many years and it was clearly the first time that many of our fans had been there. It quite brutally lived up to its reputation that night of 12 December 2012 of being the coldest ground in the UK, but Celtic scraped through with a goal scored by Adam Matthews. Once more, it was a most unimpressive performance with the only excuse possible being that Celtic had been involved in Europe and were now in the last 16 of the Champions League. They didn't look like one of the best 16 in Europe that night at Arbroath, though!

A return to Stark's Park, Kirkcaldy, for the first time this century, came next in early February. Raith Rovers held Celtic until half-time but once Celtic got going, the game ended up a 3-0 victory. It was tighter at St Mirren in early March. St Mirren had put Celtic out of the League Cup at the semi-final stage in January, so Celtic knew not to take them too lightly. All the goals came early in the 2-1 victory, but it was tough, and we were all relieved to hear the final whistle, as Celtic gave one of their infuriating performances where they couldn't kill a team off.

Another close call came in the semi-final against Dundee United at Hampden, a game won 4-3 after extra time, and we would not really have had any just cause for complaint if United had won. It was in fact a good game for the television audience to watch, but none too comfortable for Celtic fans. Once again, the full-time whistle brought some relief after Anthony Stokes had scored in extra time, and our opponents in the final were to be Hibs who had beaten Falkirk, also by the scoreline of 4-3, in another remarkable semi-final the day before.

Celtic lost the toss for colours against Hibs, and therefore had to play in black! Another oddity about this cup final was that it was the only one that has ever been played on a Sunday, but Celtic duly added to their tradition of beating Hibs in a Scottish Cup Final, as they had done in 1914, 1923, 1972 and 2001, in a competent performance with two good first-half goals from Gary Hooper and a second-half clincher from Joe Ledley. The hitherto underperforming Hooper might have joined the pantheon of Dixie Deans and Jimmy Quinn, who have scored hat-tricks in Scottish Cup Finals, but his two were good enough as Celtic, already league champions a month earlier, clinched their 36th Scottish Cup with Forster, Izaguirre, Wilson, Mulgrew, Lustig, Brown (Ambrose), Commons (Samaras), Ledley, Forrest (McCourt), Stokes and Hooper.

Celtic were less lucky in 2014. Yet they started well on 1 December 2013 with a 7-0 defeat of a dreadful Hearts team at Tynecastle, almost as a way of saying sorry for the exit from Europe the previous midweek. It was a couple of days after the helicopter crash on the Clutha bar in

Glasgow. 8 February brought Aberdeen to Parkhead in the next round, and for some reason Celtic decided to play their worst game for some time, and lost 1-2 in spite of having scored first. It was a result that turned quite a lot of supporters against Neil Lennon.

Lennon departed mysteriously in 2014 and was replaced by an unknown Norwegian called Ronnie Deila. One could hardly call Ronnie a failure (he was manager for two years and won the SPL in both years) but he was blamed by the fans for not doing better in Europe and in the two domestic trophies. This was not always fair, for he did win the Scottish League Cup in 2015, and often had more than his fair share of bad luck, particularly, it seemed, in semi-finals. 2015 against Inverness was a case in point.

The Scottish Cup campaign opened (again) at Tynecastle, but this time it was only 4-0, as distinct from last season's seven. Hearts complained about a man being sent off for a sliding tackle, but that hardly changed the game. That game had been played on 30 November 2014, and the next two Scottish Cup games were in the city of Dundee. Dens Park saw a competent 2-0 victory on 7 February 2015, but then a month later, Dundee United put up more of a show at Tannadice and earned a 1-1 draw. It was played on a poor pitch and it was not one of referee Craig Thomson's better games. An early rammy saw two men sent off (Virgil van Dijk for Celtic and the wrong one in the case of the Dundee United man!) when a quiet but stern word would have sufficed, two controversial penalties were awarded (Dundee United scored from theirs but Celtic missed) and it looked very much as if we were going out until eventually Leigh Griffiths atoned for his early penalty miss by earning Celtic's equaliser.

There was quite a lot going on between Celtic and Dundee United in those days with United having been engaged in a shocking asset-stripping exercise (involving Gary Mackay-Steven and Stuart Armstrong moving to Celtic) which guaranteed their eventual relegation, and all of Celtic's next three games were against Dundee United as well! One was in the Scottish League Cup Final, then the Scottish Cup replay and finally in the Premier League. Celtic beat a dispirited Dundee United in every one of them, winning the Scottish Cup replay 4-0 with a degree of comfort at a strangely half-empty Parkhead on Wednesday, 18 March.

This put Celtic into the Scottish Cup semi-final against our old foes Inverness Caledonian Thistle. We were on the wrong end of a couple of refereeing decisions, one of which was truly shocking, but there were also a few sub-standard performances from our players which led to the 2-3 defeat in extra time. Celtic were 1-0 up and then were denied a blatant penalty for handball by referee Steven McLean. But that was not the game changer.

The game changer came in the penalty kick awarded to Inverness and the red card to goalkeeper Craig Gordon. Technically, one supposes the referee was correct but it is a cruel rule. Lukasz Zaluska had thus to come on for one of his rare appearances and his first action was to face a penalty kick. Not surprisingly, Inverness scored. Even that need not have been fatal – it was only 1-1 – but the 11-man Inverness team beat the ten-man Celtic, with the fact that the game went to extra time possibly the crucial point in denying Ronnie Deila his treble. Still 1-1 at 90 minutes, but then Inverness scored, John Guidetti equalised for Celtic, and then tragically, Inverness scored late when a penalty shoot-out would have given Celtic a level playing field. It was also true that some of the Celtic defending was woeful, and although one can make a certain amount of excuses for the goalkeeper and the circumstances in which he came on, Zaluska did not have a good game. We all wanted Falkirk to beat Inverness in the final (ex-Celt Peter Grant and his son were involved with Falkirk) but it was the Highlanders who won the day.

It was the semi-final of 2016 which sealed the fate of Ronnie Deila, and ironically all because of a penalty shoot-out! The semi-final had been reached by undistinguished but competent performances against Stranraer, East Kilbride and Morton, and then we found ourselves against another lower-league team in the semi-final. This was the new Rangers team which one can call 'the' Rangers, Sevco, Newco or any other name that one wishes, but for brevity's sake we will call them Rangers. They were still, at this time, in the Championship (or second tier). In fact, for a neutral and the vast worldwide TV audience, it was a highly entertaining 2-2 draw which went to extra time. Celtic felt they should have won, but the game went to a penalty shoot-out.

Celtic generally don't do well in penalty shoot-outs and on this occasion Scott Brown, Callum McGregor and Tom Rogic (by no means the worst players in the world) had the misfortune to miss their penalties, and in their agony, Celtic fans demanded the resignation of Ronnie Deila, who duly said that he would go at the end of the season. But he still won the SPL a few weeks later! There was also a happy ending to the Scottish Cup when Hibs redeemed their disgraceful record since 1902 and with several ex-Celtic players on board beat Rangers in the final! And then at the end we saw Scottish Cup Final riot number three on our TV screens. In truth, it was weak stuff in comparison with 1980!

2016/17 was Celtic's 'invincible' season under new manager Brendan Rodgers, who combined tactical awareness with total (apparently) commitment to the club. We would eventually be disillusioned in the latter, but this was not yet obvious in 2017. The first game after the hated winter shutdown saw Celtic in the Scottish Cup against Albion Rovers in a game that was shifted from Cliftonhill to Airdrie. Celtic won comfortably 3-0, and then on 11 February, a few old scores were paid back when Inverness Caledonian Thistle were given a good old-fashioned 6-0 drubbing before St Mirren were similarly disposed of 4-1 a month later.

Then with the SPL well won, and the Scottish League Cup also on the sideboard, Celtic met Rangers again in the Scottish Cup semi-final on 23 April. There was no penalty shoot-out this year and although the score was only 2-0 with a goal from Callum McGregor and a penalty from Scott Sinclair, the victory was easy and at least two Rangers players might have, with justice, been red carded by referee Willie Collum. Not that it really mattered, for Celtic were comfortably in the final to meet Aberdeen.

The Scottish Cup Final on 27 May 2017 was one of the best. It was played on a stifling hot day with thunderstorms going on all round the stadium. Aberdeen were not a bad team in 2017, but Celtic were better. Jonny Hayes, then playing for Aberdeen, scored first but Stuart Armstrong equalised soon after. Kieran Tierney, who had had an outstanding season, was then taken off with a broken jaw after a collision which might have been accidental, but then again, maybe wasn't. Then at the end of an exciting second half in which Celtic were always marginally, but never overwhelmingly, on top, Tom Rogic ran through and scored an epic goal. (We were told later that a ferocious thunderstorm was in progress at the time, but no one noticed or cared!) The Celtic half of the stadium erupted in joy, and Celtic then held out against a late, spirited Aberdeen assault. The cup had been won for the 37th time and full marks to Gordon, Lustig, Simunovic, Boyata, Tierney (Rogic), McGregor, Brown, Armstrong, Roberts (Sviatchenko), Griffiths and Sinclair for winning Celtic's first treble since 2001. How nice it was to see Kieran Tierney back to enjoy the celebrations after his visit to the hospital! Broken jaw or not, Kieran was, at this stage at least, a real Celt.

Things got better. 2018 saw another treble. Brechin City were dispatched 5-0, then Partick Thistle surprised everyone by scoring late in the game to make it 3-2 after James Forrest had scored a hat-trick. But Celtic still won and then the next game was played on the Saturday of the 'beast from the east' when heavy snow hit the British Isles, paralysing much of the country for about four days.

By the Saturday, however, the snow was beginning to melt, but it was still substantial and quite a few supporters could not get to Celtic Park because of road conditions. TV, however, showed a 3-0 win over Morton with all the goals coming in the last third of the game. Dembele scored twice and Edouard once. Vive la France!

And so we came, on 15 April, to the third annual Celtic v Rangers Scottish Cup semi-final game. Rangers' players, who were naïve enough to believe the rubbish written about them in the tabloids, had apparently cheered when they heard they were to play against Celtic, and confidence was high at Ibrox, we were told! The game, however, turned out to be a thorough drubbing of the 4-0 variety. Rogic, McGregor and then two second-half penalties saw Celtic through to one of their easiest ever victories over Rangers, and Rangers players provided extra entertainment by fighting among themselves both verbally and apparently physically as well.

And so to Hampden in the sun and an easy 2-0 win over Motherwell for Celtic's 38th Scottish Cup on 19 May 2018. Two great first-half goals from Callum McGregor and Olivier Ntcham saw Celtic through with loads of unusual songs sung by the cheerful supporters about the sham that was the royal wedding that day. Even Harry and Meghan would have had to admit that Celtic were good, however, as Gordon, Lustig, Boyata, Ajer (Simunovic), Tierney, Ntcham, Brown, Forrest (Sinclair), Rogic (Armstrong), McGregor and Dembele did the business.

Was there any stopping this Celtic side? Well certainly not in the Scottish Cup of 2019. The first game kicked off, for television purposes, at the eccentric time of 5.15pm against Airdrie, and although Celtic, a little rusty perhaps from their midwinter break, took time to break them down, there was no real problem. St Johnstone were then swept aside 5-0, but a tougher nut was forthcoming in Hibs at Easter Road. On a night (another 5.15pm kick-off) that some Hibs idiot threw a bottle at Scott Sinclair, Forrest and Brown scored the goals that won the day in front of a Celtic support still disillusioned and angry at Brendan Rodgers' abrupt and treacherous departure from the club in midweek. Not long ago, Neil Lennon had been manager of Hibs. Now he was back in temporary charge of Celtic.

No Rangers in the semi-final this year, for Aberdeen had removed them, and it was Aberdeen who faced Celtic in the semi. It was a surprisingly one-sided 3-0 win but Celtic's cause was certainly made a lot easier when Aberdeen lost any sense of discipline and had two men deservedly red carded by referee Craig Thomson. Goals came – a real cracker from James Forrest, a penalty from Odsonne Edouard, then another goal from Tom Rogic, and Celtic were in the final to play Hearts.

It rained heavily most of the day (with the magic date of 25 May!) but that was of little concern to the Celtic fans who clinched their treble treble, their ninth trophy in a row and their 39th Scottish Cup thanks to Bain, Lustig, Simunovic, Ajer, Hayes (Bitton), Brown, McGregor, Forrest, Rogic (Ntcham), Johnston (Sinclair) and Edouard. After an anodyne first half, Hearts went ahead, but Edouard scored with a penalty and then with a wonderful strike as he ran on to a through ball. Joy was unconfined in the Celtic ranks and an hour or so later Neil Lennon, who had been managing the team on an interim basis, was given the job full time!

The 2020 campaign began with a 2-0 win over Partick Thistle at Firhill, goals coming from Leigh Griffiths and Callum McGregor, and then it was Clyde for the next round. That game avoided the baleful influence of Storm Ciara and Celtic won 3-0, the highlights being a great strike from Olivier Ntcham and a rare counter from Vakoun Bayo. A Ryan Christie free kick which evaded everyone was enough to win the quarter-final for Celtic at McDiarmid Park, and so it was old foes Aberdeen in the semi-final.

Season 2000/01: Winners

28/01/2001	Stranraer	away	4-1	Valgaeren, McNamara, Moravcik, og
17/02/2001	Dunfermline Athletic	away	2-2	Larsson 2
07/03/2001	Dunfermline Athletic	home	4-1	Vega 2, Larsson 2 (2 pens)
11/03/2001	Hearts	home	1-0	Larsson
15/04/2001	Dundee United	Hampden	3-1	Larsson 2, McNamara
26/04/2001	Hibs	Hampden	3-0	Larsson 2 (1 pen), McNamara

Season 2001/02: Finalists

08/01/2002	Alloa Athletic	Brockville	5-0	Balde, Wieghorst, Maloney, Petta, Sylla
26/01/2002	Kilmarnock	away	2-0	Larsson, og
25/02/2002	Aberdeen	away	2-0	Hartson, Petrov
23/03/2002	Ayr United	Hampden	3-0	Thompson 2, Larsson
04/05/2002	Rangers	Hampden	2-3	Hartson, Balde

Season 2002/03: Quarter-Finals

25/01/2003	St Mirren	home	3-0	Larsson 2, Sylla
23/02/2003	St Johnstone	home	3-0	Hartson 2 (2 pens), Smith
23/03/2003	Inverness Caley Thistle	away	0-1	

Season 2003/04: **Winners**

10/01/2004	Ross County	home	2-0	Hartson, Lambert
07/02/2004	Hearts	away	0-3	Petrov 2, Larsson
07/03/2004	Rangers	home	1-0	Larsson
11/04/2004	Livingston	Hampden	3-1	Sutton 2, Larsson
22/04/2004	Dunfermline Athletic	Hampden	3-1	Larsson 2, Petrov

Season 2004/05: **Winners**

09/01/2005	Rangers	home	2-1	Sutton, Hartson
06/02/2005	Dunfermline Athletic	away	3-0	Hartson 2, Sutton
27/02/2005	Clyde	away	5-0	Varga 2, Thompson (pen), Petrov, Bellamy
10/04/2005	Hearts	Hampden	2-1	Sutton, Bellamy
28/05/2005	Dundee United	Hampden	1-0	Thompson

Season 2005/06: **First Round**

08/01/2006	Clyde	away	1-2	Zurawski

Season 2006/07: **Winners**

06/01/2007	Dumbarton	home	4-0	Zurawski 2, Vennegoor of Hesselink, Riordan
04/02/2007	Livingston	away	4-2	Riordan 2, O'Dea, Vennegoor of Hesselink
25/02/2007	Inverness Caley Thistle	away	2-1	Pressley, Miller
14/04/2007	St Johnstone	Hampden	2-0	Vennegoor of Hesselink (1 pen)
26/05/2007	Dunfermline	Hampden	1-0	Perrier-Doumbé

Season 2007/08: **Quarter-Finals**

12/01/2008	Stirling Albion	home	3-0	Vennegoor of Hesselink, McDonald, Nakamura
02/02/2008	Kilmarnock	away	5-1	McDonald 2, Caldwell, Vennegoor of Hesselink, Samaras
09/03/2008	Aberdeen	away	1-1	Vennegoor of Hesselink
18/03/2008	Aberdeen	home	0-1	

Season 2008/09: Quarter-Finals

10/01/2009	Dundee	home	2-1	Brown, McGeady
07/02/2009	Queen's Park	home	2-1	Caldwell, McDonald
07/03/2009	St Mirren	away	0-1	

Season 2009/10: Semi-Finalists

19/01/2010	Morton	away	1-0	McGinn
07/02/2010	Dunfermline Athletic	away	4-2	Kamara, Rasmussen, Keane (pen), og
13/03/2010	Kilmarnock	away	3-0	Keane 3
10/04/2010	Ross County	Hampden	0-2	

Season 2010/11: Winners

09/01/2011	Berwick Rangers	away	2-0	Majstorovic
06/02/2011	Rangers	away	2-2	Commons, Brown
02/03/2011	Rangers	home	1-0	Wilson
16/03/2011	Inverness Caley Thistle	away	2-1	Ledley 2
17/04/2011	Aberdeen	Hampden	4-0	Mulgrew, Ledley, Commons (pen), Maloney
21/05/2011	Motherwell	Hampden	3-1	Ki, og, Mulgrew

Season 2011/12: Semi-Finalists

08/01/2012	Peterhead	away	3-0	Stokes 3
04/02/2012	Inverness Caley Thistle	away	2-0	Samaras, Brown (pen)
11/03/2012	Dundee United	away	4-0	Ledley, Samaras, Stokes, Brown (pen)
15/04/2012	Hearts	Hampden	1-2	Hooper

Season 2012/13: Winners

01/12/2012	Arbroath	home	1-1	og
12/12/2012	Arbroath	away	1-0	Matthews
03/02/2013	Raith Rovers	away	3-0	Commons (pen), Forrest, Mulgrew
02/03/2013	St Mirren	away	2-1	Ledley, Stokes
14/04/2013	Dundee United	Hampden	4-3	Commons 2, Wanyama, Stokes
26/03/2013	Hibs	Hampden	3-0	Hooper 2, Ledley

Season 2013/14: Second Round

| 01/12/2013 | Hearts | away | 7-0 | Commons 3 (1 pen), Brown 2, Ledley, Lustig |
| 08/02/2014 | Aberdeen | home | 1-2 | Stokes |

Season 2014/15: Semi-Finalists

30/11/2014	Hearts	away	4-0	van Dijk 2, Guidetti (pen), Stokes
07/02/2015	Dundee	away	2-0	Griffiths, Johansen
08/03/2015	Dundee United	away	1-1	Griffiths
18/03/2015	Dundee United	home	4-0	Denayer, van Dijk, Griffiths, Commons
19/04/2015	Inverness Caley Thistle	Hampden	2-3	van Dijk, Guidetti

Season 2015/16: Semi-Finalists

10/01/2016	Stranraer	away	3-0	Griffiths 2, Cole
07/02/2016	East Kilbride	Airdrie	2-0	Griffiths, Kazim-Richards
06/03/2016	Morton	home	3-0	Griffiths, Mackay-Steven, McGregor
17/04/2016	Rangers	Hampden	2-2	Sviatchenko, Rogic

Rangers won 5-4 on penalties

Season 2016/17: Winners

22/01/2017	Albion Rovers	Airdrie	3-0	Sinclair, Dembele, Armstrong
11/02/2017	Inverness Caley Thistle	home	6-0	Dembele 3, Lustig, Tierney, Brown
05/03/2017	St Mirren	home	4-1	Lustig, Dembele, Sinclair, Griffiths
23/04/2017	Rangers	Hampden	2-0	McGregor, Sinclair (pen)
27/05/2017	Aberdeen	Hampden	2-1	Armstrong, Rogic

Season 2017/18: Winners

20/01/2018	Brechin City	home	5-0	Forrest, Sinclair, Ntcham, Boyata, Edouard
10/02/2018	Partick Thistle	home	3-2	Forrest 3
03/03/2018	Morton	home	3-0	Dembele 2 (1 pen), Edouard
15/04/2018	Rangers	Hampden	4-0	Rogic, McGregor, Dembele (pen), Ntcham (pen)
19/05/2018	Motherwell	Hampden	2-0	McGregor, Ntcham

Season 2018/19: Winners

19/01/2019	Airdrie	home	3-0	Sinclair 2, Weah
10/02/2019	St Johnstone	home	5-0	Sinclair 3, Brown, Forrest
02/03/2019	Hibs	away	2-0	Forrest, Brown

| 14/04/2019 | Aberdeen | Hampden | 3-0 | Forrest, Edouard (pen), Rogic |
| 25/05/2019 | Hearts | Hampden | 2-1 | Edouard 2 (1 pen) |

Season 2019/20

18/01/2020	Partick Thistle	away	2-0	Griffiths, McGregor
09/02/2020	Clyde	away	3-0	Ntcham, Brown, Bayo
01/03/2020	St Johnstone	away	1-0	Christie

Also available at all good book stores

9781785315459

9781848182004

9781909178847

9781785314391

9781785311802

9781905411832

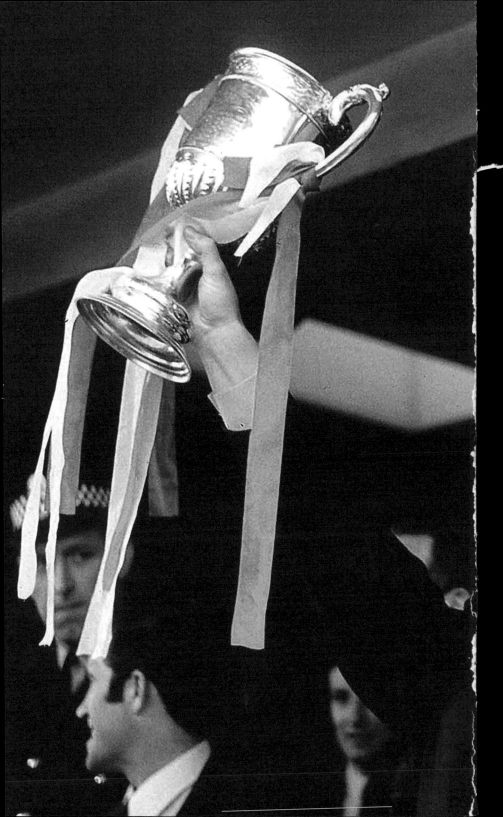